REASONING: REPRESENTATION AND PROCESS
in Children and Adults

REASONING: REPRESENTATION AND PROCESS in Children and Adults

Edited by

RACHEL JOFFE FALMAGNE

Clark University
Worcester, Massachusetts

LAWRENCE ERLBAUM ASSOCIATES, PUBLISHERS
1975 Hillsdale, New Jersey

DISTRIBUTED BY THE HALSTED PRESS DIVISION OF

JOHN WILEY & SONS

New York Toronto London Sydney

Arn

Lawrence Erlbaum Associates, Inc., Publishers
62 Maria Drive
Hillsdale, New Jersey 07642

Distributed solely by Halsted Press Division
John Wiley & Sons, Inc., New York

Library of Congress Cataloging in Publication Data
Main entry under title:

Reasoning: representation and process in children and adults.

An expansion of the material of a symposium entitled, Studies of logic, what are we studying, how, and why? at the annual meeting of the Eastern Psychological Association, Washington, D.C., April 1973.
Includes bibliographies.
1. Reasoning. 2. Syllogism. I. Falmagne, Rachel Joffe.
BC177.R33 160 75-15761
ISBN 0-470-25369-X

Printed in the United States of America

CONTENTS

Preface **ix**

INTRODUCTION, *Rachel Joffe Falmagne* **1**

1 MODELS OF DEDUCTION, *P. N. Johnson-Laird* **7**

Lexical Reasoning 9
Propositional Reasoning 14
Reasoning with Quantifiers 36
Conclusions 50
References 52

2 UNDERSTANDING CONDITIONAL REASONING WITH MEANINGFUL PROPOSITIONS, *Herman Staudenmayer* **55**

Factors in the Interpretation Process 56
Reasoning with Abstract Material 57
Reasoning with Events 59
Aim of the Study 62
Method 62
Results 69
General Discussion 75
Conclusion 77
References 78

3 LOGIC AND MODELS OF LOGICAL THINKING, *Daniel Osherson* **81**

4 **SYLLOGISTIC REASONING: LOGICAL DECISIONS FROM A COMPLEX DATA BASE,** *Russell Revlis* **93**

Schematic Model of Formal Reasoning 97
Major Findings 99
A Model of Formal Reasoning 111
Predictions from the Model 115
Speculations on Conditional Reasoning 127
References 129

5 **DEVELOPMENT OF THE COMPREHENSION OF LOGICAL QUANTIFIERS,** *Edith D. Neimark* and *Robin H. Chapman* **135**

The Experimental Task 136
Interpretation of Quantifiers in Simple Propositions 138
Interpretation of Compound Propositions 143
Summary and Conclusions 149
Appendix 150
References 150

6 **RECALL OF CLASSICAL SYLLOGISMS: A CROSS-CULTURAL INVESTIGATION OF ERROR ON LOGICAL PROBLEMS,** *Sylvia Scribner* **153**

Background 154
Study I 156
Study II 167
Discussion 169
References 172

7 **DEDUCTIVE PROCESSES IN CHILDREN,** *Rachel Joffe Falmagne* **175**

Paradigm and Theoretical Framework 176
Experiment I 179
Experiment II 184
Experiment III 190
General Discussion 196
References 199

8 **THE REPRESENTATION OF LINEAR ORDER AND SPATIAL STRATEGIES IN REASONING: A DEVELOPMENTAL STUDY,** *Tom Trabasso, Christine A. Riley,* and *Elaine Gumer Wilson* **201**

Introduction 201
Representations 202
The Task Environment 202
Serial Position Effects in Training 203
The Test Situation 205
General Research Plan 206
Method 207
Results and Discussion 209
References 228

9 **INFERENCE AS A DEVELOPMENTAL CONSTRUCTION,** *James Youniss* **231**

Transitive Inference 232
Length as a Mental Object 232
Transitivity 233
Measurement 235
Previous Empirical Findings 235
New Empirical Findings 239
Conclusions 243
References 245

10 **OVERVIEW: REASONING, REPRESENTATION, PROCESS, AND RELATED ISSUES,** *Rachel Joffe Falmagne* **247**

The Locus of Errors 248
The Reasoning Process and the Locus of Logic 253
Logical Competence: Definitional Issues 258
Reasoning and Language Comprehension, or Logic and Semantics 260
References 263

Author Index 265
Subject Index 269

PREFACE

Every book originates from a dissatisfaction and a question. This one is no exception. The dissatisfaction concerned the scarcity of cohesive sources in the area of logical reasoning in children and adults. The interest in logical thinking has undergone a tremendous development in recent years and has generated a variety of theoretical and empirical work from a variety of perspectives. Logical thinking has become a distinct subject matter for the cognitive psychologist, the developmental psychologist, and, indirectly, the psycholinguist. Yet, at a concrete level, studies of logical thinking still tend to be scattered at professional meetings and in the literature. One of the purposes of this book was to bring together and jointly discuss recent models and data covering the main subareas of logical thinking—propositional reasoning, syllogistic reasoning, and transitive inference—with the aim of providing a somewhat unified though transient picture of the current state of the area.

The questions from which this book originates are several, and concern the relationship between the Piagetian and non-Piagetian approaches to logical thinking; the notion of logical competence and the issues it entails; and the connections, both substantive and metatheoretical, between the study of reasoning and the contiguous area of psycholinguistics. The focus on those questions has been the major motivation generating this volume, and has guided the selection of chapters and the introductory and concluding discussions.

Historically, the Piagetian approach to logical thinking and the more linguistically oriented study of reasoning have developed as distinct areas with different cultural roots and, as often happens in that case, tend to be in a polemical rather than cross-fertilizing relation to each other. The rapid development of both areas and the similarity of their aims calls for some integrative effort even if preliminary. The introductory chapter in this volume presents an attempt to characterize these two traditions in terms of their respective scope and mutual relevance, and the selection of substantive chapters was intended to exemplify both.

The area of logical reasoning also has strong affinities with another of its giant neighbors, psycholinguistics. The connections are multiple and at several levels. At the substantive level, both areas focus, from their respective perspectives, on the interface between reasoning and language: topics such as lexical reasoning, generative semantics, and the logical processing involved in sentence comprehension clearly pertain to both areas. The parallelism and hopefully the complementarity of those two approaches only begins to be recognized. The models, data, and discussions in several chapters in this volume are addressed in various ways to this interdependence. At a metatheoretical level, the study of reasoning and psycholinguistics encounter strikingly similar issues, as is natural if one considers that both appeal, at the theoretical level, to a formalization of natural language input (via logic in one case, grammatical structures in the other). Some of those issues and similarities are discussed in the final overview.

The third question—or family of questions—that motivated this book is pertinent to both the Piagetian and non-Piagetian approaches to logical thinking, and concerns the notion of logical competence, the definitional issues related to that notion and the empirical issues related to its validation. Models of reasoning differ among themselves by the apparent degree of "logicality" of the reasoning process hypothesized and are sometimes opposed polemically on that ground. The range of models in this volume exemplifies various options in that regard, in the task domains considered. The status of logical competence in these various models is discussed with reference to analogous issues in psycholinguistics.

These questions, and the original dissatisfaction, first materialized in a symposium entitled "Studies of logic, What are we studying, how and why?" at the annual meeting of the Eastern Psychological Association (Washington, D.C., April 1973), the purpose of which was to provide a forum for the issues and perspectives mentioned above, and to encourage integration of empirical findings and theoretical positions. The symposium received an attention that indicated the timeliness of the topic discussed.

This volume is an expansion of the symposium material, with several additions, and is generated by the same concerns.[1]

The book is intended to serve as a source for professional reference and as a graduate textbook. It has been used as such (successfully in my opinion) in its preprint form in a graduate seminar on reasoning and semantics. Original data are presented in all chapters, and the theoretical focus of the volume as a whole is hoped to ensure its unity. At the least, the researcher and student will find in it a collection of recent models and data in the areas of propositional reasoning, syllogistic reasoning, and transitive inference; hopefully he or she will also find in it questions or viewpoints to be challenged, refined, criticized, or improved. The book is hoped to be useful to the student and researcher in cognitive development by bringing together studies of children's reasoning in Piagetian as well as non-Piagetian tasks; to the cognitive psychologist by its range of up-to-date material in the various subareas of logical reasoning; and to the student and researcher in psycholinguistics by offering, as a supplementary source, a picture of a closely connected area and a discussion of common issues.

Needless to say, the primary motivation for editing this volume was my own desire to attain some clarification and some integration, even tentative, over the issues and topics contained here; if this need is shared by others or elicited by the present attempt, then this selfish motivation has excuses. I wish to acknowledge the indirect contribution of the students in my Reasoning Seminar at Clark in this enterprise; their interest, discussions and questioning were invaluable not only for clarification and refinement of my initial conceptions, but also for some substantive amendments of it. I am indebted to Michael Acree, Stella Vosniadou, and Gary Yablick for reading and commenting the introduction and overview.

I am also indebted to Jonathan Baron, Janellen Huttenlocher, and George Miller for reading and commenting on earlier drafts of my own chapters.

Because of the congruence of this book with my own conceptual and research interests, it has represented more personal work and involvement than what an exclusively editorial role would entail. In this context, two people deserve my fondest gratitude: my daughters Catherine and Julie, whose delightful company, sense of humor, and cooperation make life and work enjoyable.

[1] The chapters by Johnson-Laird, Revlis, and Staudenmayer, and the chapter on deductive processes by Falmagne are additions to the Symposium material. The chapter by Osherson in the Symposium paper in nonexpanded form; the other chapters are expansions from the Symposium papers.

I wish to dedicate this book to my parents, Reizea Rivelis and Aron Joffe, to whom I owe my feeling that intellectual and professional pursuits are an integral, unquestioned part of the present and future, which has spared me the difficulties, doubts, and struggles faced by so many women today.

RACHEL JOFFE FALMAGNE
Worcester, Massachusetts

INTRODUCTION

Rachel Joffe Falmagne
Clark University

There are two traditions in the study of logical reasoning. One is the Piagetian tradition; the other is the study of propositional reasoning. This formulation clearly overlooks some of the issues and qualifications mentioned below, but serves its purpose of delineating two culturally distinct lines of research. It is the aim of this introduction to examine some of the divergences in focus and approach between these two traditions, to explore the question of their mutual relevance, and to indicate in preview form some issues faced by both, that will be apparent in the chapters to follow and discussed in more detail in the final overview.

The "propositional" tradition, which focuses on how people reason about verbally stated, self-contained problems such as syllogisms, has a much longer history that goes back to antiquity and has perpetuated itself through the rationalist stream of thought from Aristotle to Boole to contemporary psychological approaches. Interesting discussions of the expectations that were once attached to logic as a model of human thought, and the development, decline, or refinement of those expectations, can be found in the next four chapters in this volume.

Since its impoundment by psychology (and, evidently, before then) the "propositional" tradition has mostly focused on adult reasoning. This, in my opinion, stems from an unsupported prejudice. Historically, it is due to the fact that the recent explosion in developmental research has coincided with the sudden recognition on this side of the Atlantic of Piaget's theory, its enormous scope and its unifying integrative quality as a general theory of intelligence. The prejudice concerning children's ability to handle verbal logical problems such as syllogisms or other forms of propositional inference, is founded on Piaget's assertion that children's logic, prior to the stage of formal operations, is structurally adequate for dealing with objects and their properties but is inadequate for fully competent propositional reasoning. The claim made here that this prejudice is unsupported, at least in the radical form in which it is often expressed, is based on three considerations, which are perhaps best stated in their bold unqualified form before they are developed further in this introduction. The first one is that the data base on which Piaget's theory has been developed comes from an empirical task domain different from the "propositional" situations mentioned above, and therefore cannot a priori be generalized to these situations. An attempt to differentially characterize these two respective task domains is made below. The second, closely related consideration is that whether such a generalization is valid can only be answered on empirical grounds, that are as yet lacking, precisely because of the scarcity of empirical developmental work in the "propositional" area. Finally, the fact that adult reasoning in propositional situations is notoriously only in loose correspondence with what the ideal logical model would prescribe, calls for qualifications of what is meant by saying that the individual, from adolescence on, is in the stage of formal operations in contrast to his previous inadequacies in that respect. What is referred to here, of course, are the problems facing the validation of a competence model when its actualization at the behavioral level is imperfect; but much more crucially, the difficulty of denying such competence to other individuals whose inadequacy in performance only differs from the former by a matter of degree.

The focus of this introduction is not polemical—it cannot be, for exactly the reasons noted above about scarcity of data—but, to a large extent, conceptual; it attempts to distinguish the two domains with respect to a task analysis and the psychological processes that those tasks can be presumed to involve, in order to more clearly evaluate the comparability of the results obtained. This attempt, undoubtedly incomplete and unavoidably biased, is only hoped to serve as a stimulus for developing more adequate and refined conceptualizations.

It has been noted above that the two traditions in the study of logic differ, in particular, by the task situations investigated. A first, obvious operational difference is that, in the Piagetian case, the material the child is asked to reason about is essentially concrete (objects and properties, behavior of a physical device as in Inhelder and Piaget, 1958), whereas, in studies of the other variety the subject is asked to reason about verbal statements. However, this difference, although clear operationally, is probably a secondary one, both from a psychological viewpoint—to which

I return later—and from the conceptual viewpoint of a task analysis, in which we are presently engaged.

The genuinely fundamental difference is that, while "propositional" studies focus on the child or the adult as a logician, the Piagetian approach focuses on the child as a scientist. These are two distinct endeavors, psychologically. (We may ignore for the present purpose the epistemological status of logic, namely, the fact that it is structurally constrained to only generate empirically valid conclusions from empirically valid premises). Studying the child as a logician is essentially a psycholinguistic enterprise focusing upon the child's knowledge of language as an object. Such studies are direct descendents of the conception of logic as a formalization of natural language, factual components are kept minimal in the input of the reasoning task, and the "appropriate" behavior is for the subject to disregard this incidental information and draw conclusions from the premises in much the same manner as a linguist would judge the grammaticality of a sentence. That such judgments will ultimately be in accordance with the factual state of affairs if the premises are factually true need not concern us here, as noted above. In contrast, in the Piagetian tradition, the child is studied in his scientist's attempts to discover properties of the real world, and typically tested in situations involving either his organizing objects and events according to systematic criteria (as in the classification and seriation paradigms used by Inhelder & Piaget, 1964), or drawing inferences about a natural henomenon (as in the physics experiment described by Inhelder & Piaget, 1958). The "object of the game" is therefore different, in the same way as an empirical science differs from a formal discipline in what it aims to achieve. Such studies are traditionally referred to as approaching children's logic, and they do indeed, inasmuch as logic mediates scientific inquiry. But they also intrinsically involve, as does scientific inquiry, other functions or task requirements. One such requirement, crucial for the contrast being made here, is for the child to generate a preliminary description or encoding of the real events themselves, that is, of the empirical premises to which logic then will be applied. This is a constitutive part of what the child has to do when engaged in such situations, and a relevant description of real events is a prerequisite for appropriate inferences to be possible. A particularly obvious example illustrating this point is found in an Inhelder and Piaget billiard table experiment, in which a ball is propelled through a tube of adjustable direction with adjustable strength, and the child has to discover, through manipulation of the device, that the angle of reflection of the ball on the edge of the table equals the angle of incidence. Protocols of interviews of younger subjects reveal that, when asked to describe the outcome of a trial, they often mimick the trajectory of the ball as being a curve rather than two straight segments. It is clear that such an encoding, from which the crucial information—the angle—is missing, precludes the appropriate inference and, prior to this, the appropriate experimental manipulation.

Evidently, then, inferential attempts in such scientific situations involve an inseparable compound of logic and encoded factual information. In contrast, in the "propositional" situation in which the child is studied as a logician, the information is given to him in propositional form, and he is asked to exclusively rely on that information. Admittedly, such situations allow for modes of reasoning other than propositional, involving such resources as imagery, factual biases, or others, as has been documented in the literature and will be in this volume. Also, propositional information must clearly be encoded in some form (for example, formalized) in order to be processed, with all the resulting uncertainties, as discussed in the final overview; but the important point here is that the task *can* be solved by exclusively using the propositional apparatus (language comprehension, logic, and mapping between the two) contrary to the "scientific" tasks.

The discussion above relates to the question of *what* the subject has to do in the two respective situations. This does not prejudge the answer to the corresponding psychological question of *how* the subject does this, (although it partly constrains this answer). With respect to this psychological question, an important feature of the "scientific" situation is that, when the child has to generate systematic combinational experiments as a basis for inference, strategy, bookkeeping and memory functions operate in conjunction with the logical function per se. That is, the combinatorial "plan," if present, must be unfolded and executed. Since Piaget's notion of competence is structural rather than procedural, the bookkeeping function involved in executing the plan pertains to the performance assumptions of the theory (or should pertain there if those assumptions had been spelled out), and failures to complete the plan may therefore have to be blamed on the execution function rather than on the logical competence. What is meant by "strategy," on the other hand, is the notion that an individual may have the ability to reason propositionally, but fail to resort to it in certain contexts, for reasons related to biases, predilections or overload from other task requirements. The status of these remarks requires clarifications: they do not purport to question the validity of the inferences drawn from such situations about the logic of the child, nor do they intend to suggest the foolish ideal of a paradigm in which logic could be studied in "pure" conditions; rather, they caution against generalizations from this context to the alternative task domain, in which such biases or limitations may not be operative. When the child is presented with explicit propositional material, he may well be able to deal with it propositionally (in some cases) although he would not tend to treat factual information in that manner when reasoning about an empirical phenomenon. More generally, until those functions and processes other than logical (or, for those who like the terminology, those performance factors) have been spelled out, theoretical comparisons and oppositions between the data from both types of studies cannot be drawn hastily, although they ultimately ought to be integrated.

In both cases, however, the focus of theoretical interest is to characterize the logical competence of the child (or the adult) or, less commitedly, those processes and abilities that lead him to behave competently in the situations considered. (The notion of competence raises definitional issues that will be discussed schematically in the final overview, and it is used here in a loose sense.) Those processes can be of a widely varied nature, and both areas exhibit a comparable range of theoretical positions differing by the degree of "logicality" assumed to characterize the task and/or the reasoning process hypothesized. In theoretical positions of the first kind, the subject's behavior (in either type of task) is assumed to be generated by some logical competence and processes that unquestionably qualify as logical; positions of the other variety assume the application of some pragmatic or content bound rules on the part of the subject, or reliance on concrete models of the problem, such as imagery. Such positions are sometimes opposed polemically inasmuch as they seem to respectively impute or deny the subject some reasonably general logical knowledge.

The sample of chapters in this volume is intended to illustrate this range of perspectives within the studies of adult reasoning, of "propositional" reasoning in children, and of children's reasoning in situations associated with the Piagetian tradition. It is also intended to cover the three major areas in the study of reasoning: reasoning with propositions, with quantifiers, and transitive inference.

Thus, Johnson-Laird proposes a model of propositional reasoning in adults that operates much in the same way as a theorem-proving machine though it uses patterns of inferences other than those prescribed by standard logic. The process described consists in a linguistic analysis of the problem, whereby the linguistic form of the premises is abstracted and subsequently operated upon by applying formal rules. Staudenmeyer, on the other hand, emphasizes the influence of pragmatic factors in the content of the premises with respect to the interpretation of otherwise identical connectives; the reasoning process is therefore intrinsically content bound, via the interpretation process. With regard to syllogistic reasoning, Revlis proposes a model involving an abstract mode of representation and a process of an algorithmic nature (though involving a faulty operation), whereas Johnson-Laird describes a process whereby the subject constructs individual examples representing the information in the premise and operates on these. In the area of propositional reasoning in children, Osherson describes a model, similar in nature to Johnson-Laird's, in which reasoning operates on the form of the statements, regardless of their content, and refers to supporting data from fourth to sixth graders. Falmagne, in contrast, proposes a reasoning process relying on imagery or a functionally equivalent concrete representation, for simple quantifier problems in first graders. Finally, as regards transitive inference, Youniss appeals to a Piagetian model in which inference is motivated by the child's operational capacity and is taken as an indicator of operational competence in the child, whereas Trabasso *et al.* describe a process in which the information in the premises is mapped into an imaginal model from which the conclusion of the syllogism can be subsequently read off.

Studies from both traditions face similar empirical issues in their efforts to ascribe the subject's logical knowledge in somewhat general terms, namely the dependence of performance on a multiplicity of task variables (for example, type of material or content) and the uncertainties in encoding of the information (in whatever form it is presented). Several chapters address this "representation" issue in various ways. The chapters by Neimark and Scribner have a different status from the ones mentioned above in that they provide data on the representation of the initial information in logical tasks, rather than focus on the reasoning process proper. Such findings are of crucial importance, as will be obvious when corresponding assumptions are made in the various models presented.

The sketchy description above, contrasting the basic features of the models contained in this volume is, for heuristic purposes, phrased more categorically than is warranted. Upon closer examination the ambiguities involved in characterizing a process as "logical" or not become apparent. Among other issues, the final chapter in this volume discusses those ambiguities and examines how logical competence is embodied in various ways in the various processes described.

REFERENCES

Inhelder, B., & Piaget, J. *The growth of logical thinking from childhood to adolescence.* New York: Basic Books, 1958.

Inhelder, B., & Piaget, J. *The early growth of logic in the child.* London: Routledge & Kegan Paul, 1964.

1
MODELS OF DEDUCTION

P. N. Johnson-Laird
University of Sussex

> Beyond the obvious facts that he has at some time done manual labour, that he takes snuff, that he is a Freemason, that he has been in China, and that he has done a considerable amount of writing lately, I can deduce nothing else.
>
> *Adventures of Sherlock Holmes*
> SIR ARTHUR CONAN DOYLE

It has become a truism that whatever else formal logic may be it is not a model of how people make inferences. It perhaps provides a standard, an ideal template, against which to assess the validity of inferences; and this view has a considerable appeal until one considers just which particular logic should play the role of the paragon. Logic is not a monolithic enterprise. There are many logics. Indeed, there are an infinite number of modal logics, a mere branch of the discipline. Although the different branches may be independent of one another, a choice of logic for, say, the temporal expressions of natural language is quite likely to have implications for a choice of logic for, say, such terms as "necessary" and "possible." Many of the different linguistic suburbs—tense markers, modal terms, connectives, quantifiers, and so on—are, for a logician, independent areas of interest; and, despite the surge of interest in them (e.g., Montague, 1970; Parsons, 1972), there is as yet no single comprehensive logic of natural language (just as there is as yet no complete grammar). It may even be supposed that no single coherent logic can suffice for all the ways in which language is used (van Fraassen, 1971). Yet, in spite of this reservation, a central question endures: are there any general ways of thinking that human beings follow when they make deductions?

The tenor of much recent psychological work provides a decidedly negative answer. The content of a reasoning problem seems to matter just as much as its logical structure, determining not only how a problem is represented but also the sorts of inferences that are made. Wason and Johnson-Laird (1972) have found evidence of such effects in a variety of tasks, ranging from the testing of hypotheses to reasoning with propositions. Such findings coincide with an increasingly popular conception of inference within artificial intelligence (AI).

One of the original aims of trying to program computers to carry out intelligent activities was to devise automatic methods of theorem proving. The intention was to devise programs that would both translate natural language into expressions of the predicate calculus and operate on these expressions with general theorem-proving procedures. Because it had long been established that there could be no algorithm for proof within the predicate calculus, much of this work was of a heuristic nature. Very often, however, methods devized in a heuristic spirit turned out to be more powerful. Some methods even guaranteed, if a theorem could be proved, to find a proof sooner or later. [There was, alas, no guarantee that the method would reveal, where appropriate, that it was impossible to derive a given conclusion; and this deficiency was the heart of Church's (1936) proof that there could be no general decision procedure for the predicate calculus.] It follows that general proof procedures have one glaring disadvantage: no matter how long they grind away at a problem, there is no way of knowing whether or not they will ultimately come up with a solution. If there is proof they will sooner or later discover it; but if there is no proof, they may never find out. Therefore, the impetus behind such sophisticated methods as the resolution principle and the hyperresolution principle (Robinson, 1965, 1966) was to increase the efficiency of programs so that they would find proofs, where they existed, within a reasonable amount of computing time. However, there is another difficulty with general proof procedures. Before they can go to work on a problem, it has to be represented in the predicate calculus; and it turns out that the business of translating natural language expressions into their appropriate symbolic form is extremely taxing. Ordinary language does not wear its logical heart on its sleeve, and there are often surprising divergences between the superficial form of an expression and its underlying logic. Once again, there is no known general procedure for carrying out correct translations (see Johnson-Laird, 1970).

One reaction to these difficulties has been to try a different tack. Instead of representing putative theorems in the notation of the predicate calculus and then grinding away at them with a general proof procedure, they are represented as programs. When such programs are executed they control the process of trying to discover the proof. This idea forms the basis of Hewitt's (1970) theorem-proving language PLANNER, which has been exploited so successfully in Winograd's (1972) program for understanding natural language. One obvious advantage of the method is that it allows information and deductive procedures, pertinent to the particular content of a problem, to be taken into account in the theorem-proving process. The system therefore gains greatly in efficiency; and, if the psychological experiments are to be believed, it is also a better model of the human deductive process. There is accordingly a general tendency in both psychological and AI circles to emphasize goal-oriented inferential procedures. This tendency is also evident in recent work on uniform proof procedures, especially in the development of predicate logic as a programming language (Kowalski, 1973). The aim of this chapter, however, is to attempt to redress the balance and to examine to what extent there may be general principles of thought that are independent of any particular problem domain. In examining this topic, three main sorts of inference are discussed: lexical reasoning, propositional reasoning, and reasoning with quantifiers. A few new experimental results are presented but the emphasis is on developing models of deduction.

LEXICAL REASONING

Perhaps the most obvious sort of inference—so obvious, in fact, that it is hardly noticed in ordinary discourse—involves simple relations between such lexical items as nouns, verbs, adjectives, etc. The meanings of words are, of course, often interrelated, and a speaker's knowledge of such interrelations acts very much as a smoothing oil to help the inferential machinery revolve. If, for example, a law states that all dog owners must pay a tax, then from the statement "He owns a poodle," it may readily be inferred, "He must pay the tax." From a formal point of view such an inference is invalid: it lacks the premise, "All poodles are dogs." In daily life, however, human beings do not behave like logicians; they know that poodles are dogs, and they exploit this knowledge without a thought to the canons of formal logic.

Logicians have tended to ignore this aspect of practical reasoning, although the device of meaning postulates (see Carnap, 1956; Bar-Hillel, 1967) was developed to deal with the logical consequences of the semantic relations between words. Psychologists, however, have recently been very active in investigating such relations under the guise of studying "semantic memory." A few salient points of these studies are perhaps worth delineating (for a more extensive review, see Johnson-Laird, 1974). The overwhelming majority of studies have concerned nouns and, in particular, the relation of class inclusion between them. They have shown that where there is a hierarchy of class inclusion, such as *poodle: dog: animal,* it may take time to grasp the transitivity of the relation. It may take time, in other words, to recover the fact that a poodle is an animal. A variety of competing theories have been proposed to explain this phenomenon (e.g., Collins & Quillian, 1969; Landauer & Meyer, 1972; Schaeffer & Wallace, 1970). None of these theories is entirely satisfactory, if only because there are occasions in which the transitive relation is easier to retrieve than its constituents, e.g., "a poodle is a mammal" is harder to verify than "a poodle is an animal" even though mammals are included in the class of animals (Rips, Shoben, & Smith, 1973). Nevertheless, it remains true that not all semantic relations are obtainable from the lexicon with the same ease. It is necessary to work, albeit for a few hundredths of a second, to retrieve more recondite relations. And such work, of course, has the logical form of an inference. Indeed, when Graham Gibbs and I gave subjects an inferential task, involving such material as

> Flowers are killed by this chemical spray.
> Therefore, roses are killed by this chemical spray.

We obtained results comparable to more conventional studies of semantic memory. In certain cases (e.g., *python: snake: reptile*) a transitive inference took longer than inferences involving its constituents; in other cases (e.g., *pine: conifer: tree*) a transitive inference took less time than the inferences involving its constituents.

What sort of semantic relations are there between the meanings of words? The simple relations include synonymy (e.g., *automobile–car*), antonymy (e.g., *man–woman*), and class inclusion (e.g., *dog–animal*); and these relations give rise to corresponding relations between sentences in which the words occur. It is no accident that studies of semantic memory have concentrated on class inclusion: it is a potent relation because it leads to transitive inferences. Similar transitive hierarchies can be generated by the relation of spatial inclusion and sometimes by the relation *part of*. However, the obvious source of transitive relations is comparative adjectives, e.g., *"larger than," "better than,"* and expressions of the general form *"more x than."* It is a simple matter to infer that if *a* is larger than *b*, and *b* is larger than *c*, than *a* is larger than *c*. However, so much controversy has arisen over various details of the process (see Huttenlocher & Higgins, 1971; Clark, 1971) that certain broader issues have been ignored in the quest to explain experimental findings. One such issue, the representation of the transitivity of a relational term, is considered below.

There are other patterns of lexical inference apart from transitivity. An intransitive relation (**R**), for instance, permits an inference of the form

$$a\mathbf{R}b \textit{ and } b\mathbf{R}c \qquad \therefore \textit{not } (a\mathbf{R}c)$$

The relation *"next in line to"* is obviously intransitive because if *a* is next in line to *b*, and *b* is next in line to *c*, then it follows that *a* is not next in line to *c*. A nontransitive relation, however, permits neither the transitive nor the intransitive inference; for example, if *a* is next to *b*, and *b* is next to *c*, then nothing follows about whether *a* is next to *c*—the items may be arranged in a circular fashion or in a line.

Another aspect of the logic of relations concerns symmetry. A relation is symmetrical if it permits an inference of the form

$$a\mathbf{R}b \qquad \therefore b\mathbf{R}a$$

The relation *next to* is symmetrical because if *a* is next to *b*, then it follows that *b* is next to *a*. A relation is asymmetrical if it permits an inference of the form

$$a\mathbf{R}b \qquad \therefore \textit{not } (b\mathbf{R}a)$$

The relation *on the right of* is clearly asymmetrical. A relation is nonsymmetrical if it permits neither of these inferences; the relation *nearest to* is clearly nonsymmetrical.

There are still other logical properties of relational terms, such as reflexitivity and connectivity, but their role in ordinary language appears to be negligible. However, because transitivity and symmetry are independent attributes, the lexicon already contains a variety of relations. They are exemplified in Table 1 by a set of spatial expressions.

The semantic representation of relational terms must include information about their transitivity and symmetry. For example, the representation of "beyond" must permit a transitive inference, whereas the representation of "nearest to" must prevent it. What has yet to be determined is precisely how this representation is effected. It is possible that each relational term has stored with it in the mental lexicon a simple tag indicating a transitivity value and another tag indicating a symmetry value. Where a term **R** is tagged as transitive, it permits an inference of the form

$$a\mathbf{R}b \textit{ and } b\mathbf{R}c \qquad \therefore a\mathbf{R}c$$

This conception evidently requires inference schemata to be separately specified as adjuncts to the lexicon. A more plausible system, however, renders the transitivity of a relation self-evident from its semantic specification,

TABLE 1
Spatial Expressions as Exemplars of the Logical Sorts of Binary Relations in Ordinary Language

	Transitive	Symmetric
In the same location as [as *x* as]	+	+
Beyond [more *x* than]	+	–
Not beyond [not more *x* than]	+	o
Next in line to	–	+
Directly on top of	–	–
Nearest to	–	o
Next to	o	+
On the right of	o	–
At	o	o

+transitive = transitive; –transitive = intransitive; o transitive = nontransitive;

+ symmetric = symmetric; – symmetric = asymmetric; o symmetric = nonsymmetric.

i.e., the conclusion *a***R***c* would be self-evident from the joint representation of *a***R***b* and *b***R***c*. A way of representing quantified statements (e.g., "All bankers are prudent men") with just this property is described below. The best evidence for this sort of representation for simple relational terms is provided by inference about spatial relations. Consider the following inference:

The box is on the right of the chair.
The ball is between the box and the chair.

Therefore, the ball is on the right of the chair.

The most likely way in which such an inference is made involves setting up an internal representation of the scene depicted by the premises. This representation may be a vivid image or a fleeting abstract delineation—its substance is of no concern. The crucial point is that its formal properties mirror the spatial relations of the scene so that the conclusion can be read off in almost as direct a fashion as from an actual array of objects. It may be objected, however, that such a depiction of the premises is unnecessary, that the inference can be made by an appeal to general principles, or rules of inference, which indicate that items related by *between* must be collinear, etc. However, this view—that relational terms are tagged according to the inference schemata they permit—founders on more complex inferences. An inference of the following sort, for instance, seems to be far too complicated to be handled without constructing an internal representation of the scene

> The black ball is directly beyond the cue ball. The green ball is on the right of the cue ball, and there is a red ball between them.
>
> ---
>
> Therefore, if I move so that the red ball is between me and the black ball, then the cue ball is on my left.

Even if it is possible to frame inference schemata that permit such an inference to be made without the construction of an internal representation, it is most unlikely that this approach is actually adopted in making the inference. The only rules of inference that are needed are a procedure for setting up a joint representation of separate assertions and a procedure for interrogating the joint representation. Much of the work can be done by the semantic information in the lexicon; and the same principle of allowing lexical information to specify directly the logic of a relation can apply equally well to abstract terms with meanings that are difficult or impossible to visualize directly. With concrete or abstract terms, the structure of a joint representation is isomorphic to its logic in a way that is exemplified below in the analysis of quantified inference.

Perhaps the most potent source of lexical inferences is the set of verbs of a language. The same sorts of relation obtain between them as between other lexical items—relations such as antonymy (e.g., *open–shut*), and class inclusion (e.g., *assassinate–murder–kill*). However, verbs can often be used to express relations between several arguments, rendering even the simple analysis of a relation and its converse (e.g., *buy–sell*) a complicated matter. The additional complexity of verbs does, indeed, lead to some interesting problems. Consider the following typical sorts of inference that depend on the meanings of verbs:

> Pat forced Dick to refrain from swearing.
> ∴ Dick refrained from swearing.
> ∴ Dick did not swear.
>
> Sam managed to prevent Dean from pretending to be naive.
> ∴ Sam prevented Dean from pretending to be naive.
> ∴ Dean did not pretend to be naive.
> ∴ Dean was not naive.
>
> John regretted that he had no chance to lie.
> ∴ John had no chance to lie.
> ∴ John did not lie.

These examples illustrate ways in which inferences may be drawn about the truth or falsity of a clause occurring as the complement of a verb. For example, if someone *forces* x to do z, then it may be inferred that x did z, whereas if someone *prevents* x from doing z, then it may be inferred that x did not do z. The validity of these inferences depends on the meaning of the verbs and, in particular, on the fact that their semantic representation contains a conjunction of separate elements of meaning. The essentially conjunctive nature of many verbs is perhaps more evident in the semantics of causal verbs:

He moved the table.
∴ He did something and consequently the table moved.

He showed us the picture.
∴ He did something and consequently we could see the picture.

He gave her the book.
He had the book and he did something and consequently she had the book.

The logic of these inferences can largely be captured by treating the concept of cause as a special sort of conjunction (see Miller & Johnson-Laird, 1975). Of course, it is very much more than a simple conjunction and seems to involve the following conditions in ordinary language (*pace* Dowty, 1972):

a caused *b* if and only if: (i) *a* happened;
(ii) *b* happened;
(iii) it is not possible for *a* to happen and *b* not to happen afterward.

The important point, however, is that it is seldom necessary to take the analysis so far in order to explain the inferential properties of causal verbs. A conjunctive analysis usually suffices.

In short, lexical reasoning is noteworthy not for the novelty of its patterns of inference but for the speed and smoothness with which its inferences occur. They are sometimes so immediate as to pass unnoticed. Their patterns include simple relational schemata and, especially in the case of verbs, simple propositional inferences.

PROPOSITIONAL REASONING

It has been realized since antiquity that one source of inferential relations is the manner in which sentences, or clauses, are combined. Language provides a variety of connectives, such as "and," "or," and "if," that can be used to combine clauses expressing propositions, e.g., "The boat has gone, *or else* it has been sunk *and* no trace of it can be found." To know what these connectives mean is tantamount to knowing how to draw certain inferences on the basis of the formal patterns in which they occur. For example, a speaker can hardly be said to have fully grasped the meaning of "or" unless he appreciates the validity of an inference such as

The boat has gone or else it has been sunk.
It has not been sunk.
Therefore, it has gone.

The logic of connectives has been most fully explored in the development of the propositional calculus. There are, in fact, a variety of different calculi and a variety of different ways of formulating them. However, a brief and informal exposition of the standard calculus will suffice here. If lower case letters are allowed to range over propositions, then the calculus can be formalized by specifying what counts as a well-formed formula, and by stating a set of axioms such as

1. $(p \text{ or } p) \rightarrow p$
2. $p \rightarrow (p \text{ or } q)$
3. $(p \text{ or } q) \rightarrow (q \text{ or } p)$
4. $(p \rightarrow q) \rightarrow [(r \text{ or } p) \rightarrow (r \text{ or } q)]$

where the arrow is a sign for material implication. In addition to the axioms, two rules of inference are necessary. The first rule of inference allows new formulas to be generated by substituting any well-formed formula for a propositional variable in an expression, and the second rule of inference, the so-called law of *modus ponens,* may be stated as follows:

From a formula A together with a formula *if* A *then* B, the formula B may be deduced.

It is fairly simple to show that these axioms and rules suffice to derive all the formulas that are true on the logical interpretations of the connectives.

What does such a system state about the reasoning of intelligent but logically naive persons? The answer must surely be: very little. However, it is worth dwelling on the system for a moment because at least one influential psychologist, Piaget, has used it as the basis of a model of reasoning (Beth & Piaget, 1966) and because the contrast between it and ordinary deduction is instructive.

Among the more obvious difficulties of using the propositional calculus as a model of ordinary deduction is the fact that its connectives can stand only between fully fledged propositions. In ordinary language simple constituents, such as noun phrases, may be linked by a connective. A sentence such as

Mark and Anne are excellent riders

is easily translated into a form suitable for the calculus:

Mark is an excellent rider and Anne is an excellent rider.

However, there is no comparable procedure for dealing with such sentences as:

Mark and Anne make a splendid couple.

This sentence must be treated as a single proposition. Another difficulty, of course, is that the calculus is truth functional: the meaning of its connectives is defined purely in terms of the truth value they give to a complex proposition as a function of the truth values of its constituents. The multifarious connectives of ordinary language (e.g., *because, before, although*) cannot be completely captured in a purely truth-functional calculus. Nor, indeed, can the logic of commands or questions be immediately accommodated within its essentially assertive framework.

A further divergence between logical calculi and the inferential machinery of everyday life concerns their respective functions. Calculi are devised primarily for deriving logical truths. The aim of practical inference, however, is not to prove theorems but to pass from one contingent statement to another. Therefore, practical inference is likely to involve few, if any, axioms but a relatively large number of rules of inference. A formulation of the calculus that is therefore more appropriate abandons axioms in favor of a system of rules analogous to Gentzen's method of "natural" deduction, an approach that has had some influence in the development of theorem-proving programs (e.g., Amarel, 1967; Reiter, 1973). A system of natural deduction involves the specification of rules of inference in a schematic form. The rule of *modus ponens,* for example, is stated in the following schema:

$$\frac{A \qquad \textit{If A then B}}{\therefore B}$$[1]

where the premises appear above the line and the conclusion appears below it. A parsimonious system, of course, stipulates the minimum number of such schemata from which all the others can be derived. For instance, negation and disjunction may be taken as primitive, inference rules stipulated for them, and the remaining connectives simply defined in terms of negation and disjunction. From a psychological point of view, however, it would be foolish to seek parsimony at the expense of plausibility. What is needed is a set of psychologically basic patterns of inference.

Any decision about whether a pattern of inference is psychologically basic is ultimately an empirical matter. It is necessary to find out whether the inference is in the immediate repertoire of mature but logically naive persons. An inference schema can hardly be considered as basic if most people are incapable of carrying it out or can only do so in a matter of minutes, subsequently giving a detailed resumé of a whole chain of deductions they have carried out to make the inference. Unfortunately, there is not enough evidence to determine the definitive set of basic patterns of inference. What can be done, however, is to build up a plausible first approximation to it, taking care not to include any inferential schema known to cause difficulty to logically naive subjects. The fact that an inference is feasible for the majority of people suggests that it is basic but is hardly a decisive proof: the inference may be the result of combining several other inferences. Only those inferences that seem *prima facie* to be basic are therefore included in the following set, but in many cases the final decision must depend on further investigations.

Some extremely simple inferences are considered first. It is obvious that from a clause expressing the meaning A one can immediately deduce a clause expressing the same meaning, A. (This way of writing in terms of clauses expressing meanings is excessively cumbersome; from now on I shall write simply of propositions, although it must not be forgotten that I am dealing with inferences expressed in natural language.) Similarly, the conclusion A can be immediately deduced from a proposition of the form A or A. These inferences are summarized in the following schemata:

$$\frac{A}{\therefore A} \tag{1}$$

$$\frac{A \text{ or } A}{\therefore A} \tag{2}$$

Although inferences of this sort may sometimes rely on complex lexical inferences, their structure is very simple and can hardly be derived from anything more basic. The question is whether these inferences may not be too trivial to be useful. In fact, they do have a role to play, and a model of propositional inference is defective without them.

The same may be said about some further schemata. The first pair permit a proposition to be inferred from its occurrence in a conjunction:

$$\frac{A \text{ and } B}{\therefore A} \tag{3a}$$

$$\frac{A \text{ and } B}{\therefore B} \tag{3b}$$

The second pair permit a disjunction to be inferred from either one of its constituents:

$$\frac{A}{\therefore A \text{ or } B} \tag{4a}$$

$$\frac{A}{\therefore B \text{ or } A} \tag{4b}$$

The third pair permit a conjunction to be inferred from the independent occurrence of its constituents:

$$\frac{A \qquad B}{\therefore A \text{ and } B} \tag{5a}$$

$$\frac{A \qquad B}{\therefore B \text{ and } A} \tag{5b}$$

And the final pair permit negated conjunctions to be deduced:

$$\frac{A \text{ and not } -B}{\therefore \text{ not both } A \text{ and } B} \tag{6a}$$

$$\frac{\text{not } -A \text{ and } B}{\therefore \text{ not both } A \text{ and } B} \tag{6b}$$

A real problem with these simple patterns of inference is to find a suitable way to curb their productivity. As a number of authors have recently pointed out, there are constraints on what can reasonably be expressed in the form of a conjunction or a disjunction. It may be true, for example, that boys eat apples, and that Mary threw a stone at the frog, but the conjunction

Boys eat apples and Mary threw a stone at the frog

is, as Lakoff (1971) argues, barely acceptable. It is customary to suit an utterance to its context, and this principle applies to the relations between clauses as well as to the relations between sentences. Hence, if a speaker follows one clause with another explicitly specifying what seems to have been taken for granted, then he creates an extremely odd conjunction, e.g.,

> John ran out of the house and he got out of bed (Johnson-Laird, 1969a).
> All of John's children are bald and John has children (Karttunen, 1973).

The existence of constraints on the topics of conjunctions and disjunctions can hardly be doubted. Indeed, the constraints on "but" proved sufficient for that conjunction to be used by Bendix (1966) as the basis of a semantic test. However, there is no adequate explication of a complete set of constraints. One solution is therefore to do away with the simple inference schemata that give rise to the free combination of propositions in conjunctions and disjunctions. Unfortunately, it is impossible to do without these rules of inference. They are needed in order to make such deductions as

> It is frosty.
> If it is foggy or frosty, then the game will be canceled.
> ---
> Therefore, the game will be canceled.

For the time being, schemata (1) to (6) shall be called "auxiliary inferences," for reasons that will become clear when the method of curbing their power is described.

In contrast to the auxiliary inferences, there are a number of primary patterns of inference that have no restrictions placed on them. There is among them the familiar pattern exemplified in the following inference:

> John is intelligent or he is rich.
> He is not rich.
> ---
> Therefore, he is intelligent.

There is good reason to suppose that its underlying schema

$$\frac{A \text{ or } B \qquad \text{not} - A}{\therefore B} \tag{7a}$$

$$\frac{A \text{ or } B \qquad \text{not} - B}{\therefore A} \tag{7b}$$

is basic. A study by Hill (cited in Suppes, 1965) found that 82% of a sample of 6-year-old children were able to make the inference correctly.

Johnson-Laird and Tridgell (1972) found that it led to errors only when the negative occurred in the disjunctive premise, e.g.,

> John is intelligent or he is not rich.
> He is rich.

With premises of this sort, some of their adult subjects inferred that John was not intelligent, whereas other subjects considered that no conclusion followed from the premises. Such a finding suggests, however, not that the schema is intrinsically difficult but that an unusual placement of negative information can disturb its smooth execution.

The patterns of inference in (7) are valid both for an inclusive disjunction, where both constituent propositions can be true, and for an exclusive disjunction, where this possibility is ruled out. There is a further rule of inference that applies only to exclusive disjunctions, e.g.,

> Either Mary is a plagiarist or else she is a genius (but not both).
> She is a genius.
>
> ---
> Therefore, she is not a plagiarist.

The real force of this inference derives from the exclusivity of the two propositions in the disjunction. It is therefore plausible that the basic inferential schema should be formulated in the following way:

$$\frac{\textit{Not both A and B} \qquad A}{\therefore \textit{ not} - B} \tag{8a}$$

$$\frac{\textit{Not both A and B} \qquad B}{\therefore \textit{ not} - A} \tag{8b}$$

The main candidate for a basic pattern of inference involving the conditional is *modus ponens:*

$$\frac{A \qquad \textit{If A then B}}{\therefore B} \tag{9}$$

There is considerable evidence to suggest that this schema is basic, whereas a closely related pattern, known as *modus tollendo tollens*, is not (see Wason & Johnson-Laird, 1972). The latter inference has the following form:

$$\frac{\textit{Not} - B \qquad \textit{If A then B}}{\therefore \textit{ not} - A}$$

Intelligent subjects can make inferences of this sort but they tend to do so with a greater difficulty than with *modus ponens* and it is natural to suppose that they are carrying out a sequence of inferential steps rather than a single inference. They may, in fact, be arguing in the following way:

> If the safe is locked, then this light is on.
> This light is not on.
>
> ---
>
> Suppose the safe is locked.
> It follows then that the light is on (by *modus ponens*).
> But the light is not on (from the premise).
> Therefore, the assumption leads to an impossible, contradictory state of affairs.
> Therefore, the assumption is false: the safe is not locked.

This sort of argument is, of course, a *reductio ad absurdum* and requires an inferential schema of the form

$$\frac{A \textit{ implies } (B \textit{ and not } -B)}{\therefore \textit{ not } -A} \tag{10}$$

It is certainly true that logically naive persons can argue by a *reductio* (Evans, 1972); and it can be accepted as basic instead of *modus tollendo tollens,* although a completely convincing justification for this choice cannot be established at present.

There are two subsidiary points about the *reductio* schema in (10). First, a conditional may equally well have been used in place of the implication, because if one proposition can be derived from another, then this fact can be expressed by a conditional

$$\frac{A \textit{ implies } B}{\therefore \textit{ If } A \textit{ then } B} \tag{11}$$

Second, where a *reductio* is used to establish the falsity of a negative proposition, it is necessary to be able to eliminate the resulting double negation, e.g., "It isn't the case that 5 is not odd" becomes "5 is odd." A simple schema makes this elimination possible:

$$\frac{\textit{not not } -A}{\therefore A} \tag{12}$$

Its seeming simplicity, however, may be deceptive. At least one school of logicians, the intuitionists, have excluded this rule from their canon. These logicians, represented by Heyting (1956), are primarily worried about certain sorts of mathematical reasoning. In particular, they are concerned with inferences involving infinite sets and argue that such inferences must involve constructive and intuitive principles. They claim that it is not sufficient, in order to demonstrate the existence of a mathematical property, to show that its universal denial leads to a contradiction. Hence, the intuitionists reject the law of the excluded middle, i.e., the principle that either a proposition or its negation is true. They consequently reject the related principle for eliminating double negations. The relation between the intuitionist and the classical calculus of propositions is not so straightforward as might be imagined; Gödel (1933) has shown that the classical calculus can nevertheless be treated as contained within the intuitionistic calculus! It shall be assumed here, however, that the elimination of double negations is a feature of ordinary reasoning.

The dozen inference schemata that have now been stated constitute a plausible set of psychologically basic patterns of deduction. There are other forms of inference that, although probably not basic, are well within the competence of most people, and a way must certainly be found for incorporating them into the model. One example of such an inference is the *simple dilemma,* e.g.,

The President is dishonest or he is incompetent.
If the President is dishonest, then he will be forced to resign.
If the President is incompetent, then he will be forced to resign.

Therefore, the President will be forced to resign.

Such an argument places an adversary literally on the horns of a dilemma, because no matter which of the alternatives he chooses from the initial disjunction, he is forced to accept the same conclusion. The rhetorical force of such arguments was, indeed, recognized by Cicero (see Kneale & Kneale, 1962; p. 178). However, the argument can be considered, for psychological purposes, as merely a special case of a more general pattern of inference:

$$\frac{A \text{ or } B \qquad \text{If } A \text{ then } C \qquad \text{If } B \text{ then } D}{\therefore C \text{ or } D}$$

If C is substituted for D in this schema, then the derived conclusion becomes C or C, and this conclusion, in turn, is immediately reducible to C by an auxiliary inference. It is feasible that the simple dilemma is derived in this way from the more general argument. A comparable chain of inference, which indeed is not logically independent of the general dilemma, is the so-called *hypothetical syllogism.* This pattern of inference makes explicit the transitivity of conditional propositions

$$\frac{\text{If } A \text{ then } B \qquad \text{If } B \text{ then } C}{\therefore \text{If } A \text{ then } C}$$

Obviously, a way must be found to insure that the model permits such inferences to be drawn.

There are a number of simple equivalences that cannot be established by the present rules of inference, e.g., "Neither John can come nor Mary can leave" is equivalent to "John can't come and Mary can't leave." It would be a simple matter to introduce schemata for them, but it would be slightly odd to treat such relations by way of rules of propositional inference. A more sensible solution is to assume that inferences based on synonymy are just special cases of the schema $A / \therefore A$, and that synonymy is established on linguistic grounds. In other words, the complete mechanism of lexical inference is at the disposal of the propositional machinery. Indeed, it may be said that reasoning with propositions is simply a matter of grasping the meaning of those lexical items that happen to be connectives. This view is certainly suggested by considering the question of how patterns of inference are acquired in the first place. Where, indeed, do they come from? And how are they fitted together into a coherent system? One plausible conjecture is that the basis of the whole process is the acquisition of the truth conditions of the various connectives. Perhaps this notion should be broadened to include the extensional conditions for commands and questions, etc.; however, for the sake of simplicity only the truth conditions of assertions shall be considered here.

In the standard formalizations of the propositional calculus, including the method of natural deduction, nothing explicit is said about the truth conditions of the various connectives. When the calculus has been axiomatized, a *theorem* is defined as a formula that can be derived from the axioms by the rules of inference. This sort of definition, and the equivalent sort for the method of natural deduction, is essentially formal: it provides purely syntactic criteria, pertaining solely to the manipulation of symbols, for what counts as a theorem. It is also possible, however, to define a *valid* formula—a formula that is a logical truth. The usual way of carrying out such a definition, as demonstrated below, is to set up a semantical model in the spirit of Tarski (1956). This model may be treated as a mathematical entity involving certain marks on paper, such as "T" and "F," or alternatively it may be interpreted so as to involve certain concepts, such as truth and falsity. Logically speaking, a crucial issue is whether the calculus is complete. A proof of its completeness amounts to showing that the set of formulas derivable from the axioms is one and the same as the set of valid formulas defined by the semantical model. It is a fairly simple matter to show that the standard formalizations of the propositional calculus are, indeed, complete.

The issue of completeness has no obvious counterpart in the psychological modeling of inference. The reason it disappears is, in my view, simply that the whole system is semantically based. The conditions in which conjunctions, disjunctions, etc., are true and false are learned and, from these conditions, the basic patterns of inference are derived. A competent adult therefore has at his disposal both the inference schemata and their underlying semantic basis.

The development of a semantical model for the propositional calculus typically involves the following sorts of conditions:

1. A negative proposition, *not A*, is true if and only if *A* is false.
2. A conjunction, *A and B,* is true if and only if *A* is true and *B* is true.
3. A disjunction, *A or B*, is true if and only if *A* is true or *B* is true.

There are two difficulties, however, one linguistic and the other metalinguistic, in regarding such principles as part of a psychological basis for the semantics of connectives.

The metalinguistic difficulty is caused simply by the lack of any obvious psychological correlate of the logician's distinction between an object language and a metalanguage. In the truth conditions above, the reader will have noticed that the connectives themselves actually occur as part of their own definitions. Logically, there is nothing objectionable in this practice because the conditions for the object language connectives are being stated in a quite separate language, the metalanguage. However, it is rather unfortunate that this metalanguage turns out to be ordinary English. If it is claimed that learning the truth conditions of ordinary connectives amounts to learning rules of the sort illustrated above, then a vicious circle is created because these rules presuppose a knowledge of the meaning of ordinary connectives. This problem seems to have been overlooked by many of the linguists engaged in setting up semantical bases for natural language (e.g., Keenan, 1970). Its solution presumably involves some more abstract form of mental representation for metalinguistic information about natural language.

The linguistic difficulty with the semantical rules concerns the interpretation of conditional statements and it goes to the heart of the problem of using the propositional calculus as the basis of a psychological model. Conditionals in ordinary language are, of course, capable of a great many different sorts of interpretation. They may be used to state temporal, causal, or logical relations between propositions. It is only relatively rarely that they fit the requirements of the calculus, for example, in conveying a material implication. Such an implication is true provided its antecedent is false or provided its consequent is true, e.g., "If this picture isn't by Picasso, then it's by Braque." The majority of everyday conditionals, however, are not rendered true merely by establishing that their antecedents are false. A statement such as "If this picture is by Picasso, then it was painted in 1910" is simply irrelevant—neither true nor false—if the picture in question turns out not to be by Picasso. It is one of the fictions of the propositional calculus as a model of ordinary deduction that propositions always have a truth value. The calculus does not permit truth-value gaps.

The distinction between a material implication and a conditional with a truth-value gap may be considered trivial. In fact, however, it leads to a clear divergence between the logical calculus and ordinary inference. The following bizarre inference for instance, counts as valid if conditional statements are treated as material implications:

> You can't both hate Mailer and admire him.
> If you hate Mailer, then you will soon give up reading his work.
> If you admire Mailer, then you will read his entire works.
> ---
> Therefore, if you hate Mailer you will read his entire works, or if you admire Mailer you will soon give up reading his work.

The validity of the argument turns simply on the fact that a material implication is true whenever its antecedent is false, and one of the two conditional antecedents in the conclusion must be false according to the first premise.

A more plausible account of conditionals should permit them to lack a truth value. The semantical rule for the conditional connective might then be stated as

> A conditional *if A then B* has a truth value if and only if *A* is true; and it is true if and only if *B* is true.

The trouble with this analysis, however, is that it leaves out of account the strong intuition that there should usually be some sort of connection between *A* and *B* in order for a conditional of the form *If A then B* to be true. It also, of course, runs entirely counter to the evaluation of many conditionals that, *ex hypothesi,* have antecedents that are false or as yet unfulfilled, e.g., such counterfactual conditionals as "If Hitler had been a successful painter, then World War II would not have occurred," and such conjectural conditionals as "If the Russians invade West Germany, then World War III will occur." Evidently, these conditionals are not truth functional.

What happens when you evaluate a conditional appears to depend on whether or not you already assent to its antecedent, and whether or not you already assent to its consequent. As Ramsey (1950) pointed out long ago, if you have no view about the antecedent, then for the sake of argument you add it to your set of beliefs and then consider whether or not the consequent is true. This judgment is in turn reflected back to your evaluation of the conditional as a whole. In contrast, if you happen already to believe that the antecedent is true, then your task is simply to evaluate the consequent. A problem arises, however, if you happen already to believe that the antecedent is false. Its solution, as Stalnaker (1968) has shown, is simply to add the antecedent to your beliefs for the sake of argument and then to make minimal changes in your other beliefs in order to maintain consistency. The way is then clear for you to evaluate the consequent in the light of these hypothetical assumptions. Your decision about the consequent must obviously take into account any views you have about a causal connection, or any other sort of connection, between the antecedent and consequent.

Your prior attitude to the consequent of the conditional obviously plays a part in these proceedings. If you happen already to believe that it is true and can continue to do so in the light of your treatment of the antecedent, then you may very well assent to the conditional even if there appears to be little connection between its antecedent and consequent. In contrast, if you happen already to believe that the consequent is false and continue to do so in the light of your treatment of the antecedent, then you must evaluate the conditional as false. Finally, if you have no prior views about the consequent, your evaluation of it must depend on what connections, if any, you establish between it and the antecedent.

This unified approach to the evaluation of conditionals can be precisely formulated in terms of a semantical model resting on the notion of a "posible state of affairs" (see Stalnaker, 1968). Its details are not of concern here because their psychological realization is more plausibly thought of as a set of procedures for making assumptions, eliminating inconsistencies, and so on. The crux of the matter is simply that although such connectives as the conditional are not truth functional, their role in deductions can nevertheless be modeled by inference schemata. Rules of inference may, indeed, be learned by considering truth conditions but they can be applied without reference to them.

The present set of inference schemata are still deficient as a psychological model, because the power of the auxiliary rules of inference has yet to be curbed. The method that shall be adopted here depends on the idea of modeling the machinery of ordinary deductive inference by a set of computer-like procedures, an idea that goes back to the work of Miller, Galanter, and Pribram (1960), and Newell, Shaw, and Simon (see Newell & Simon, 1972). This conception of a program of interrelated deductive procedures has many advantages, not least that it provides a straightforward way of making auxiliary inferences dependent on primary inferences. The basic idea is simply that an auxiliary inference can be made only as

TABLE 2
The Set of Auxiliary Inferences

	Premises	Conclusions
1.	*A*	*A*
2.	*A* or *A*	*A*
3.	*A* and *B*	*A*
	A and *B*	*B*
4.	*A*	*A* or *B*
	A	*B* or *A*
5.	*A B*	*A* and *B*
	A B	*B* and *A*
6.	*A* and not *B*	Not both *A* and *B*
	Not *A* and *B*	Not both *A* and *B*
11.	*A* implies *B*	If *A* then *B*
12.	Not not *A*	*A*

a necessary precursor to a primary inference: it is an auxiliary aid that prepares the way for a primary inference. An example of the process may clarify the relation between the two sorts of inference.

Suppose that the deductive program is given the goal to make an inference from two premises of the form:

A and C
If A then B

It is obvious that no initial conclusion can be derived using a primary inference because instead of a simple categorical premise *A*, required by *modus ponens,* there is only the conjunction *A and C*. However, because this conjunction is linked to a constituent of the conditional, i.e., they contain the proposition *A* in common, a subgoal can be set up to derive *A* from the first premise, *A and C*. The primary inferences are no help here but an auxiliary inference allows the inference to be made. Once the auxiliary inference is made, the way is clear to deduce the conclusion *B* using a primary inference.

It may be helpful at this point to summarize the two sorts of inference schemata. The auxiliary inferences are stated in Table 2. The primary inference schemata, however, are more conveniently summarized in the form of Table 3. This format enables procedures to be devised that allow access to the table by way of a premise or by way of a conclusion.

TABLE 3
The Set of Primary Inferences

Complex premise	Categorical premise: *A*	Not *A*	*B*	Not *B*
7. *A* or *B*		*B*		*A*
8. Not both *A* and *B*	Not *B*		Not *A*	
9. If *A* then *B*	*B*			? (Not *A*)

The cell entries give the form of the conclusion deduced from that particular combination of complex and categorical premise. The "?" refers to the *modus tollendo tollens* inference, which may be made directly but, as was argued in the text, is likely to involve a more complex procedure.

A more general statement of the relation between primary and auxiliary inferences is given in Fig. 1. This flow diagram is a simplified model of informal propositional inference. Its power is limited because the program terminates as soon as it succeeds in making a primary inference. However, its general principle is instructive. When a primary inference fails, a test is made to see whether it has failed because there has been a mismatch between the categorical premise and the relevant constituent of the complex

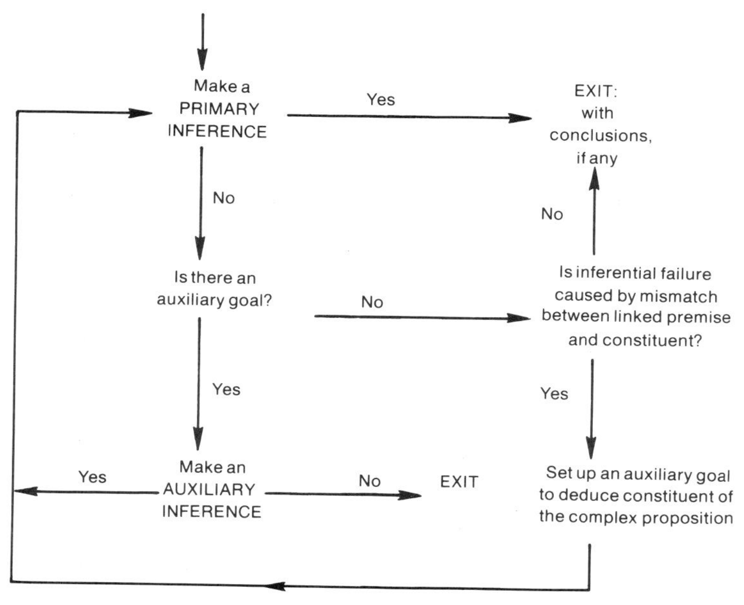

FIG. 1. A simplified model of propositional inference.

premise. If there is such a mismatch, an auxiliary goal is set up to infer the constituent from the categorical premise. If there is no such mismatch, the program can go no further. It is only when an auxiliary goal is set up that it becomes possible to try an auxiliary inference; and an auxiliary goal is only set up in order to try to make a primary inference. An everyday corollary of this relation is that auxiliary deductions do not normally occur in isolation, e.g., it is odd to argue "John's children are grown up," therefore, "John's children are grown up or it is raining in Manchester."

The model described in Fig. 1 is, of course, much less flexible than a human reasoner. Even if it were equipped to deal systematically with several premises, it would be unable to make certain complex deductions in more than one way. For example, faced with premises of the following form:

not D
C or D
A
If A and C then B

the program could deduce the conclusion *B* by proceeding in this fashion:

Make a primary inference from *not D*, and *C or D,* to *C*.
Attempt a primary inference from *C*, and *If A and C, then B*.
Set up an auxiliary goal to infer *A and C*.
Make an auxiliary inference from *A*, and *C*, to *A and C*.
Make a primary inference from *A and C,* and the conditional premise, to *B*.

However, if it attempts to proceed in this fashion,

Attempt a primary inference from *A*, and *If A and C, then B*.
Set up an auxiliary goal to infer *A and C*.

its failure is abrupt because in this case the auxiliary goal cannot be achieved by either a primary or an auxiliary inference. A human reasoner is unlikely to have too much difficulty in completing the chain of inference. What defeats the program is its lack of ability to set itself complex auxiliary goals requiring several inferences for their satisfaction. It cannot, in attempting to deduce *A and C*, set about trying to derive first *A*, and then *C*. Because this procedure is likely to place a considerable load on working memory, it will be interesting to know whether children are capable of it. Indeed, once a suitable modification to the program is made, a danger of the opposite sort is encountered. The program has no limit on the degree of recursion that can occur, whereas a human reasoner can presumably

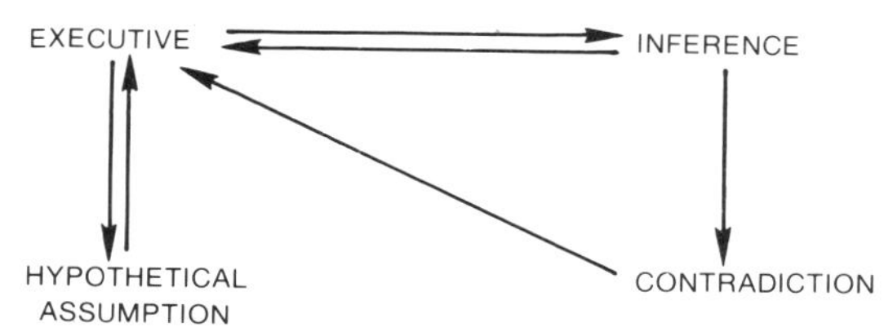

FIG. 2. The interrelations between the four components of the complete model of propositional inference.

tolerate only a certain degree. Such a limit can easily be introduced into the program, but what is humanly tolerable is an empirical matter that has yet to be determined.

A further severe limitation of the model is that it is totally incapable of making certain sorts of inference. It cannot make a deduction by a *reductio ad absurdum;* it cannot construct a hypothetical syllogism; and it cannot resolve a dilemma. These inferences require, first, a procedure that makes hypothetical assumptions and, second, a procedure that is sensitive to contradictions. In order to incorporate these procedures, however, it is necessary to consider the organization of a more complete model of deduction.

The complete model consists of four main components: an executive that controls the various attempts to make inferences, an inferential component that carries out primary and auxiliary inferences, a component for making hypothetical assumptions, and a component for detecting contradictions. The interrelations between these components are summarized in Fig. 2. The executive component, which is shown in Fig. 3, organizes the process of inference. When there are premises but no particular inferential goal, then the executive sets up a goal to make a deduction from the premises and then passes control to the inferential component. If an inference is made, then generally a new goal is created to try to deduce something from its conclusion. However, if no inference can be made, the executive passes control to the procedure that makes hypothetical assumptions. Only when the executive component runs out of premises to try does it cease to make any further attempts at inference.

The inferential component closely resembles the simplified model of inference. It has, as Fig. 4 shows, two main modifications. First, whenever a primary inference is made, control passes to the procedure for detecting contradictions. Second, a routine has been introduced for setting up complex auxiliary goals, thus remedying a major defect of the simplified model.

The procedure for making hypothetical assumptions will be grossly inefficient if it selects them at random, because it may take a long time to discover a fruitful assumption. The obvious heuristic is to find a proposition,

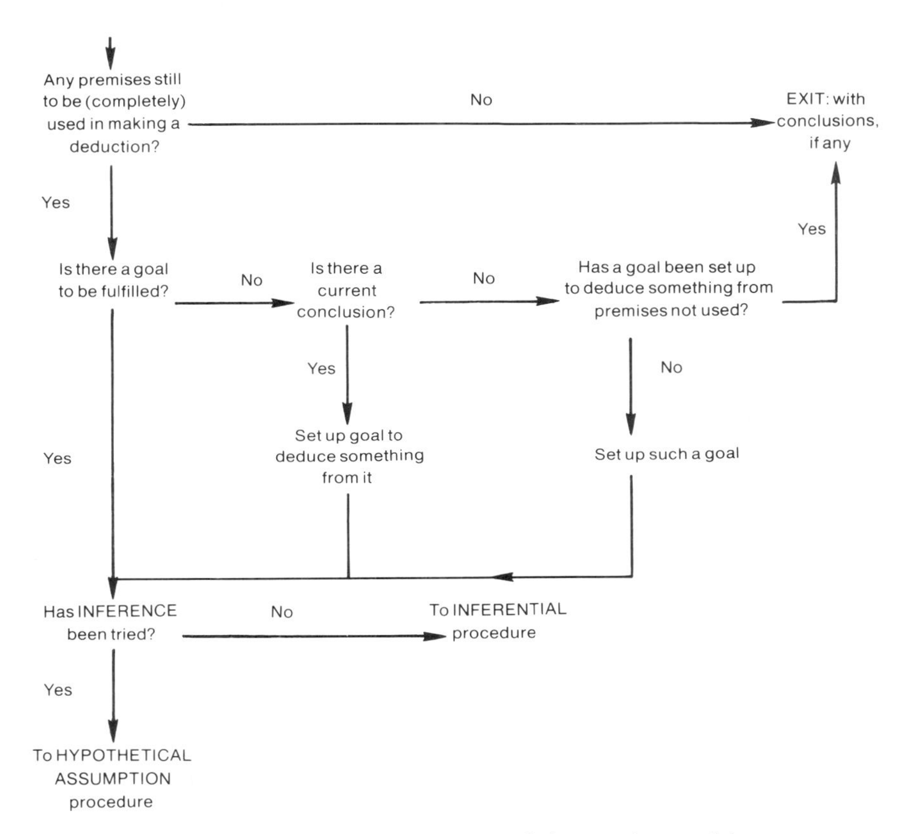

FIG. 3. The executive component of the complete model.

either a premise or a conclusion previously inferred, with an overall form that corresponds to one of the complex propositions of a primary inference, and then to assume an appropriate categorical premise (see Osherson, this volume). The form of this categorical premise can easily be ascertained by examining the primary inference decision table. For example, suppose that there is a premise of the form *If A or C, then B,* then it is clear from Table 3 that a conclusion can be drawn from this premise provided there is a categorical assertion of its antecedent. Therefore, it is this antecedent, *A or C,* that must be assumed. When one returns with this assumption to the inferential program, a primary inference yields the conclusion *B*.

It is important to keep track of an assumption because, unless it can be independently inferred, any conclusion based on it cannot be asserted categorically: all that can be asserted is that the assumption implies the

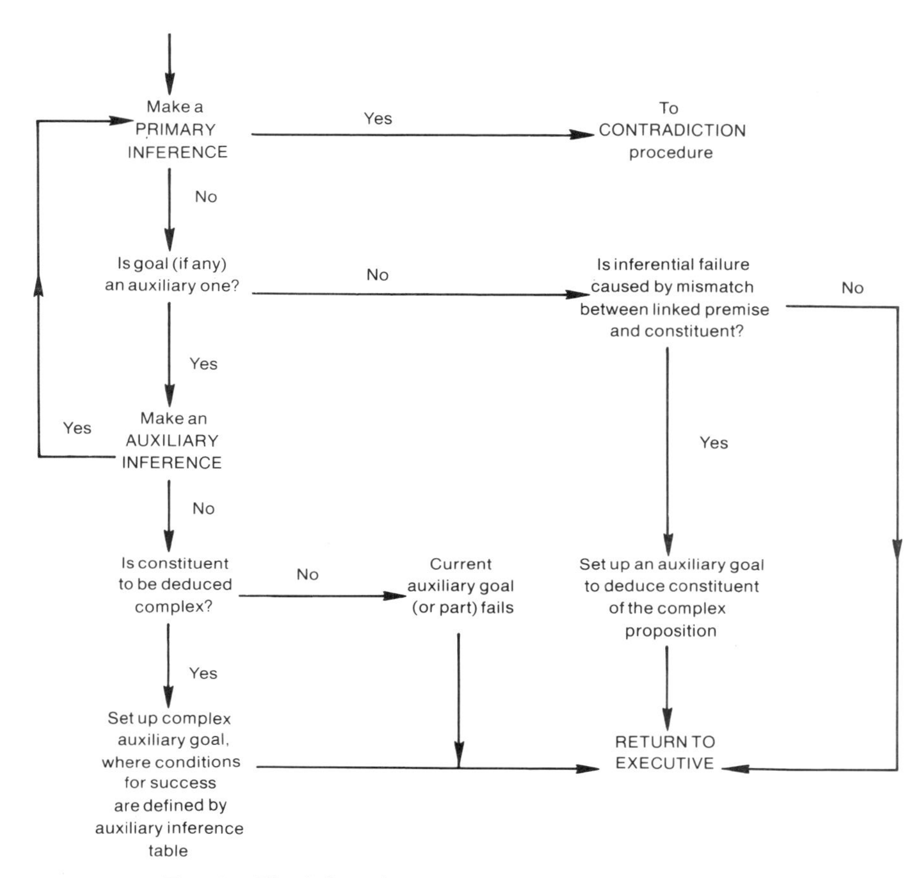

FIG. 4. The inferential component of the complete model.

conclusion. Where an assumption *A* implies a conclusion *B*, the program concludes, by an auxiliary inference, *If A then B,* One obvious moral is that it is no use making an assumption if it leads to no more than this initial deduction. For example, with a premise of the form. *If A then B,* the assumption of *A* can be used to deduce *B*, but if nothing else follows, the auxiliary inference leads merely to *If A then B,* a conclusion that is no more than what was known from the start. The hypothetical procedure has accordingly the capability of setting up a series of goals once an assumption has been made. The first goal is both to deduce a conclusion from the hypothetical assumption and to make a further inference from this conclusion. A failure to achieve this goal is made manifest if the hypothetical procedure is reentered with it, for such an event can only occur if the program has failed to make a primary inference. However, if at least an initial conclusion has been drawn, then a second goal can be set up to deduce a contradiction to it. In other words, the first goal may lead to a hypothetical syllogism, and the second goal to a *reductio ad absurdum.*

If the hypothetical procedure is reentered with the second goal, then it too must be abandoned in favor of a third goal. This situation may arise, for example, in the case of premises with the form of a dilemma:

A or B
If A then C
If B then D

The program may have proceeded as follows:

Assume *A*.
Make the primary inference *A*, *if A then C,* therefore *C*.
Attempt to deduce something from *C* (first hypothetical goal).
Attempt to deduce *not C* (second hypothetical goal).

Evidently, what is needed at this point is another assumption, but not just any assumption will do. A useful heuristic is to find another premise in which the original assumption also occurs and then to make a hypothetical assumption of its remaining major constituents:

Find A or B
Assume B

The third hypothetical goal is to deduce something from this assumption. This goal is fulfilled in the example:

Make the primary inference *B, If B then D,* therefore *D*.

Subsequently, the conclusion based on the assumption of *B* will be combined with the conclusion based on the assumption of *A*, and the combination will have the same logic as the premise in which both *A* and *B* occurred. Because this premise was *A or B,* the final conclusion will be *C or D*. The machinery for generating this conclusion, and the other sorts of hypothetical conclusion, is more conveniently located in the procedure for detecting contradictions. The procedure for making hypothetical assumptions is summarized in Fig. 5.

Whenever a primary inference is made, control passes to the procedure for dealing with contradictions that is summarized in Fig. 6. Contradictions that stem from an assumption are taken to imply the negation of that assumption, according to the *reductio* schema. If no assumption has been made, however, it follows that the premises are inconsistent. A conclusion cannot be categorically asserted unless it is established that it is not based

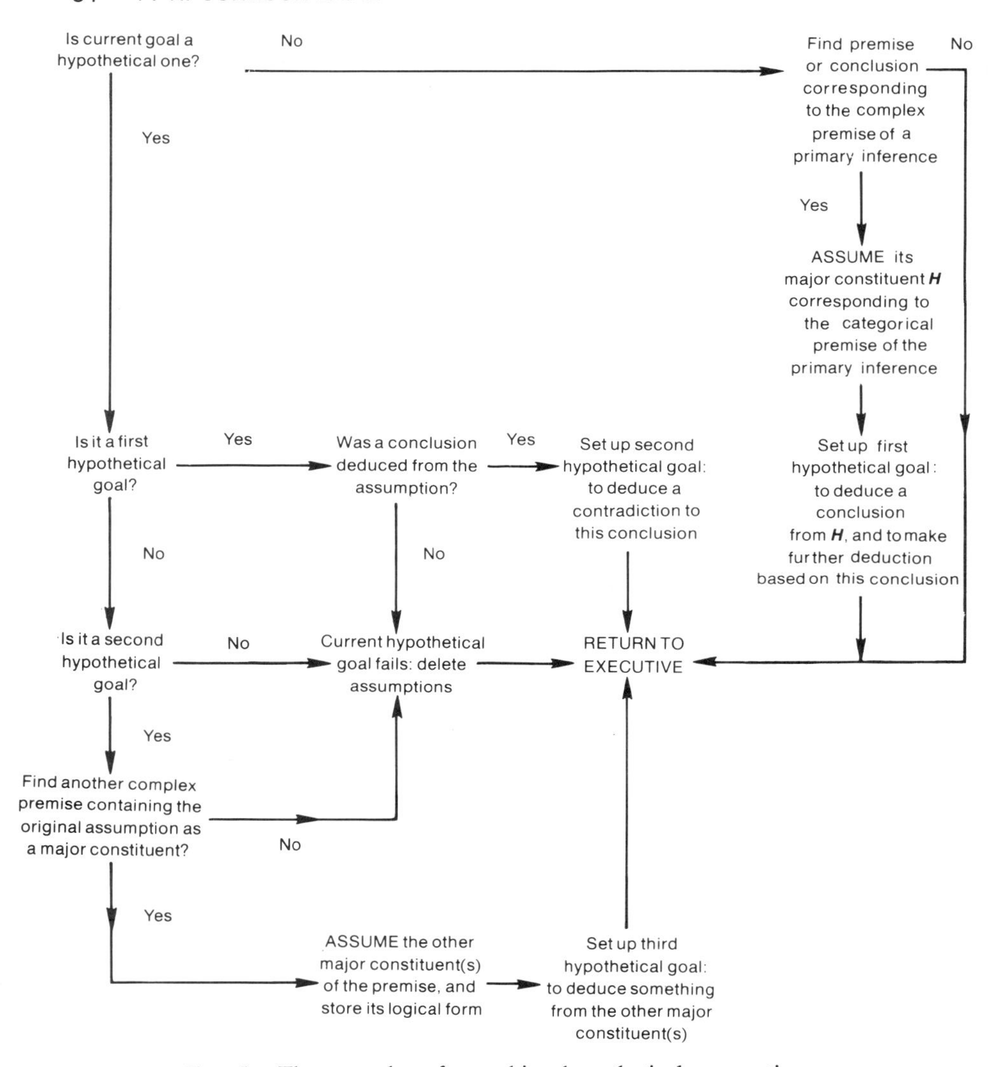

FIG. 5. The procedure for making hypothetical assumptions.

on an assumption. Where an assumption has been made, a conditional conclusion is drawn only if more than an initial consequence has been derived from it. Alternatively, if separate conclusions have been drawn from separate assumptions, then the conclusions may be combined according to the logical relations that originally obtained between the respective assumptions. This routine insures in the case of our previous example that the conclusion to the general dilemma is *C or D*.

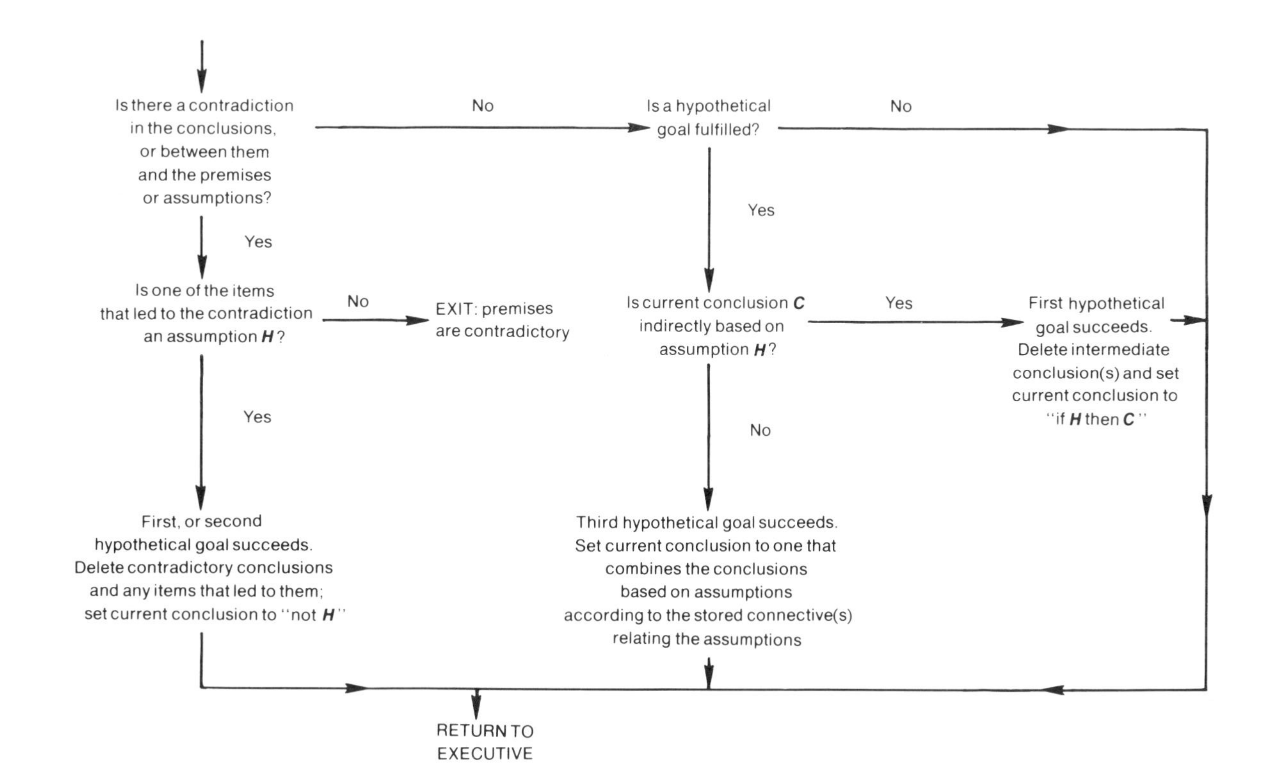

FIG. 6. The procedure for contradictions.

The description of the model is complete, but how is it to be tested empirically? There are three potential methods. First, a correspondence between the model and intelligent but logically naive subjects can be sought. It should be capable of inferences within their competence and it should be incapable of inferences outside their competence. This test may not be particularly stringent because what little evidence there is about human competence in propositional inference has been taken into account in the formulation of the model. Second, a detailed correspondence between the performance of the model and the performance of human reasoners can be sought. Do they go about the business of inference in the same way? Do they, for example, check each time they make a primary deduction to see whether it has yielded a contradiction? The methodology of making such tests of the model is not obvious, although human retrospections are likely to provide some useful evidence. Indeed, they already suggest one weakness of the model. Human reasoners seem to have the ability to gather a rapid global impression of premises and to use it to control their initial attempt at deduction. They do not appear to find it necessary, for example, to attempt a *reductio ad absurdum* before attempting a dilemma. The model's serial ordering of hypothetical goals may therefore be too strong an assumption.

If it proves possible to modify the model so as to increase its power of simulation, then a third method of testing may become feasible. This method involves using a model to make predictions about the relative difficulties of different sorts of inference. Such an approach is, unfortunately, some way off.

REASONING WITH QUANTIFIERS

The valid patterns of relational and propositional deduction do not exhaust the set of general structural rules of inference that human reasoners customarily follow. A new set of principles is required for inference with quantifiers. These terms include the familiar items "all," "some," "none," "many," "few," etc., and a wide range of implicit quantifiers, e.g., "usually," "often," "certain," "possible," and "permissible." Logically speaking, it is possible to develop the usual apparatus of axioms and rules of inference for quantifiers and to raise the customary question of completeness with respect to an appropriate semantical model. Psychologically speaking, however, matters are less clear-cut. Despite the many experimental studies of the syllogism, going back at least 70 years (see the work of Störring, cited in Woodworth, 1938), it is only very recently that actual models of syllogistic inference have been proposed (Erickson, 1973; Revlis, this volume). The majority of theories are about factors that create difficulty in dealing with syllogisms (e.g., Woodworth & Sells, 1935; Chapman & Chapman,

1959; Ceraso & Provitera, 1971). Indeed, the concentration of interest on the syllogism, that traditional but minor province of quantified inference, is symptomatic of the backward state of knowledge in this area.

The model of propositional inference incorporated the mechanism for lexical inference, and they must both in turn be contained within any model of quantified inference. Inferences based on synonymity are a very salient feature because the disposition of quantifiers allows the same basic fact to be expressed in a variety of ways, e.g.,

> Not all the critics admired all of his films.
> Some of the critics did not admire all of his films.
> Some of the critics did not admire some of his films.
> All the critics did not like all of his films.

A similar flexibility extends to terms that are implicit quantifiers, e.g.,

> You are not compelled to vote.
> You are allowed not to vote.
> It is not necessary for you to vote.
> It is possible for you not to vote.

There are at least two alternative ways in which these sorts of semantic relation may be handled. The first alternative is parasitic on a speaker's knowledge of how to give a surface form to an underlying semantic content. I have elsewhere specified a set of grammatical transformations that derive such synonymous sentences from a common underlying form (Johnson-Laird, 1970); and a number of other linguistic accounts of the synonymities involving quantifiers have been proposed (cf. Leech, 1969; Seuren, 1969; Lakoff, 1970; Jackendoff, 1972). Here is not the place to try to weigh up the respective merits of these accounts; what they appear to have in common is the realization that the behavior of quantifiers with negation conforms only in a covert and complicated way to the behavior of these items in a logical calculus. As in logic, one quantifier within the scope of a negation, e.g., "Not all of his films were admired," is equivalent to the alternative quantifier outside the scope of the negation, e.g., "Some of his films were not admired." The complexities arise because of the lack of clear devices in natural language for marking the scope of operators. Sometimes, for example, the scope of negation is indicated by the choice of quantifier, as in the contrast between the following sentences:

> I did not like any of his films.
> I did not like some of his films.

And sometimes scope is indicated by word order—although rarely definitively, because in a sentence such as "None of the critics like some of his films" the first quantifier is within the scope of the second.

The second approach to the problem of synonymity is to provide a direct semantic representation or model for each sentence. The equivalence between sentences is then established by noting that they give rise to the same representation rather than by first reducing the sentences to a common underlying linguistic structure, and then providing a semantic interpretation for it. The direct approach is relatively unexplored for natural language, although Julian Davies at Edinburgh (personal communication) has written a computer program with this sort of facility for quantifiers. The contrast between the two alternative approaches resembles, in many ways, the contrast between an intensional and an extensional semantics. For example, the linguistic approach is well suited to accounting for relations between sentences, whereas the direct approach is well suited to accounting for the relations between sentences and what they describe in the real world. It is too soon either to determine which approach makes the better psychological sense or to grasp the extent to which they are empirically distinguishable.

A more important question is whether it is possible to devise a general model of inference with quantifiers along the lines of the model for propositional inference. In fact, can that model be extended to take into account the internal structure of clauses and their quantifiers? The remainder of this paper is devoted to this problem, but because there is virtually no empirical data apart from the results of experiments on syllogisms, the main aim is to develop a model of how people cope with such syllogisms as the following typical example (from Lewis Carroll):

All prudent men shun hyenas
All bankers are prudent men
∴ All bankers shun hyenas

Psychological studies of the syllogism have been dogged by the baleful tradition of scholastic logic. Not that this logic is necessarily bad—it has simply been bad for psychologists, blinding them to some rather obvious points. Most introductory texts give a standard account of the syllogism, describing its four figures and its 64 moods, and concluding that there are 256 syllogisms. A psychologist, however, should recognize that there are exactly twice this number, because there is nothing God-given about the assumption, underlying the four traditional figures, that the predicate of the conclusion occurs in the first premise. A psychologist might be interested, for example, in the evaluation of a syllogism of the form

All bankers are prudent men
All prudent men shun hyenas
∴ All bankers shun hyenas

This syllogism, of course, is in a figure that does not correspond to any of the traditional four.

The early experimenters (e.g., Wilkins, 1928; Woodworth & Sells, 1935; Sells, 1936) relied on tasks that required given syllogisms to be evaluated rather than on tasks that insured a syllogistic inference was made. They selected the syllogisms from what they thought was a population of 256 in an arbitrary way. (More recent studies have sometimes added the further vice of presenting pooled data from syllogisms of the same mood but different figures, a habit that unfortunately has made it difficult to use the results in constructing a model of inference.) Nevertheless, the pioneering studies led to the important idea of an "atmosphere" effect in which negatives and the quantifier "some" exert a potent bias on the form of an acceptable conclusion to a syllogism—or so, at least, the protagonists of the theory believed.

In order to test the theory and, more importantly, to develop a theory of syllogistic reasoning a systematic study of syllogisms is required. There are 512 possible syllogisms but there are only 64 different combinations of premises (of which 27 yield valid inferences). If experimental subjects are asked to state what follows from each different premise combination, there is a strong presumption that they will be forced to make an inference; and, of course, the population of premise combinations is of a manageable size. Two recent studies, one of which is reported here have tested the ability of intelligent subjects to perform this task. The first study investigated only the 27 valid premise combinations. The second study, carried out in collaboration with Huttenlocher, investigated all 64 pairs of premises. In both these studies, the syllogisms were presented with a sensible everyday content but a content that lacked any perceptible bias toward particular forms of conclusion, e.g.,

> Some of the parents are scientists.
> None of the drivers are parents.

The patterns of inference that were made in both experiments were very similar, even though the experiments were carried out with different materials on opposite sides of the Atlantic. This discussion shall therefore concentrate on the second and more comprehensive study.

The most salient feature of the results is that there is a very wide divergence in the relative difficulty of syllogisms. To take two extreme examples, all 20 subjects presented with premises of the form

Some B *are* A
All B *are* C

correctly deduced a conclusion of the form *Some* A *are* C or its equivalent *Some* C *are* A. However, when these same subjects were presented with premises of the form

All B *are* A
No C *are* B

none of them gave the correct response, *Some* A *are not* C. Perhaps part of the fascination of syllogisms to psychologists is that the manipulation of a handful of variables can yield such very large differences in performance.

The results also demonstrated the inadequacy of the atmosphere hypothesis as a complete account of what goes on in syllogistic reasoning. As there is no point in belaboring this point, amply confirmed in another recent study (Mazzocco, Legrenzi, & Roncato, 1974), it can simply be stated that 40% of the conclusions drawn by the subjects are in accordance with the hypothesis, 8% of their conclusions are incompatible with the hypothesis, and the remaining 52% of their responses are neither compatible nor incompatible with the hypothesis because they consisted almost entirely of the response that no conclusion could be drawn from the premises. It may be objected that the atmosphere hypothesis, in fact, accounts for most of the results if one ignores those syllogisms for which no conclusion was drawn from the premises. However, this objection merely begs the question: how is it that subjects realize that no conclusion follows? The atmosphere hypothesis cannot explain this phenomenon.

There was one striking and unexpected aspect of the results. Certain figures of the syllogism exerted a strong influence on the form of the conclusion that subjects inferred, and this influence did not depend on the logic of particular syllogisms. Where the premises were of the form below where A–B designates the order in which terms A and B were mentioned, regardless of the quantifiers used),

A–B
B–C

85% of the conclusions that were drawn had the form A–C. Where the premises were of the form

B–A
C–B

86% of the conclusions that were drawn had the form C–A. In the case of the other two sorts of syllogisms, however, there were only slight biases, as the following percentages show:

B–A	A–B
B–C	C–B
A–C (54%)	C–A (67%)

Although the "figural" effect provides an important clue to how people make syllogistic inferences, it is not the whole story. There is an interaction between the figure and the mood of the premises; and the main goal of a model of syllogistic inference must be to account for this interaction.

Why has this figural effect never been noticed before? The answer is simply because of the neglect of half the possible syllogisms, a neglect fostered by relying on a traditional account of the logic of syllogisms. Indeed, it is a pity that psychologists have not gone back to Aristotle, because the first of his figures has the form

All A *are* B
All B *are* C
∴ *All* A *are* C

This form of syllogism is the only one that Aristotle considered to be perfect, perhaps because the transitivity of the connection between its terms is obvious at a glance (see Kneale & Kneale, 1962, p. 73).

Aristotle's method of validating syllogisms involved their "reduction," by way of a variety of transformations, to the pattern of his perfect syllogism. Subsequent recipes for syllogistic inference have tended to be more mysterious. They are mechanical procedures that work, but their workings are in no way intuitive. It is natural to wonder how such procedures have been established as infallible. One possibility is that they have been tested by exhaustive searches for counterexamples. Another possibility, however, is simply that people, even logically naive people, are capable of syllogistic inference and, with sufficient care, can elucidate a syllogism of any form. This possibility obviously demands that a model of syllogistic inference be able to account for both valid and invalid deductions.

The essence of the model to be developed here is that an initial representation of the premises is set up, from which a conclusion may be read off. This initial representation, however, may be subjected to a series of tests. Where it is submitted to all of these tests, any ultimate conclusion corresponds in all cases to a valid inference. Where some of the tests are omitted, the conclusion may or may not be valid. The syllogisms that are easy to solve turn out either not to permit tests of the initial representation or else not to require their initial conclusions to be modified. The syllogisms that are difficult to solve do permit tests of the initial representation and invariably these tests call for a modified conclusion.

It is impossible from mere introspection to determine how the different sorts of syllogistic premises are mentally represented. They may be represented in a format resembling Euler's diagrams (see Erickson, 1973; Revlis, this volume; Neimark & Chapman, this volume). However, one difficulty with this representation is that it cannot account for the "figural" effect because, for example, the representation of *Some* A *are* B is identical to the representation of *Some* B *are* A. It is unfortunate that, in developing his interesting set-theoretic model of syllogistic inference, Erickson (1973) has overlooked the possibility of a "figural" effect by neglecting half the possible syllogisms. The fact that human reasoners often show a pronounced "figural" bias in stating their conclusions, even where such a bias is logically unwarranted, demonstrates the need to modify any simple representation of premises in the form of Euler's circles. However, instead of attempting such a modification, an entirely different format has been chosen for the present model. The model assumes that human reasoners represent a class by imagining an arbitrary number of its members. For example, a class of artists is represented by a set of elements that are tagged in some way as artists. The nature of the elements and their tags is immaterial—they may be vivid visual images or ghostlike verbal tags. The crucial point is simply that they are discrete elements. A statement such as "All the artists are beekeepers" relates two separate classes and it is represented in the following way:

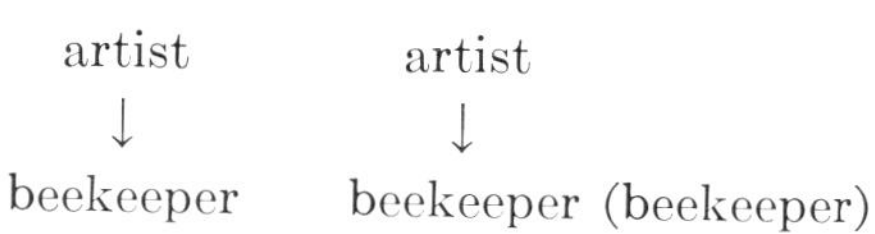

where representatives of one class are mapped onto representatives of the other class, and the parenthetical item indicates that there may be beekeepers who are not artists. This representation is similar, but not isomorphic, to an Euler diagram. The discrepancy arises from the function of the arrows, which may be interpreted as pointers within a list-processing language. In other words, although the mapping represented by a single arrow is logically symmetrical, i.e., $a \rightarrow b$ is equivalent to $a \leftarrow b$, the two expressions are not psychologically equivalent. Intuitively, the item at the tail of the arrow can be thought of as having stored with it the address in memory of the item at the head of the arrow. Therefore, a fundamental assumption of the model is that it is easier to read off information from such representations proceeding in the direction of the arrows. It is possible to proceed in the opposite direction, but it is harder because it will be necessary to search memory for the item at the tail of the arrow. The model is accordingly very far from making the assumption that subjects tend readily to convert statements (*pace,* Chapman & Chapman, 1959). It does not even assume that they make valid conversions spontaneously during syllogistic reasoning, e.g., from "Some artists are bricklayers" to "Some bricklayers are artists." There is good reason to suppose that such pairs of statements are not always equivalent in ordinary discourse. The former statement, as Hintikka (1973, p. 69) has emphasized, presupposes that the field of search includes all artists, whereas the latter statement presupposes that the field of search includes all bricklayers. This divergence may even lead to a rather special interpretation of the predicate term, suggesting in the second example above, for instance, that some bricklayers are artists in their manner of laying bricks.

In general, a universal affirmative statement, *All* A *are* B, is represented in the following way:

$$\begin{array}{lll} a & a & \\ \downarrow & \downarrow & \\ b & b & (b) \end{array}$$

where the parenthetical item (b) indicates that there may be a b that is not a. The number of a's and b's in the representation is, of course, entirely arbitrary—we may just as well have linked 15 a's to 15 b's and included 30 parenthetical b's; for convenience, we have chosen two a's in representing each of the different sorts of premise. A particular affirmative statement, *Some* A *are* B, is represented in the following way:

$$\begin{array}{ll} a & (a) \\ \downarrow & \\ b & (b) \end{array}$$

where (a) indicates that there may be an a that is not b, and (b) indicates that there may be a b that is not a.

The representation of a negative statement involves a negative link: there is no mapping of the sort defined above and, moreover, none can be established by any subsequent manipulations of the representation. The representation of a universal negative statement *No* A *are* B requires an arbitrary number of negative mappings, which are here indicated by stopped arrows:

$$\begin{array}{ll} a & a \\ \underline{\downarrow} & \underline{\downarrow} \\ b & b \end{array}$$

If there is a negative link beetween a and b, neither of them may be involved in any positive links from a to b, or from b to a. A particular negative statement, *Some* A *are not* B, is represented by

$$\begin{array}{cc} a & (a) \\ \underline{\downarrow} & \downarrow \\ b & b \end{array}$$

where the positive mapping, $(a) \rightarrow b$ indicates that some a may be b.

The logic of these representations is as follows, where $a \in \mathsf{A}$, $b \in \mathsf{B}$, and R stands for the relation of identity

All A *are* B:	$(a)(\exists b) \quad (a\mathbf{R}b)$
Some A *are* B:	$(\exists a)(\exists b) \quad (a\mathbf{R}b)$
No A *are* B:	$(a)(b) \ \neg (a\mathbf{R}b)$
Some A *are not* B:	$(\exists a)(b) \quad \neg (a\mathbf{R}b)$

On the plausible assumption that A and B are never empty classes in ordinary language, these expressions seem to capture the obvious inferential properties of quantifiers. The logic of sentences in which the copula is replaced by some other relation (e.g., "All the artists married beekeepers") is easily accommodated by this notation.

It is a simple matter to write a program that sets up a representation for the first premise of a syllogism. The representation of the second premise is a more complicated matter because one term — the middle term of the syllogism — will have already been represented. The logical work, in fact, commences with the representation of the second premise because it is grafted onto the representation of the first premise. The process is perhaps best described by way of an example.

Suppose that the first premise of a syllogism is of the form *Some* A *are* B, and can accordingly be represented as

$$\begin{array}{cc} a & (a) \\ \downarrow & \\ b & (b) \end{array}$$

A crucial distinction is whether or not the middle term is the quantified item in the second premise. The representation of the premise *All* B *are* C simply involves mapping the existing members of B onto representative elements of C:

$$\begin{array}{ccc} a & (a) & \\ \downarrow & & \\ b & (b) & \\ \downarrow & \downarrow & \\ c & c & (c) \end{array}$$

The valid conclusion *Some* A *are* C may be read off from this representation, proceeding in the direction of the arrows. However, if the second premise is *All* C *are* B then it is necessary to set up some representative elements of C and to map them onto B. It is also necessary to allow that there may be other *b*'s that are not *c*'s; therefore, an initial representation of this syllogism is

$$\begin{array}{ccc} a & (a) & \\ \downarrow & & \\ b & (b) & (b) \\ \uparrow & \uparrow & \\ c & c & \end{array}$$

Because the mappings do not proceed in a uniform direction, there is no firm anchor on which to base the inference; and the model predicts that subjects will tend to be divided between concluding (invalidly) *Some* A *are* C and concluding (invalidly) *Some* C *are* A.

Both the representations that have been described reflect an initial bias of the model toward establishing transitive mappings. This feature has been introduced in order to account for the subjects' bias toward drawing conclusions where, in fact, none are warranted. Because many subjects are capable of a more sophisticated syllogistic performance, the model assumes that once an initial representation of the premises has been created, it may be submitted to tests before any attempt is made to read off a conclusion. These tests can be characterized as efforts to test to destruction any initial transitive mappings. The initial phase is analogous to a process of verification; the testing phase is analogous to a process of falsification and, as with falsification, it is often overlooked by subjects (see Johnson-Laird & Wason, 1970).

The procedure for falsifying a mapping involves trying to modify the representation of the second premise so that it is no longer connected to items that are themselves involved in a mapping relation. The procedure has no effect on the first illustrative syllogism but it is possible to modify the initial representation of the second illustrative syllogism from

$$\begin{array}{ccc} a & (a) & \\ \downarrow & & \\ b & (b) & (b) \\ \uparrow & \uparrow & \\ c & c & \end{array}$$

to

$$\begin{array}{ccc} a & (a) & \\ \downarrow & & \\ b & (b) & (b) \\ & \uparrow & \uparrow \\ & c & c \end{array}$$

The critical link has been broken; and because both its presence and its absence are consistent with the interpretation of the premises, it follows that no valid conclusion can be deduced from them.

The predictions of the model for the two illustrative syllogisms are summarized below, together with the numbers of experimental subjects (out of 20) deducing the predicted conclusions:

Some A *are* B	*Some* A *are* B
All B *are* C	*All* C *are* B
∴ *Some* A *are* C: 16	∴ *Some* A *are* C: 5
	∴ *Some* C *are* A: 5
	No conclusion follows: 9

A simple set-theoretic model does not account for the results with the first of these syllogisms because it predicts a response of *Some* A *are* C as often as a response of *Some* C *are* A.

Certain features of the present model can only be illustrated by considering the representation and testing of negative premises. Consider premises of the form

No B *are* A
All C *are* B

The first premise is represented as

$$\begin{array}{cc} a & a \\ \bar{\uparrow} & \bar{\uparrow} \\ b & b \end{array}$$

The second premise, of course, requires an additional b to be introduced and, when such an introduction occurs, the model bears in mind the universal nature of the first premise:

$$\begin{array}{ccc} a & a & a \\ \bar{\uparrow} & \bar{\uparrow} & \bar{\uparrow} \\ b & b & (b) \\ \uparrow & \uparrow & \\ c & c & \end{array}$$

It is a straightforward matter to read off the conclusion, *No* C *are* A, but a more difficult matter to read off the conclusion *No* A *are* C.

The initial representation of the premises

No B *are* A
All B *are* C

is set up in a similar way:

$$\begin{array}{ccc} a & a & \\ \bar{\uparrow} & \bar{\uparrow} & \\ b & b & \\ \downarrow & \downarrow & \\ c & c & (c) \end{array}$$

However, the mappings do not proceed in a uniform direction and the model predicts that subjects will be divided between the (invalid) conclusions *No* A *are* C and *No* C *are* A.

The falsification tests of a negative mapping consist in trying to establish that a transitive link can be set up between the elements in the representation. The only constraint on this maneuvre is that elements cannot be linked in inconsistent ways such as these in the following example:

$$\begin{array}{ccc} a & a & \\ \bar{\uparrow} & \bar{\uparrow} & \\ b & b & b \\ \uparrow & & \uparrow \\ c & & c \end{array}$$

because these links imply inconsistencies, such as that *c* both is and is not an *a*. The first syllogism survives the falsification tests unmodified. The second syllogism does not. Its initial representation

$$\begin{array}{ccc} a & a & \\ \bar{\uparrow} & \bar{\uparrow} & \\ b & b & \\ \downarrow & \downarrow & \\ c & c & (c) \end{array}$$

allows the following links to be established:

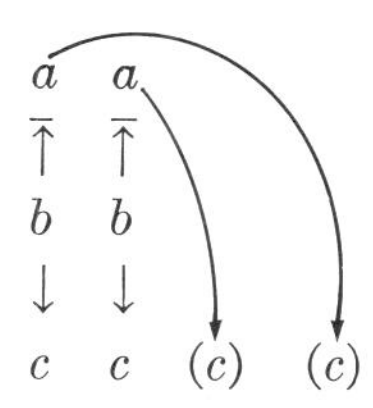

It is always possible to add new parenthetical items provided there are existing ones; it is never possible to add any items to a set that contains no parenthetical items. The distinction, in fact, corresponds to the traditional notion of a distributed term (no parenthetical items) and an undistributed term (parenthetical items). The new links in the representation are, of course, consistent. Yet subjects initially predisposed to conclude *No* A *are* C may find this second representation, which suggests *All* A *are* C, such a contrast that they may judge that no conclusion follows from the premises. More astute subjects, however, can appreciate that it is impossible to add further *a*'s to the representation and therefore that *Some* C *are not* A.

The predictions of the model for the two negative syllogisms are summarized below, together with the number of experimental subjects (out of 20) deducing the predicted conclusions:

No B *are* A		*No* B *are* A	
All C *are* B		*All* B *are* C	
∴ *No* C *are* A:	13	∴ *No* C *are* A:	4
∴ *No* A *are* C:	3	∴ *No* A *are* C:	3
		No conclusion follows:	4
		∴ *Some* C *are not* A:	7

The main features of the model of syllogistic inference have now been illustrated, and it should be obvious that it has the sort of flexibility needed to match the diversity of subjects' deductions. To generate quantitative predictions, however, would require the specification of various parameters and the estimation of their values from the experimental results. The exercise would not be very rewarding. A more appealing possibility is to try to derive assumptions about the relative value of these parameters from the processing properties of the model itself. The point can be illustrated by considering the figural effect in terms of the processing of lists. When the arrows in a representation lie in a uniform direction, they largely determine the direction in which conclusions are read off from it. It is possible to proceed in the opposite direction but at the cost of having to search memory for the items that are the tails of arrows. This asymmetry, which is reflected in human performance, is a simple consequence of the structure of lists. At a later stage of development of the model, it may be possible to derive some of fine-grain aspects of performance from similar sorts of information-processing considerations.

The reader familiar with the problems of manipulating Euler's circles can appreciate the computational advantage of the present style of representation. An Eulerian representation of, for example, *Some* A *are* B requires four separate diagrams to be created. When such representations are combined, the combinatorial consequences can become psychologically embarassing, particularly where several premises are involved, e.g.,

Some A *are* B
All B *are* C
All C *are* D

An Eulerian deduction from these premises involves considering at least $4 \times 2 \times 2 = 16$ different combinations of diagram, whereas the list representation is simply

$$\begin{array}{llll} a & (a) & & \\ \downarrow & & & \\ b & (b) & & \\ \downarrow & \downarrow & & \\ c & c & (c) & \\ \downarrow & \downarrow & \downarrow & \\ d & d & d & (d) \end{array}$$

from which it is easy to infer *Some* A *are* D. It may be that in making such inferences human reasoners break the problem down into a series of syllogisms; but it is also feasible that they set up a complete representation of several premises in this way.

There are, of course, alternative models of syllogistic inference that can be couched in the list format. Mark Steedman (personal communication) has devised a model, involving a more elegant representation, in which invalid inferences arise not from a failure to test initial and improper representations of the combined premises but from actual errors in the representations of single premises. In particular, the model assumes that parenthetical items are often neglected so that universal premises come to be interpreted as *All and only* A *are* B. The list representations may also be extended in order to deal with quasi-numerical quantifiers (e.g., "many," "most," "few") and with statements involving several quantifiers. A statement such as "Some of the tenants will not vote for all the representatives" may be represented in the following way:

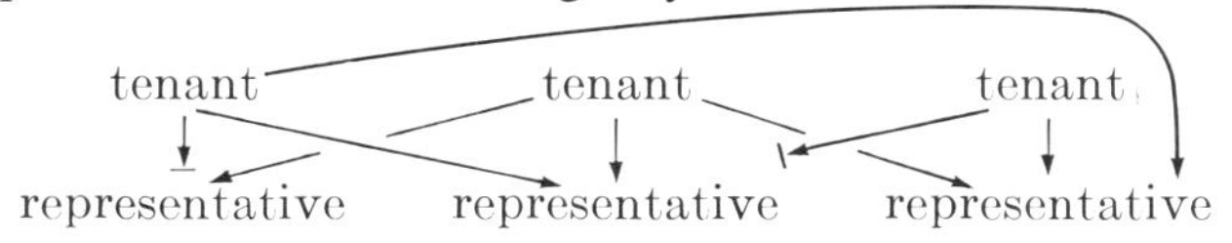

where the mapping represents the relation *votes for*. The combination of these diagrams is a complicated affair, but from the few studies of inference with such statements (Johnson-Laird, 1969b) it seems that untrained human reasoners have fairly restricted powers with them, too. It is likely that the list representation is sufficiently flexible to form part of a general model of quantified inference.

CONCLUSIONS

In an attempt to formulate models of deduction that operate on different aspects of the structure of statements, two essential inferential processes have been discerned: the transformation of information and the combination of information from separate sources. The transformation of information occurs primarily in lexical inferences and in the majority of auxiliary inferences. The combination of information occurs in three-term series problems, in inferences about complex spatial relations, in primary propositional inferences, and in syllogisms. When information is transformed, the process is usually governed by essentially linguistic rules. When information is combined, however, the process often seems to involve the creation of an internal "model" of the world. This procedure seems to be necessary for syllogistic inference; and it has the great advantage that the transitivity of relational terms can be made a direct consequence of their representation rather than an indirect consequence of an additional rule of inference. Indeed, it is seldom that it can be conclusively demonstrated that the transformation of information does not proceed by the construction of internal models.

What of the role of content? Do different contents introduce perhaps difference principles of inference? It is certainly noticeable that a listener is able to draw on general knowledge to allow a speaker to leave many things unsaid. The sorts of inference that a listener can make are illustrated in the following examples culled from current work in a variety of disciplines:

He went to three drugstores.
Therefore, the first two drugstores didn't have what he wanted. (Abelson & Reich, 1969)

The mirror shattered because the child grabbed the broom.
Therefore, the child hit the mirror with the broom and broke it. (Bransford & McCarrell, 1972)

The policeman held up his hand and the cars stopped.
Therefore, the policeman was directing the traffic. (Collins & Quillian, 1972)

Harry is enjoying his new job at the bank, and he hasn't been to prison yet.
Therefore, Harry may be tempted to steal some of the money in the bank. (Wilson, 1972)

John gave Mary a beating with a stick.
Therefore, John wanted to hurt Mary. (Schank, Goldman, Rieger, & Riesbeck, 1973)

Janet needed some money. She got her piggybank and started to shake it.
Therefore, Janet got her piggybank and shook it in order to get some money from it. (Charniak, 1973)

Of course, the man may have visited three drugstores in order to enforce a protection racket; and the mirror may have shattered because it was balanced on top of the broom; and so on. The inferences are therefore plausible rather than valid. What appears to happen, however, is that people exploit a communal base of knowledge that includes such assumptions as:

Drugstores are shops that have certain sorts of goods.
People visit shops in order to buy goods.
If one shop does not have an item that it normally stocks, then another shop of the same sort may have it.

This knowledge will be automatically elicited by any utterance with a relevant topic, and it can be used by the inferential machinery in order to make good any gaps in the explicit discourse. The procedure relies on a convention that a speaker will draw attention to any special circumstances that render communal assumptions inappropriate.

If discourse is supplemented by common sense assumptions, it is unnecessary to postulate special rules of inference to deal with specific topics, although the content of statements may exert a selective bias on the availability of different rules of inference (see Wason & Johnson-Laird, 1972). The simple answer is to revert to Sherlock Holmes, who was himself a model of deduction. What he exploited, very much in the manner of PLANNER, were two special sources of information: an acute perceptual attention to detail, and an extensive specialized knowledge—the sort of knowledge to be expected in an individual who contributed to the literature on both cigar ash and tattoos. It was knowledge that was the foundation of his exceptional ability. The structure of his inferences was, indeed, elementary.

ACKNOWLEDGMENTS

This work was supported by a grant for scientific assistance from the Social Science Research Council. I am indebted to George Miller for some extremely useful ideas about the structure of the lexicon. I am also grateful to Keith Oatley and Mark Steedman for helpful discussions on spatial and syllogistic inference, to Gerard

Kempen for his work in programming part of the model of propositional inference, and to Janellen Huttenlocher for allowing me to describe some joint research. My interest in inference was originally stimulated by Peter Wason, and I would like to acknowledge here my debt to him.

REFERENCES

Abelson, R. P., & Reich, C. M. Implication modules: a method for extracting meaning from input sentences. *First international joint conference on artificial intelligence.* Washington, D.C., 1969.

Amarel, S. An approach to heuristic problem solving and theorem proving in the propositional calculus. In J. F. Hart & S. Takusu (Eds.) *Computer science and systems,* Toronto: University of Toronto Press, 1967.

Bar-Hillel, Y. Dictionaries and meaning rules. *Foundations of Language,* 1967, **3,** 409–414. Reprinted in Y. Bar-Hillel, *Aspects of language: Essays and lectures on philosophy of language, linguistic philosophy and methodology of linguistics.* Jerusalem: The Magnes Press, The Hebrew University. Amsterdam: North-Holland Publ., 1970.

Bendix, E. H. *Componential analysis of general vocabulary: The semantic structure of a set of verbs in English, Hindi and Japanese.* The Hague: Mouton, 1966.

Beth, E. W., & Piaget, J. *Mathematical epistemology and psychology.* Translated by W. Mays. Dordrecht-Holland: Reidel, 1966.

Bransford, J. D., & McCarrell, N. S. A sketch of a cognitive approach to comprehension: some thoughts about understanding what it means to comprehend. Paper presented at the Conference on Cognition and the Symbolic Processes, Pennsylvania State University, October 1972.

Carnap, R. *Meaning and necessity: A study in semantics and modal logic.* (2nd ed.) Chicago: Chicago University Press, 1956.

Ceraso, J., & Provitera, A. Sources of error in syllogistic reasoning. *Cognitive Psychology,* 1971, **2,** 400–410.

Chapman, L. J., & Chapman, J. P. Atmosphere effect re-examined. *Journal of Experimental Psychology,* 1959, **58,** 220–226.

Charniak, E. Jack and Janet in search of a theory of knowledge. *Third international joint conference on artificial intelligence.* Stanford: Stanford Research Institute, 1973.

Church, A. A note on the Entscheidungs Problem. *Journal of Symbolic Logic,* 1936, **1,** 40–41.

Clark, H. H. More about "Adjectives, comparatives, and syllogisms": a reply to Huttenlocher and Higgins. *Psychological Review,* 1971, **78,** 505–514.

Collins, A. M., & Quillian, M. R. Retrieval time from semantic memory. *Journal of Verbal Learning & Verbal Behavior,* 1969, **8,** 240–247.

Collins, A. M., & Quillian, M. R. How to make a language user. In E. Tulving & W. Donaldson (Eds.), *Organization of memory.* New York: Academic Press, 1972.

Dowty, D. R. On the syntax and semantics of the atomic predicate CAUSE. In P. M. Peranteau, J. N. Levi, & G. C. Phares (Eds.), *Papers from the eighth regional meeting, Chicago Linguistic Society.* Chicago: Chicago Linguistic Society, 1972. Pp. 62–74.

Doyle, A. C. *The adventures of Sherlock Holmes.* London: J. Murray, 1917.

Erickson, J. R. A set analysis theory of behavior in formal syllogistic reasoning tasks. Paper presented to the Loyola Symposium on Cognition, Chicago, May 1973.

Evans, J. St. B. T. Deductive reasoning and linguistic usage (with special reference to negation). Unpublished doctoral dissertation, University of London, 1972.

Gödel, K. Zur intuitionistischen Arithmetik und Zahlentheorie. *Ergebnisse eines mathematischen Kaloquiums,* 1933, Heft iv, 34–38. Translated by M. Davis, On Intuitionistic Arithmetic and Number theory. In M. Davis (Ed.), *The undecidable: Basic papers on undecidable propositions, unsolvable problems and computable functions,* Hewlett, N.Y.: Raven Press, 1965.

Hewitt, C. PLANNER: a language for manipulating robots and proving theorems in a robot. Project MAC Artificial Intelligence Memo No. 168, Massachusetts Institute of Technology, 1970.

Heyting, A. *Intuitionism, an introduction.* Amsterdam: North-Holland Publ., 1956.

Hintikka, J. *Logic, language-games and information: Kantian themes in the philosophy of logic.* Oxford: Clarendon, 1973.

Huttenlocher, J., & Higgins, E. T. Adjectives, comparatives, and syllogisms. *Psychological Review,* 1971, **78,** 487–504.

Jackendoff, R. *Semantic interpretation in generative grammar.* Cambridge, Mass.: MIT Press 1972.

Johnson-Laird, P. N. "&" *Journal of Linguistics,* 1969, **6,** 111–114. (a)

Johnson-Laird, P. N. Reasoning with ambiguous sentences. *British Journal of Psychology,* 1969, **60,** 17–23. (b)

Johnson-Laird, P. N. The interpretation of quantified sentences. In G. B. Flores D'Arcais & W. J. M. Levelt (Eds.) *Advances in psycholinguistics.* Amsterdam: North-Holland, 1970.

Johnson-Laird, P. N. Experimental Psycholinguistics. In M. R. Rosenzweig & L. W. Porter (Eds.) *Annual Review of Psychology,* Vol. 25. Palo Alto, Calif.: Annual Reviews Inc., 1974.

Johnson-Laird, P. N., & Tridgell, J. When negation is easier than affirmation. *Quarterly Journal of Experimental Psychology,* 1972, **24,** 87–91.

Johnson-Laird, P. N., & Wason, P. C. A theoretical analysis of insight into a reasoning task. *Cognitive Psychology,* 1970, **1,** 134–148.

Karttunen, L. Presuppositions of compound sentences. *Linguistic Inquiry,* 1973, **4,** 169–193.

Keenan, E. L. *A Logical Base for a Transformational Grammar of English.* University of Pennsylvania, Transformations and Discourse Analysis Papers, No. 82, 1970.

Kneale, W., & Kneale, M. *The development of logic.* Oxford: Clarendon, 1962.

Kowalski, R. Predicate logic as programming language. Memo No. 70, Department of Computational Logic, School of Artificial Intelligence, University of Edinburgh, 1973.

Lakoff, G. Linguistics and natural logic. *Synthese,* 1970, **22,** 151–271.

Lakoff, R. If's, and's, and but's about conjunction. In C. J. Fillmore & D. T. Langendoen (Eds.), *Studies in linguistic semantics.* New York: Holt, Rinehart & Winston, 1971.

Landauer, T. K., & Meyer, D. E. Category size and semantic memory retrieval. *Journal of Verbal Learning & Verbal Behavior,* 1972, **11,** 539–549.

Leech, G. N. *Towards a semantic description of English.* London: Longmans, Green, 1969.

Mazzocco, A., Legrenzi, P., & Roncato, S. Syllogistic inference: The failure of the atmosphere effect and the conversion hypothesis. *Italian Journal of Psychology,* 1974, **1,** 157–172.

Miller, G. A., Galanter, E., & Pribram, K. H. *Plans and the structure of behavior.* New York: Holt, Rinehart & Winston, 1960.

Miller, G. A., & Johnson-Laird, P. N. *Perception and language,* 1975, in press.

Montague, R. English as a formal language. In B. Visentini *et al.* (Eds.), *Linguaggi nella società e nella tecnica.* Edizionidi Comunità, Milan, 1970.

Newell, A., & Simon, H. A. *Human problem solving.* Englewood Cliffs, N. J.: Prentice-Hall, 1972.

Parsons, T. A semantics for English. Mimeo., 1972.

Ramsey, F. P., General propositions and causality. In F. P. Ramsey (Ed.) *Foundations of mathematics and other logical essays.* London: Routledge & Kegan Paul, 1950.

Reiter, R. A semantically guided deductive system for automatic theorem-proving. In *Third international joint conference on artificial intelligence.* Stanford: Stanford Research Institute, 1973.

Rips, L. J., Shoben, E. J., & Smith, E. E. Semantic distance and the verification of semantic relations. *Journal of Verbal Learning & Verbal Behavior,* **1973, 12,** 1–20.

Robinson, J. A. A machine-oriented logic based on the resolution principle. *Journal of Association for Computing Machinery,* 1965, **12,** 23–41.

Robinson, J. A. Automatic deduction with hyper-resolution. *International Journal of Computer Mathematics,* 1966, **1,** 227–234.

Schaeffer, B., & Wallace, R. The comparison of word meanings. *Journal of Experimental Psychology,* 1970, **86,** 144–152.

Schank, R., Goldman, N., Rieger, C. J., & Riesbeck, C. Margie: memory, analysis, response generation, and inference on English. *Third international joint conference on artificial intelligence.* Stanford: Stanford Research Institute, 1973.

Sells, S. B. The atmosphere effect: an experimental study of reasoning. *Archives of Psychology,* 1936, **29,** 3–72.

Seuren, P. A. M. *Operators and nucleus: A contribution to the theory of grammar.* Cambridge, England: Cambridge University Press, 1969.

Stalnaker, R. C. A theory of conditionals. *American Philosophical Quarterly, Monograph No. 2.* In Nicholas Rescher (Ed.) *Studies in Logical Theory,* 1968, 98–112.

Suppes, P. On the behavioral foundations of mathematical concepts. In L. N. Morrisett & J. Vinsonhaler (Eds.), *Mathematical learning. Child Development Monograph,* 1965, **30**(1), 60–96.

Tarski, A. The concept of truth in formalized languages. In *Logic, semantics, metamathetics: Papers from 1923 to 1938.* Translated by J. H. Woodger. London and New York: Oxford University Press, 1956.

van Fraassen, B. C. *Formal semantics and logic.* New York: Macmillan, 1971.

Wason, P. C., & Johnson-Laird, P. N. *Psychology of reasoning: structure and content.* Cambridge, Mass.: Harvard University Press, 1972.

Wilkins, M. C. The effect of changed material on the ability to do formal syllogistic reasoning. *Archives of Psychology,* 1928, **16**(102).

Wilson, D. Presuppositions II. University College London, Mimeo, 1972.

Winograd, T. *Understanding natural language.* New York: Academic Press, 1972. Also published as the whole of *Cognitive Psychology,* Part 1, 1972, **3,** 1–191.

Woodworth, R. S. *Experimental psychology.* New York: Holt, 1938.

Woodworth, R. S., & Sells, S. B. An atmosphere effect in formal syllogistic reasoning. *Journal of Experimental Psychology,* 1935, **18,** 451–460.

2
UNDERSTANDING CONDITIONAL REASONING WITH MEANINGFUL PROPOSITIONS

Herman Staudenmayer
New School for Social Research

The relation between logic and thinking has been a philosophical issue in Western thought since the time of Plato and Aristotle. On one side are those who argue that logic deals with the processes of thinking and reasoning (e.g., Kant, 1781; Mill, 1874); on the other side are those who argue that the rules of logic are not applicable in characterizing the processes and complexities of thinking (e.g., Nagel, 1956; Boole, 1854). A brief historical summary of proponents of both positions may be found in Henle (1971).

Many philosophical and psychological interpretations of thinking still maintain that human reasoning cannot be represented adequately by the rules of logic. This argument is largely based on pointing to the existence of fallacies. The mistake inherent in this argument is the failure to distinguish the reasoning process from the resulting evaluations that are observed. Correct evaluations are formally, and in some sense arbitrarily, defined, and any deviation from these evaluations is considered to be fallacious reasoning. Furthermore, correct evaluations are defined with respect to the formal operators or forms used in the premises, without any regard for the material on which these operators work, thereby disregarding the semantic material in the premises as well as the demand characteristics and nature of the task. The individual's interpretation of what he is reasoning about and why he is reasoning in that situation are therefore assumed to have no effect on resulting evaluations. Multiple or varied interpretations of the same material or task situation are disallowed; this is a serious restriction considering the plethora of meanings in natural language.

Those who argue that the rules of logic underly the processes in thinking and reasoning distinguish between the process involved in the interpretation (of implicative statements, for example) and the process involved in making or evaluating inferences. The interpretative process is conceptualized as being more inductive than deductive (Mill, 1874) in that the likelihood of accepting or rejecting an interpretation is based on personal knowledge, presuppositions about context, linguistic structure of the sentence, and beliefs about task demands. Henle (1962, 1971) has reemphasized the importance of judging the results of the reasoning process according to the interpretations or codes used by the individual rather than those intended by the investigator. Once the interpretation of the premises is taken into account, the process of evaluating inferences is deductive, as are the formal operations of logic, in that certain inferences necessarily follow given interpretations. Viewed in this way, the rules of logic can be used to characterize the processes of thinking and reasoning. The burden of this viewpoint lies in identifying the factors involved in the interpretation process and in demonstrating how they affect specific inferences in the evaluation process. The aim of this study is to identify such factors and demonstrate the effects of some of them on the evaluation process.

FACTORS IN THE INTERPRETATION PROCESS

In reasoning and language comprehension, there are both linguistic and nonlinguistic factors that influence the manner in which an individual may glean information from sentences expressing implication. Such a sentence contains linguistic information about the content of and relation between the antecedent (p) and consequent (q) propositions. Specifically, the content of the propositions can be abstract or symbolic, or semantically concrete and meaningful. Also, the semantic relation between concrete propositions can express, for example, nominal class inclusion, attribute description, or causality. And finally, there is the connective logically joining the propositions which may be the conditional *if . . . then . . .* ; some semantic equivalent, such as *since, because,* or *cause,* or even a logically different connective, such as the biconditional *if and only if.*

These variables are linguistic in that they explicitly contribute to the structure of the sentence and, taken independently, all have some denotative or dictionary meanings as assigned by semantics. [Because syntax and semantics are conceptually as well as practically difficult to separate (cf. Lakoff, 1971), they are not separated here and instead the joint concept is referred to as the linguistic structure of the sentence.] The complete interpreted meaning of a sentence is usually not entirely given by the denotative meaning in the linguistic structure of the sentence. Instead, the complete meaning of an expression usually encompasses connotation as well. Connotative meaning is interpreted not from the linguistic structure of the sentence but from nonlinguistic, pragmatic factors pertaining to the use of the sentence (Wittgenstein, 1958). These pragmatic factors include not only factual or empirical knowledge of the world and contextual presuppositions but also the generic concept of the speech act, which incorporates the speaker and the hearer as well as their interpreted possible worlds as variables that may affect reasoning, language comprehension, and thinking (cf. Stalnaker, 1970).

Essential to the psychological study of reasoning is the consideration of the active process by which inferences are made. Pragmatic factors, it is argued, must be considered primary to this process and consequently to any general theory of reasoning, language comprehension, and thinking having psychological validity. Therefore, in addition to the factors emphasized here, others to be recognized are responses bias strategies, emotional involvement, social attitudes about certain material, and interpretation of the nature of the task *per se*. These particular factors are reviewed and discussed in the context of syllogistic reasoning in the chapters by Revlis and by Johnson-Laird, this volume, and are discussed no further here.

REASONING WITH ABSTRACT MATERIAL

When the content of the propositions is abstract the interpretation of the sentence cannot be readily attributable to the semantic relation between propositions or to pragmatic contextual factors unless one assumes that individuals generate concrete examples and solve the problem by analogy. The interpretation of abstract, context-free sentences can instead be attributable to several other factors affecting reasoning. For one, the interpreted meaning of the sentence may be attributed to the connective as defined formally or linguistically. The meaning traditionally assumed for the connective *if . . . then . . .* is represented by the conditional truth table (COND). For the COND the joint occurrence of the propositions are defined to be $pq+$, $p\bar{q}-$, $\bar{p}q+$, and $\overline{pq}+$, where $+$ symbolizes *can occur* and $-$ symbolizes *cannot occur*. Many logicians (e.g., Reichenbach, 1947; Strawson, 1952) have observed that *if . . . then . . .* may not have the same meaning as assumed in formal logic for the operation symbolized by "$\rightarrow$" or its notational equivalent "$\supset$." Yet, this meaning has been traditionally assumed the only "correct" one for the conditional sentence *if p then q,* for the sake of expediency and to remove ambiguity. However, empirical tests by Wason (1966, 1968) using the selection task have clearly shown that most individuals do not evaluate *if p then q* according to this formal specification. Wason concluded that individuals regard conditions in which the antecedent is denied, i.e., $\bar{p}$, to be irrelevant in the task situation. Consequently, the predicted truth function is $pq+$, $p\bar{q}-$, and $\bar{p}q$ and $\bar{p}\bar{q}$ both irrelevant. Taplin (1971), using a syllogistic task, has confirmed Wason's suggestion that the interpretation of the conditional sentence is not necessarily COND. Taplin, however, noted that most individuals did consider all propositional contingencies relevant and that the truth table describing the evaluations was the biconditional (BIC) defined as $pq+$, $p\bar{q}-$, $\bar{p}q-$, and $\bar{p}\bar{q}+$.

Thus, both Wason and Taplin have shown that *if p then q* is not always interpreted in a manner equivalent to the COND. If individuals, naive about specifications in formal logic, do not interpret *if p then q* according to the COND, especially with abstract material, it is not valid to conclude that they are reasoning fallaciously. They are illogical only in the sense that they do not interpret the connective according to one unique specification which, from the psychological evidence, is arbitrary. When reasoning with *if p then q* is evaluated according to the interpretation each individual gives to the sentence, the inferences may be perfectly consistent and logical with respect to that interpretation (cf. Henle, 1962, 1971).

Other factors that may influence the interpretation of *if p then q* in reasoning tasks are: (1) response bias, for example, the atmosphere effect suggested by Woodworth and Sells (1935) for categorical syllogistic reasoning, or the matching bias suggested by Evans (1972) to account for Wason's findings in the selection and evaluation tasks; (2) task characteristics, such as the number of response alternatives in the conditional sentence reasoning task employed by Taplin and Staudenmayer (1973); and (3) the instructions about the nature of the task (e.g., Taplin & Fujii, 1973).

In addition, as noted above, the possibility exists that individuals may generate concrete, meaningful examples to mediate reasoning with abstract material. In this situation, the linguistic structure of the sentence limits the types of analogies that may be generated. For example, the linguistic structure of the proposition "It is an *X*" implies that *X* is a nominal class; likewise, the structure of the proposition "It is (has) *X*" implies that *X* is an attribute; and lastly, the structure "*X* occurs" implies that *X* is an event. The structure of the sentence also restricts the possible semantic relation between propositions as well as the connective that is semantically consistent. For example, if both propositions contain nominal classes, the relation between propositions is restricted to one of several possible class relations, such as "*p* is a subset of *q*." This being the case, such connectives as *if . . . then . . .* and *since* are appropriate, whereas *cause* is not. When the contents of both propositions are events, then clearly the semantic relation cannot be one between nominal classes but it can be one where one event causes the other, i.e., causality.

In summary, these "nonlogical" factors must be considered in evaluating reasoning. However, their existence does not warrant the rejection of logic as a model of reasoning. Rather, these factors interact with the logical form in that they influence the interpretation of the task and the material employed. Once this interpretation is established, the rules of logic may very well describe the particular operations carried out in the making of inferences. Wundt long ago pointed out the necessity of considering the global structure of knowledge and the variety of processing strategies an individual possesses and uses to interpret information (Blumenthal, 1970). The requirements of the task as well as the information an individual is asked to make inferences about are not dealt with in isolation but rather become the focal point of the total picture within an interactive, global knowledge and processing system.

REASONING WITH EVENTS

Everyday use of implicative statements is not likely to involve abstract propositions or even norminal classes. Most likely, expressions will be either promises, threats, commands, or predictions. These various types of conditional expressions have a certain commonality in that they most often consist of two events related by a connective, e.g., "If it rains, then he will take his umbrella." Furthermore, conditional sentences used to relate events involve a temporal successive relation, unlike sentences with abstract material or nominal and descriptive classes, in which the temporal relation is not applicable. Temporal succession is important in reasoning with events because it can be used to establish the cause–effect asymmetry in causal relations. Overall, then, the predominant cases of everyday implicative reasoning involve events temporally successive that may, in addition, be interpreted to be causally related.

The concept of causality is not one for which philosophers have a consensus (cf. Nagel, 1961, pp. 316–324). In dealing with the psychological properties of causality in reasoning, the definition of "cause" must be broad enough to incorporate relations that are commonly interpreted as causal. The necessary conditions for mechanical causation as presented by Aronson (1971) fulfill this requirement. The three conditions are here rewritten to apply explicitly to events in the conditional sentence that have a semantic causal relation between p and q. First, the effect q is a change brought about by another external event. If things were unaltered or left alone, the change in q would not be realized by itself. Second, at the time the effect occurs, there is contact, some kind of contingency, between the object (instrument) described in the causal event p and the object in q. Third, before the occurrence of q, the object in p that makes contact with the effect object possesses some form of energy that is transferred to the effect object when the contingency is realized and manifested as q. To illustrate these three points of external force, contingency, and transfer of energy, consider the conditional sentence "If the switch is turned on then the light will go on." There is an external event, turning the switch, which is contingent in terms of time and electrical circuit and which allows for the transfer of electrical energy to light energy.

There is an additional property of p that must be considered by any theory dealing with the interpretation of sentences with connected, meaningful propositions. This property is the pragmatic, logical condition within p in relation to the realization of q. There are four such logical conditions defined by combining *necessary* or *not necessary* with *sufficient* or *insufficient*. Each of these conditions can be described by a unique truth table, pertaining to the joint occurrence of two propositions, p and q, in the two valued propositional calculus of formal logic.

To understand how an individual may process and make judgments about these logical conditions it seems helpful to represent the information in the propositions of the conditional sentence by a notation recently used by Kintsch (1972) to represent information units in memory. Each proposition contains a relation, usually a verb, that requires or allows certain cases, such as agent, object, instrument, recipient, etc., to accompany that verb (cf. Fillmore, 1968). Within this framework, judgments of the sufficiency and necessity of p as a whole are reducible to judgments of the component cases. When a specific value for a case is contained in a proposition, e.g., "I turn the switch," then the question reduces to: Is "I" the only value of agent that can be substituted for the agent case? The same is true for the objective case, e.g., "Is the switch the only object I can turn?" When the linguistic structure of the sentence is such that a generic value for a case is used or implied elliptically, e.g., "The switch is turned," then that particular case, here the agent case, does not allow for a judgment of *not necessary* for p. If no cases are judged *not necessary,* then the proposition is *necessary*. And last, if additional restrictions or qualifying assumptions are introduced into the premises, e.g., the circuits in the switch are working, then p is judged *insufficient*.

Keeping these considerations in mind, let us examine in detail the four logical conditions of p and how they map onto truth tables. First, p can describe a condition that is *sufficient but not necessary* for the occurrences of q, "If I turn the switch on then the light will go on." This sentence specifies a unique agent who manipulates the object in p that transfers energy to the object in q. Obviously, someone else could also turn the switch and the effect, q, would be the same. This interpretation, that someone else can turn the light on, is an instance of q having an alternative cause, formally $\bar{p}$, to one explicitly specified in the proposition p; therefore, p is *not necessary*. *Sufficient* implies that no qualifying assumptions are expressed or acknowledged, so that if I turn the switch the light will definitely go on. This first condition is described by the COND, where the joint occurrence of pq is possible and the joint occurrence of $p\bar{q}$ is impossible.

Second, p can describe a condition that is both *sufficient and necessary* for the occurrence of q, e.g., "If the switch is turned on then the light will go on." Again, *sufficient* implies that switch turning always leads to the light going on. *Necessary* implies that there are no alternatives to p that can lead to q. In this sentence, the agent case is not explicitly stated, making it impossible to make a judgment of *not necessary* on the basis of the agent. This second condition is described by the BIC as the joint occurrences of pq and $\overline{pq}$ are possible.

Third, p can describe a condition that is *necessary but insufficient* for the occurrence of q. This situation usually results from the conjunction of two or more qualifying conditions in p. In the example, one might add the restriction "The light bulb is not burned out," making switch turning *insufficient*. In so doing, the joint occurrence of both $p\bar{q}$ and pq are possible. That is, the light may or may not go on when the switch is turned, depending on the state of the light bulb. Given that this condition is also *necessary,* such an interpretation can be described by a truth table where pq and $p\bar{q}$ are +, $\bar{p}q$ is —, and $\overline{pq}$ is +. This truth function is referred to as "reversed conditional" (REV COND) because the truth values of the $p\bar{q}$ and $\bar{p}q$ contingencies have been interchanged with respect to the COND.

The fourth and last condition is one in which p is both *not necessary and insufficient*. This means that q can be realized by alternatives to p as well as p and that p alone is not always enough for q. The truth table describing this condition is one in which all four contingencies of the two propositions are possible, namely, $pq+$, $p\bar{q}+$, $\bar{p}q+$, and $\overline{pq}+$.

The interpretation of the logical condition of p in meaningful sentences is not entailed in the linguistic structure of the sentence. Rather, this information must be inferred from nonlinguistic, pragmatic factors, such as factual or empirical knowledge (e.g., lightbulbs must not be burned out for the light to go on) and presuppositions about context (e.g., I am or am not alone in the room).

AIM OF THE STUDY

The central thesis of this study is that pragmatic, contextual presuppositions are primary and necessary considerations for understanding how people interpret the complete meaning of a semantic, causal relation and make inferences from implicative statements, specifically, from the conditional sentence *if p then q*, and the causal sentence *p causes q*. The study aims to show that the evaluations resulting from the conditional sentence reasoning task can be influenced by manipulating certain structural variables in the sentence, namely, the content of the propositions and the meaningfulness of the relation between propositions. The truth functions (either COND or BIC) ascribed to conditional and causal statements in various sentences will be inferred, thereby indicating whether a particular presupposition about the necessity of p has or has not been made by an individual. To arrive at a COND interpretation the individual must search his memory, centered at q, for alternatives to p that allow the realization of q. Finding just one such alternative is enough to interpret the conditions in $\bar{p}$ as *not necessary*. Logically, these alternatives to p are subsumed under $\bar{p}$ and the joint occurrence of $\bar{p}q$ is thus a real possibility. In contrast, the BIC interpretation is one in which q is realized by only p. Therefore, p is *necessary* since $\bar{p}$ always leads to the realization of $\bar{q}$.

METHOD

Subjects

Volunteers were recruited from the University of Colorado undergraduate pool. The subjects were divided into eight experimental conditions with about 50 subjects in each group. The subjects were run in groups of average size about 25, randomly assigned to the experimental conditions. A postexperimental query determined whether subjects had any formal instruction in logic at the college level. Those subjects having had such training were removed from all analyses.

Procedure

Each test item was contained on a slide and projected onto a screen at the front of the classroom. Each slide portrayed a set of three statements labeled *A*, *B*, and *C*, where *A* and *B* constituted the premises and *C* the conclusion. A typical example of such an item is

A. If the switch is turned on then the light will go on.
B. The switch is turned on.
C. The light goes on.

The first premise was always the implicative sentence. The second premise was either the antecedent or the consequent, affirmed or denied; and the conclusion was the other proposition, affirmed or denied, giving the eight forms of the conditional argument presented in Table 1. The tenses of the verbs in the second premise and the conclusion were consistent with the principle of temporal succession. In other words, if the second premise contained the antecedent, affirmative or negative, it was in the present tense, as was the consequent in the conclusion. If the second premise contained the consequent, it was in the present tense, while the antecedent in the conclusion was in the past tense. The task for the subjects was to read and interpret the two premises and, on the basis of this knowledge, to evaluate (on a response sheet provided) the occurrence of the conclusion as always true (True), always false (False), or sometimes true and sometimes false (Sometimes).

This response mapping allows for both determinate (True or False) and indeterminate evaluations of the conclusion. An example of an indeterminate evaluation is one in which the subject interprets the premises according to the COND and is given *If p then q* and q as premises. For this case, both p or $\bar{p}$ are both possible occurrences, and the "Sometimes" response is appropriate for either conclusion. If the subject interprets these same premises according to the BIC, a determinate response is appropriate; "True" when the conclusion is p and "False" when the conclusion is $\bar{p}$.

TABLE 1
Eight Forms of the Conditional Arguments with Response Entries of True (T), False (F), and Sometimes (S) for Three Truth–Table Mappings

First premise[a]	Second premise	Conclusion	COND	BIC	REV COND
If p, then q	p	q	T	T	S
If p, then q	p	$\bar{q}$	F	F	S
If p, then q	$\bar{p}$	q	S	F	F
If p, then q	$\bar{p}$	$\bar{q}$	S	T	T
If p, then q	q	p	S	T	T
If p, then q	q	$\bar{p}$	S	F	F
If p, then q	$\bar{q}$	p	F	F	S
If p, then q	$\bar{q}$	$\bar{p}$	T	T	S

[a]The first premise for groups reasoning with the explicit causal connective consistently read "p causes q."

The eight forms of the conditional argument were randomly assigned within each block of eight trials for 12 blocks, giving a total of 96 trials. The content of the premises was the same within a block, changing between blocks. Presentation of items was paced, each item being exposed for 20 sec. The twelve replications on each form of the argument were presented to determine whether subjects were statistically consistent within each of the eight forms. A binomial test was used for this purpose, and for each form the criterion point at which the null hypothesis that there is equal likelihood of a response in each of the three response categories was rejected was $\alpha = .05$. If a subject was found not to be consistent at this criterion level (i.e., eight or more responses out of the 12 replications of any argument where not in one of the three response categories) on all eight forms of the argument, then he was initially classified as statistically inconsistent. Otherwise, the analysis proceeded to the next step, which was to infer a truth table that could account for the subject's evaluations of the arguments. To simplify the discussion from here on, only those subjects who responded consistently to all eight forms of the argument are considered. Therefore, that response which a subject used eight or more times on a given form of the argument was used to make an inference about his possible truth function.

The patterns of responses corresponding to the three truth functions investigated in this study, namely, COND, REV COND, and BIC, are presented in Table 1. The method by which truth tables have been inferred from the subject's responses is discussed in the remainder of this section. Comprehension of this step by step method is not essential to understanding the results of this study and may be bypassed by the reader.

To understand the method of inferring a truth table in the two valued propositional calculus from the evaluations made by a subject, consider two questions. First, what is the space of possible truth tables for the conditional sentence expressed in the first premise? Any one truth table represents judgments about the possibility that joint events resulting from the four possible combinations of p or $\bar{p}$ with q or $\bar{q}$ can occur given *if p then q*. Because the assignments of values are in principle independent, there are $2^4 = 16$ possible truth tables, as shown in Table 2. Each corresponds to a particular assignment of *can occur* (+) and *cannot occur* (—) to the joint events in the cells of the 2×2 table of $\{p,\bar{p}\} \times \{q,\bar{q}\}$. Second, on the basis of his responses to the eight forms of the argument, how can it be determined whether the subject has a truth table or whether he is contradictory between arguments in his evaluations and no truth table can be inferred? Furthermore, if a subject is noncontradictory in his evaluations of the forms of the argument, how can we determine which one of the possible 16 truth tables he has?

TABLE 2

Sixteen Possible Truth Tables in the Two-Valued Propositional Calculus

Truth–table	Truth functions[a]															
contingency	1	2	3	4	5	6	7	8	9	10	11	12	13	14	15	16
pq	+	+	+	+	+	+	+	+	–	–	–	–	–	–	–	–
$p\bar{q}$	+	+	+	+	–	–	–	–	+	+	+	+	–	–	–	–
$\bar{p}q$	+	+	–	–	+	+	–	–	+	+	–	–	+	+	–	–
$\overline{pq}$	+	–	+	–	+	–	+	–	+	–	+	–	+	–	+	–

[a]The following are labels for the truth functions: 2, inclusive disjunction; 3, reversed conditional; 5, conditional; 7, biconditional; 9, alternatie denial; 10, exclusive disjunction; 4, 6, 11, 13, affirmation; 8, 12, 14, 15, conjunction; 1 and 16 are best described as "anything can occur" and "nothing can occur," respectively.

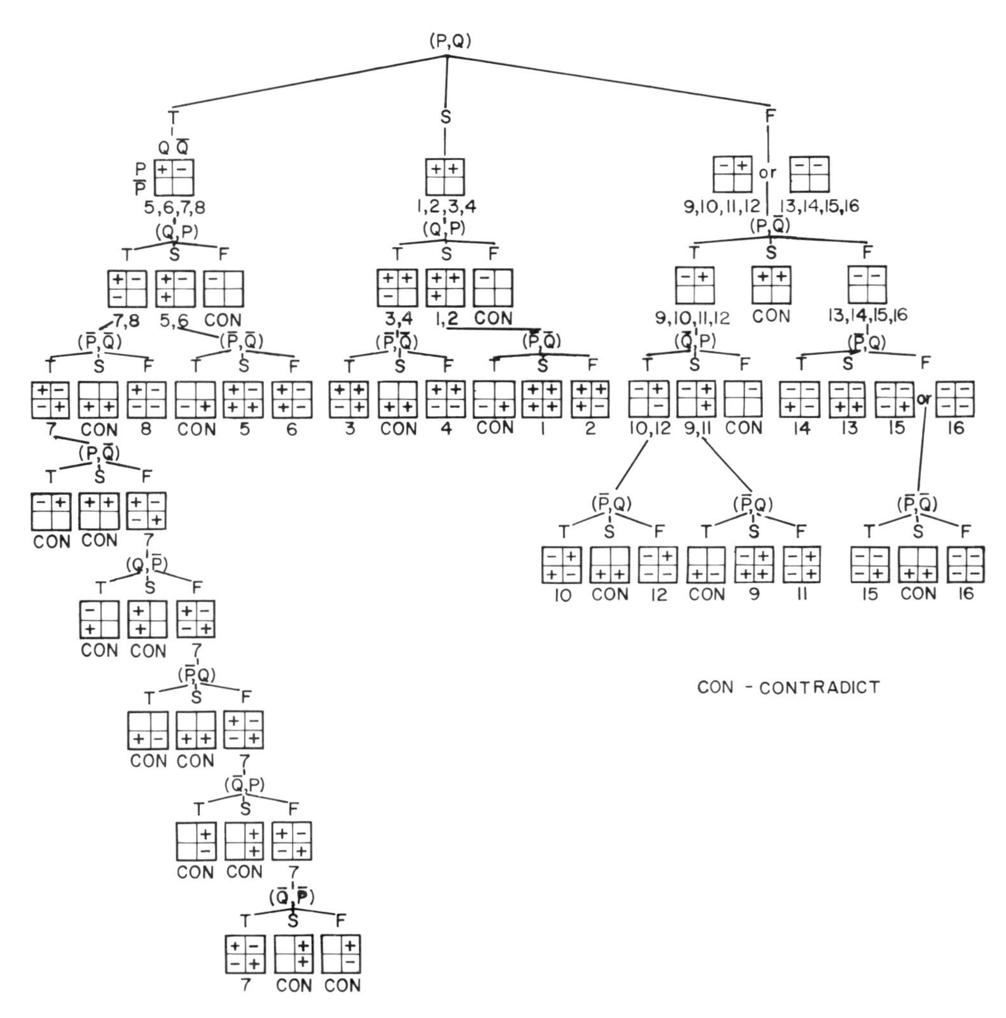

FIG. 1. Decision tree for inferring any one of 16 possible truth tables in the propositional calculus from three responses, True (T), False (F), and Sometimes (S), in the conditional sentence reasoning task.

The system for inferring a truth table in the conditional sentence reasoning task may be understood with the aid of Figure 1. The figure is a decision tree with two-tuples of the form of the argument (second premise, conclusion) serving as test nodes for the decisions about the possibility of these joint events occurring. Successively refined partitions of the set {1, 2, . . . , 16} of possible truth tables are the outcomes of the decisions.

This tree, although not unique, is sufficient to infer a particular subject's truth table from his responses. Each terminal node either corresponds exactly to one truth function or indicates that the subject is contradicting himself across arguments and no truth table can be inferred. Arbitrarily, the first test node in the tree represents the form of the argument where p is affirmed as the second premise and q is affirmed as the conclusion to be evaluated; in graph notation, simply (p, q). The subject's response to this argument, "True" (T), "False" (F), or "Sometimes" (S), gives us his judgments about the joint occurrence of the two events and also defines a path in the tree. As indicated in Fig. 1, a "True" response narrows the possibilities for the subject's truth table from 16 to four, namely {5, 6, 7, 8}, as numbered in Table 2. Only two further tests with (q, p) and $(\bar{p}, \bar{q})$ are necessary to determine which one of these four possible interpretations the subject is using. The remaining forms of the argument are exhaustively tested to see whether the subject contradicts himself at any point. This latter test for contradiction between arguments is explicitly shown only for the leftmost major branch of the tree diagram, where the noncontradictory pattern of responding leads to a BIC.

It may be helpful at this point to follow this leftmost branch using a concrete example to explicate the various notational conventions in Figure 1 along the way. An omnipresent first premise is the conditional sentence, "If the switch is turned on, then the light will go on." The first form of the argument examined is one in which p is affirmed as the second premise, namely, "The switch is turned on," and q is affirmed as the conclusion to be evaluated, namely, "The light goes on"; this is represented by (p, q) at the top of the tree. The path to the leftmost branch is reached if a "True" response is given, which means that it is always true that the light will go on (q) given the switch is turned (p). The 2×2 table under the T in the path tabulates this evaluation of the occurrence of the joint events. The occurrence of q given p is represented by a plus in that cell. And, because p always leads to q, this entails that p never leads to $\bar{q}$, allowing the placement of a minus in that cell representing the joint events, $p\bar{q}$. From the two cell entries, the number of 16 possible truth tables in Table 2 is reduced to four, {5, 6, 7, 8}. To make inferences about the entries in the remaining two cells, additional forms of the argument must be examined. The second node, (q, p) tests the argument; given the light is on, was the switch turned on? A response of "True" indicates that the light will not go on if the switch is not turned. This warrants a minus to be entered in the $\bar{p}q$ cell, indicating that the joint events $\bar{p}q$ cannot occur. With three cells filled, only two possible truth functions remain, {7, 8}. The third node, $(\bar{p}, \bar{q})$, tests the argument: given the switch was not turned, is the light off? A response of "True" indicates that the joint events $\overline{pq}$

always occur, represented by a + in that cell (i.e., it is always the case that not turning the switch will result in the light not going on.)

At this point, after examining only three forms of the argument, all truth-table contingencies have been evaluated, with the resulting truth table being {7} or BIC. The remaining five arguments are examined to determine whether there is a contradiction between arguments. The fourth node, $(p, \bar{q})$, is such a test. Here, the argument is: given the switch is turned, does the light remain off? A "False" response indicates that the joint events $p\bar{q}$ never occur. This evaluation is in agreement with the BIC and therefore this response is necessitated for the evaluations to be noncontradictory with prior evaluations. Given this response, the procedure for evaluating a truth table is repeated for the reamining nodes. However, if a "True" or "Sometimes" response is made to the $(p\bar{q})$ argument (yielding a "+" in the corresponding cell) there is a contradiction between this argument and prior arguments (which have led to a "—" in the same cell). Whenever there is such a contradictory response, the inference procedure is terminated and no truth table is inferred. Instead, the resulting truth-table classification is CONTRADICTORY.

Design

The conditions in this experiment were aimed at understanding some factors that might influence the interpretation of premises made by subjects in reasoning with events. Four variables differentiated conditions: semantic content (abstract versus concrete), form of the connective (*if . . . then . . .* versus *cause*), semantic relation (anomalous versus causal), and the pragmatic relation of the antecedent to the consequent (*necessary* versus *not necessary*).

The first group reasoned with abstract material jointed by the conditional connective *if . . . then . . .* (*abs–cond*). Predication within the propositions was such that the content of p and q, although abstract, could only be interpreted as events. The transitive verb "occurs" was selected as the predicate in each proposition because it can only take a predicate phrase depicting an event as grammatical subject. Sentences were of the form "If X occurs, then Y occurs," where X and Y represent letters of the alphabet.

The second group reasoned with abstract material joined by the causal connective *cause* (*abs–cause*). Again, the content of the propositions, although abstract, could only be interpreted as events because of the restrictions in the verb "cause" that connects the two events. Sentences were of the form X *causes* Y with the same restrictions on the assignment of letters to X and Y as in the previous *abs–cond* group. The verb "cause" was selected because it is a dimension word (Austin, 1962, p. 71) that encompasses the more specific transitive verbs, such as "makes," "push," "knocks," "turns," etc., that are more commonly used to express causality.

The third and fourth groups reasoned with identical material except for the form of the connective joining the propositions. The semantic relation between concrete propositions was anomalous. The third group dealt with an anomalous semantic relation between events connected by the conditional connective (*anom–cond*). Sentences were of the form "If she waters the tropical plant then the light will go on." The fourth group had the semantically anomalous relation connected by the causal connective (*anom–cause*). Sentences were of the form "Her watering the plant causes the light to go on." These sentences were generated by arbitrarily recombining antecedent and consequent propositions from the sentences used in the groups in which the semantic relation was meaningfully causal. These 12 sentences were made up by the investigator to comply with the three requirements of mechanical causality specified earlier, dealing with events common to everyday experience. These groups are described next.

The fifth and sixth groups both reasoned with a meaningful, causal relation between events joined by the conditional connective. The two groups differed in the pragmatic features (and associated logical structure of p). The fifth group (*not nec–cond*) had p a *not necessary* condition for q. Sentences were of the form "If I turn on the switch then the light will go on." In this example, as noted above, it is not necessary that "I" turn on the switch because the light will go on if "you" or "someone else" turns on the switch. The sixth group (*nec–cond*) was identical to the fifth except that p was a *necessary* condition for a. Sentences were of the form "If the switch is turned on then the light will go on." In this sentence the agent case is unspecified, thus not allowing a judgment of *not necessary* on this basis.

The material for the seventh group (*not nec–cause*) was identical to that used for the fifth except for the form of the connective. The events were causally related with p *not necessary* for q, connected by the explicit causal connective. Sentences for this condition were of the form "My turning the switch on causes the light to go on." The eighth group (*nec–cause*) was parallel to the sixth except for the form of the connective. The events were causally related with p *necessary* for q, connected by the causal connective. Sentences for this group were of the form "Turning the switch on causes the light to go on."

RESULTS

The responses for each subject were analyzed individually. The first step in the analysis was to determine whether the subject was statistically consistent within each of the eight argument types. To be classified as consistent a subject had to be consistent for all eight arguments; i.e., for each of these he had to give the same response eight times or more across the

TABLE 3

Percentage of Subjects Inferred in Each Truth-Table Classification

	Statistically consistent				Statistically inconsistent			
Condition	COND	REV COND	BIC	CONTRA-DICTORY	COND	BIC	CONTRA-DICTORY	*N*
Abs–cond	26.8	4.9	36.6	2.4	9.8	9.8	9.8	41
Abs–cause	8.0	18.0	60.0	2.0	4.0	6.0	2.0	50
Anom–cond	13.8		39.7	12.1	17.2	5.2	12.1	58
Anom–cause	20.4		42.9	4.1	10.2	8.2	14.2	49
Not nec–cond	37.0		29.6	3.7	9.3	14.8	5.6	54
Not nec–cause	20.0		34.5	5.5	9.1	12.7	18.2	55
Nec–cond	7.7		44.2	5.8	11.5	11.5	19.2	52
Nec–cause	5.9		31.4	7.8	7.8	27.5	19.6	51

12 replications. If one to four arguments were inconsistent, the subject was classified as "statistically inconsistent." Furthermore, the subjects inconsistent on five or more arguments were eliminated from any further analyses. Fifteen subjects, distributed over the eight experimental conditions, were eliminated for this reason.

The next step was to infer a truth table for each subject that could describe the pattern of evaluations of the arguments. The inferences made about the truth values for each truth-table contingency were according to the method described above. Based on the evaluations, each subject in each group was initially classified into one of five categories, COND, REV COND, BIC, CONTRADICTORY (i.e., statistically consistent within any one argument but logically contradictory between arguments), or inconsistent (i.e., statistically inconsistent within arguments). Those subjects who were initially classified as "inconsistent" were further classified into one of the other four categories on the basis of only those forms of the argument on which they were statistically consistent. Inconsistent subjects for whom no one unique truth function could be inferred from the remaining consistent arguments were pooled with the inconsistent subjects who had been reclassified as CONTRADICTORY. For purposes of group comparisons, the REV COND subjects were pooled with the BIC subjects; the rationale behind this pooling is that both truth-table mappings have *p necessary,* although they differ on sufficiency. The results for each of the eight experimental groups are presented in Table 3.

Two types of statistical analyses comparing results between groups were performed, both of which employed χ^2. The first analysis dealt with the logical consistency of subjects in different experimental groups. The subjects were classified into two categories based on prior tabulations. One category, called "consistent and noncontradictory," contained those subjects who were statistically consistent in their evaluations of all eight forms of the argument and interpreted the sentences as either COND or BIC (includes REV COND). The other category, called "inconsistent or contradictory," included the remaining subjects, who were inconsistent on one or more arguments or who were statistically consistent but CONTRADICTORY.

The second analysis dealt with the particular interpretation subjects made or tended to make for the sentences. The subjects were again classified into two categories based on their truth-table interpretation, COND or BIC. In this classification, however, the question of consistency was ignored so that subjects who were consistent were combined with those who were inconsistent on some arguments but still could be inferred to be COND or BIC on the remaining arguments. For brevity, the second analysis will be referred to as the "truth-table analysis" and the first analysis will be referred to as the "consistency analysis."

Each of these analyses is applied to the results from those experimental groups which address the effects of a particular variable on the interpretation and evaluation of the sentences. The variables in this study are analyzed and discussed in the following order: meaning of the connective, content of the propositions, semantic relation, and the pragmatics of the antecedent.

Meaning of the Connective

To determine the difference in the meaning of the connectives *if . . . then . . .* and *cause,* independent of content and relations between propositions, the results of the four groups reasoning with *if . . . then . . .* were combined and compared to the combined results of the four groups reasoning with *cause.* The analysis on consistency indicated that the number of subjects who evaluated *if . . . then . . .* consistently (59.5%) did not differ statistically from the number of subjects who evaluated *cause* consistently (60.2%), $\chi^2(1) = 0.02$, $p = .858$. However, the comparison on truth tables, COND versus BIC, was significant, $\chi^2(1) = 14.68$, $p < .001$. For *if . . . then . . .* 40.7% of subjects were COND and 59.3% were BIC, whereas for *cause* only 23.3% were COND and 76.7% were BIC. The conclusion about the meaning of the conectives is that *cause* is more likely to be interpreted as BIC than is *if . . . then . . .*, ignoring the effects of other variables.

Content of the Propositions

The content of the propositions, abstract or concrete, has been suggested as an important factor in accounting for fallacies in syllogistic reasoning (Wilkins, 1928). To analyze what the effect might be in this task, the combined results of *abs–cond* and *abs–cause* were compared to the combined results from the other six groups in the study, all reasoning with concrete propositions although not always meaningfully related. The number of consistent subjects (78.0%) was significantly higher with abstract material than with concrete material (54.5%), $\chi^2(1) = 16.23$, $p < .001$. The analysis on truth tables was inconclusive, $\chi^2(1) = 3.58$, $p = .055$. With abstract material, 25.0% of subjects were COND and 75.0% were BIC; with concrete material, 36.3% were COND and 63.7% were BIC. The effects of different material lies mostly in the consistency with which subjects evaluate arguments. This finding seems to characterize the essence of Wilkins' (1928) hypothesis. With abstract material, subjects are more consistent relative to concrete material. The effect of material on the interpretation, COND or BIC, indicates that concrete material leads to greater variance in the interpretation of the sentences, although not quite enough to be statistically significant at $\alpha = .05$.

When the effects of content are separately analyzed for the connectives, there is an interaction in terms of truth-table interpretations. For *if . . . then . . .*, the number of COND subjects is 41.7% with abstract material and 40.5% with concrete propositions; there is no difference, $\chi^2(1) = 0.02$ $p = .864$. However, for *cause* the relative number of COND subjects reasoning with abstract material (12.5%) is half the number in concrete groups (26.6%). This difference was statistically significant, $\chi^2(1) = 4.01$, $p = .042$. Therefore, there is an interaction between the specific connective and the content of the material with respect to the particular interpreted meaning of the sentence, COND or BIC. The strong tendency for subjects to interpret *cause* as BIC is not so readily overcome with concrete material.

Semantic Relations

The previous findings raise the question: what is it about concrete material that leads to greater inconsistency? To answer this question the following hypothesis is proposed. The interpretation of concrete propositions is affected by factors other than the meaning of the connective alone. These factors open the door to many possible meanings of a sentence, all of which are potential interpretations that subjects can make. One such factor is the semantic relation between propositions. Given our knowledge of the world, some relations represent information that is consistent with this knowledge, e.g., lights are turned on with switches, whereas other relations are inconsistent with this knowledge and therefore semantically anomalous, e.g., lights are not turned on by watering plants. With semantically anomalous relations subjects may either ignore the content and treat the propositions as abstract or make the anomalous meaningful in a hypothetical world. Which of these strategies subjects may employ in this study can be tested. If subjects treat semantically anomalous propositions no different from abstract propositions, no difference in consistency or truth-table evaluations is expected by comparing the combined results of the *abs–cond* and *abs–cause* groups with the combined results of the *anom–cond* and *anom–cause* groups. If in fact there are no differences in this comparison, then it can be hypothesized that multiple meanings of a sentence are dependent on the existence of a semantically meaningful relation as defined in our everyday knowledge of the world. However, if subjects make anomalous relations meaningful in a hypothetical world, then the expected comparisons should differ. In addition, no differences are expected between groups reasoning with a semantically anomalous relation and groups reasoning with a semantically meaningful relation.

The results of the consistency analysis showed subjects reasoning with abstract material to be more consistent (78.0%) than those reasoning with semantically anomalous propositions (57.9%), $\chi^2(1) = 8.99$ $p = .003$. The truth-table analysis comparing the same groups was also significant, $\chi^2(1) = 3.93$ $p = .044$. With abstract material the interpretations were 25.0% COND and 75.0% BIC; with the anomalous relation the interpretations were 39.3% COND and 60.7% BIC. The increase in COND interpretations is consistent with the earlier finding of great variance in interpretation with concrete material. These findings warrant the rejection of the hypothesis that subjects treat concrete propositions anomalously related as if they were abstract.

The results of the comparison between subjects reasoning with an anomalous relation with those reasoning with a semantically causal relation showed them to be equally consistent, $\chi^2(1) = 0.75$ $p = .609$. With the anomalous relation 57.9% were consistent and with the causal relation 52.8% were consistent. There was also no difference in the truth-table analysis, $\chi^2(1) = 0.50$, $p = .514$. With the anomalous relation the interpretations were 39.3% COND and 60.7% BIC and with the causal relation the interpretations were 34.7% COND and 65.3% BIC. These findings support the hypothesis that semantically anomalous relations are not necessarily meaningless when allowance is made for a shift to hypothetical, possible worlds where the contextual pragmatics can also be represented in terms of the logical condition of p. The semantic relation, defined to be semantically meaningful in our everyday world, therefore cannot be used to explain the greater inconsistency in reasoning resulting from sentences with concrete material.

Pragmatics of the Antecedent

There was one factor manipulated in this study to influence the interpretation of sentences either toward COND or toward BIC. By introducing a specific agent into the implicative sentence the presupposition that someone else could perform the causal act is invited. If the presupposition is made, the logical condition of p is *not necessary,* a condition consistent with the COND. When the agent is omitted, the presupposition is precluded and the logical condition of p is *necessary,* a condition consistent with the BIC. To test the effect of this manipulation a comparison of the combined results of *not nec–cond* and *not nec–cause* with the combined results of *nec–cond* and *nec–cond* was made. The truth-table analysis confirmed the expectation in that 45.1% of the subjects were COND with *p not necessary,* whereas only 22.4% were COND with p necessary. The statistical comparison was significant, $\chi^2(1) = 9.40$ $p = .002$.

Although this finding demonstrates that the presupposition about alternative agents can be induced by manipulating the case structure in the sentence, there is reservation about the extent to which this presupposition is made by subjects because 54.9% of subjects did not make it. This is not so surprising, because the presupposition, to have an effect on the interpretation, must also include an assumption about the context in which the events occur. Specifically, in the example about turning on the light, the assumption must entail more than one person in the room. A study investigating context and the particular effects it has on the presuppositions is currently being carried out in our laboratory (Staudenmayer & Garcia, 1975).

GENERAL DISCUSSION

A review of previous formulations of the relation between the rules of logic and reasoning indicated a general misunderstanding as to the role of the rules of logic in reasoning and in thinking in general. At the heart of the misunderstanding was the erroneous assumption that the symbolic operators in formal logic (and the forms of the syllogism in syllogistic reasoning) could be mapped, on a one-to-one basis, onto linguistic connectives and onto the processing operations individuals used to make evaluations in reasoning. This conceptualization completely ignored two possibilities: (1) the possibility that subjects might interpret symbolic operators or linguistic connectives to mean something other than their formal definition (Reichenbach, 1947: Strawson, 1952; Taplin & Staudenmayer, 1973); and (2) the possibility that subjects might not accept the demands of the task and consider certain evaluations to be irrelevant (Wason, 1966) or reason according to the least demanding or most parsimonious strategy (Ceraso & Provitera, 1971). Any attempt to refute the hypothesis that thinking and reasoning follow the rules of logic cannot succeed if it ignores these possibilities in judging evaluations simply because the hypothesis is misunderstood.

However, a theory based on this hypothesis which carefully distinguishes between the interpretation process and the evaluation process in reasoning seems viable. Viable to the extent, at least, that refutation of the theory must consider and encompass the distinction.

The present study has been concerned with demonstrating the feasibility of developing such a logical theory of reasoning. The burden of investigation within this theoretical framework rests on the identification of factors that affect the process by which an individual interprets premises. The theory entails the possibility of multiple interpretations of the same lexical information. These different interpretations can result from an individual's predisposed strategy, his interpretation of and reaction to the task demands, the structural and semantic variables in the implicative sentence, and the contextual presuppositions made to complete the meaning of the statement.

The results of this reasoning study support this approach with respect to implicative statements. The unique patterns of evaluations described by the COND and BIC have been reliably predicted for many individuals on the basis of certain manipulations in the implicative sentence. In addition, the connective between propositions interacted with content of the propositions and the semantic relation between propositions in affecting the consistency of evaluations. In evaluating human reasoning and thinking, none of these factors can be ignored because they all have some effect on the interpretation of the premises and the evaluation of conclusions, some more so than others depending on the task demands. It is a necessary prerequisite for psychologists to understand the interpretation process in order to model reasoning. To reemphasize the point stated so well by Henle (1962, 1971), the more rudimentary operations involved in evaluating a conclusion from an interpreted code can be studied only after that code is known.

One proposed explanation for the BIC interpretation of conditional sentences has been that subjects who interpret an implicative statement as BIC do so because they assume it to be a causal statement. Although the BIC is consistent with a causal interpretation wherein p is *necessary and sufficient,* it is also possible for a causal relation to be interpreted as COND when p is judged *not necessary but sufficient.* When the logical condition of p is ambiguous, as is the case with abstract material, the subject may very well generate concrete examples that reflect a causal relation with p *necessary* to mediate evaluations. Assuming p *necessary* rather than *not necessary* is the prevailing tendency among subjects, especially when the connective is explicity "cause." However, this finding should not be mistakenly interpreted to mean that subjects who evaluate abstract conditional sentences as BIC do so because they infer a causal relation between p and q. Such an explanation is erroneous because it assumes that p in causal relation is always interpreted to be necessary. This need not be the case, as evidenced by the finding that about one-fifth of the subjects evaluated sentences with the causal connective as COND. These findings are consistent with the principle of invited inference, suggested by Geis and Zwicky (1971), in that subjects will interpret the BIC unless made aware of alternative possibilities.

Another finding was that a larger percentage of subjects reasoning with abstract material were consistent when compared to those reasoning with anomalously related propositions. This finding is consistent with the argument that a semantically anomalous relation confuses subjects more than no semantic relation at all, as in abstract sentences. Wason and Shapiro (1971), in discussing similar relations in a selection task, have offered a similar explanation. They have noted that it may be the concrete relation between terms, rather than the terms themselves, which is beneficial. They have proposed to test this hypothesis by using sentences made up of propositions with abstract content, letters and numbers, with the relation between propositions expressed by verbs that restrict the possible interpretations of the abstract content, e.g., "Every time I go to K I travel by 3," where letters are restricted to a place and numbers to a mode of transport. Furthermore, traveling to a place by transport makes sense with respect to our knowledge of the world. The results of this study also suggest that subjects can make sense out of anomalous relations even though they are meaningless in everyday knowledge of the world. Possibly, they shift to a hypothetical world in which they organize the propositions in some meaningful manner.

The results also show that subjects reasoning with meaningful propositions causally related are more inconsistent than those reasoning with abstract material. This finding appears counterintuitive in light of the emphasis on semantic relations in this study and similar speculations by other authors. Wason and Shapiro (1971), for example, have hypothesized that thematic material, unlike abstract material, forms a coherent unified whole that is part of our knowledge system. When this representation is activated by appropriate cues, the solution to a problem may be simply read off by reference to this stored information. Other studies (Johnson-Laird, Legrenzi, & Legrenzi, 1972; Lunzer, Harrison, & Davey, 1972) have shown empirically that subjects perform logically better when reasoning with thematic material in the selection task developed by Wason.

Then why would more subjects reasoning with meaningful relations be inconsistent than those reasoning with abstract material? Should the semantic relations not help subjects to evaluate the arguments consistently?

With abstract material, an individual can follow a fixed strategy for evaluating arguments without having to consider other possible interpretations implied by inferring different contextual presuppositions from the semantic relation. When presuppositions lead to different interpretations of the logical condition of *p* between successive problems, the individual will be classified inconsistent or contradictory when his performance is evaluated across problems. Unfortunately, this study did not tap one individual's evaluations of each of the 12 problems separately, although such an investigation is in progress (Staudenmayer & Garcia, 1975).

CONCLUSION

Central to the theory in this study is the separation of two important aspects in the psychological investigation of reasoning and thinking. First, there is the process by which implicative sentences are interpreted, and second, there is the process by which arguments are evaluated. The interpretive aspect of reasoning is more of an inductive (Mill, 1874; Henle, 1971) or practical process wherein the strength or likelihood of accepting or rejecting an interpretation is a personal factor, such that different individuals may reach different conclusions about the plausibility of any proposition or combination of propositions. The point here is that this inductive process that determines the plausibility of accepting an interpretation is influenced by general knowledge, presuppositions about context, linguistic variables in the sentence, and predisposed strategy or bias for reasoning. According to Mill, Henle, and others, once an individual accepts the most plausible interpretation for him, the evaluations follow consistently and logically. In Mill's (1874) words, "What remains to be performed afterward is merely deciphering our own notes [p. 142]." The rules of logic, it is argued, capture the essence of this deductive process used to decipher or evaluate those notes.

ACKNOWLEDGMENTS

This research was supported by Research Grants MH 14314-06 and NSF GB340-77X awarded to Lyle E. Bourne, Jr., to whom the author expresses special thanks not only for his financial support, but more important, for his suggestions and criticisms in the conceptualization and development of this study in an earlier form submitted as a Ph.D. dissertation to the University of Colorado. I am grateful to Rachel Falmagne for editorial suggestions improving the presentation in the manuscript.

REFERENCES

Aronson, J. L. On the grammar of "cause." *Synthese,* 1971, **22,** 414–430.

Austin, J. L. *Sense and sensibilia.* London and New York: Oxford University Press, 1962.

Blumenthal, A. L. *Language and psychology: Historical aspects of psycholinguistics.* New York: Wiley, 1970.

Boole, G. *An investigation of the laws of thought.* New York: Macmillan, 1854.

Ceraso, J., & Provitera, A. Sources of error in syllogistic reasoning. *Cognitive Psychology,* 1971, 2, 400–410.

Evans, J. St. B. T. Interpretation and matching bias in a reasoning task. *Quarterly Journal of Experimental Psychology,* 1972, **24,** 193–199.

Fillmore, C. J. The case for case. In E. Bach & R. T. Harms (Eds.), *Universals in linguistic theory.* New York: Holt, Rinehart, & Winston, 1968, 1–90.

Geis, M., & Zwicky, A. M. On invited inferences. *Linguistic Inquiry,* 1971, **2,** 561–566.

Henle, M. On the relation between logic and thinking. *Psychological Review,* 1962, **69,** 366–378.

Henle, M. Of the scholler of nature. *Social Research,* 1971, **38,** 93–107.

Johnson-Laird, P. N., Legrenzi, P., & Legrenzi, M. S. Reasoning and a sense of reality. *British Journal of Psychology,* 1972, **63,** 395–400.

Kant, I. *Critique of pure reason,* 1781. Translated by Max Muller, New York: Doubleday, 1966.

Kintsch, W. Notes on the structure of semantic memory. In E. Tulving & W. Donaldson (Eds.), *Organization of memory*. New York: Academic Press, 1972, 249–309.

Lakoff, G. On generative semantics, In D. D. Steinberg & L. A. Jakobovits (Eds.), *Semantics*. Cambridge, England: Cambridge University Press, 1971, 232–296.

Lunzer, E. A., Harrison, C., & Davey, M. The four card problem and the generality of formal reasoning. *Quarterly Journal of Experimental Psychology*, 1972, **24**, 326–339.

Mill, J. S. *System of logic*. New York: Harper, 1874.

Nagel, E. *Logic without metaphysics*. Glencoe, Ill.: Free Press, 1956.

Nagel, E. *The structure of science*. New York: Harcourt, 1961.

Reichenbach, H. *Elements of symbolic logic*. New York: Dover, 1947.

Stalnaker, R. C. Pragmatics. *Synthese*, 1970, **22**, 272–289.

Staudenmayer, H., & Garcia, R. Contextual effects in the interpretation and evaluation of meaningful conditional sentences. Paper presented at the third meeting of the Epistemics group, Urbana–Champaign, Illinois, February, 1975.

Strawson, P. F. *Introduction to logical theory*. London: Methuen, 1952.

Taplin, J. E. Reasoning with conditional sentences. *Journal of Verbal Learning & Verbal Behavior*, 1971, **10**, 218–225.

Taplin, J. E., & Fujii, M. S. Ambiguous sentence interpretation in a deductive reasoning task. Paper presented at the 81st Annual Convention of the American Psychological Association, Montreal, Canada, 1973.

Taplin, J. E., & Staudenmayer, H. Interpretation of abstract conditional sentences in deductive reasoning. *Journal of Verbal Learning & Verbal Behavior*, 1973, **12**, 530–542.

Wason, P. C. Reasoning. In B. Foss (Ed.), *New horizons in psychology*. Harmondsworth, England: Penguin, 1966.

Wason, P. C. Reasoning about a rule. *Quarterly Journal of Experimental Psychology*, 1968, **20**, 273–281.

Wason, P. C., & Shapiro, D. Natural and contrived experience in a reasoning problem. *Quarterly Journal of Experimental Psychology*, 1971, **23**, 63–71.

Wilkins, M. C. The effect of changed material on ability to do formal syllogistic reasoning. *Archives of Psychology*, 1928, No. 102.

Wittgenstein, L. *Philosophical investigations*. (3rd ed.) Translated by G. E. M. Anscombe. New York: Macmillan, 1958.

Woodworth, R. S., & Sells, S. B. An atmosphere effect in formal syllogistic reasoning. *Journal of Experimental Psychology*, 1935, **18**, 451–460.

3
LOGIC AND MODELS OF LOGICAL THINKING[1]

Daniel Osherson
University of Pennsylvania

Mathematical logic, in the opinion of many, began to take its modern form in the work of the nineteenth century Irish mathematician, George Boole. Boole (1854) considered his logical calculus to be of more than formal interest, however, and his treatise *The Laws of Thought* was "designed, in the first place, to investigate the fundamental laws of those operations of the mind by which reasoning is performed." Boole was clearly making psychological claims, and as he himself pointed out, these claims stood in need of empirical test. So far as I know, no one has yet performed the crucial experiments. Mathematical logic made rapid advances after Boole's contribution; his logical calculus was abandoned in its original form and psychology apparently ceased to take his psychological claims seriously.[2]

Regardless of the fate of either his logical or psychological theories, Boole's work raises a critical question for current research on logical thinking. That question is: What relevance has the work of formal logicians to the psychological explanation of reasoning about logical matters? The

[1] This is an essentially unrevised version of a paper given at the Annual Meeting of the Eastern Psychological Association, Washington, D.C., April 1973.

[2] See Lewis and Langford (1959) for a brief history of logic. Henle (1962) discusses the history of the controversy over the relation between logic and natural thought. It may also be mentioned here that Piaget (1955) has expressed a similar interest in uniting logical and psychological investigation. See especially his series *Etudes d'épistémologie génétique* (Presses Universitaires de France).

possibilities are that logical systems may serve (1) in models of logical competence, (2) in models of logical performance, (3) or in both. As a model of logical competence, a logical system must be responsible for generating all the statements that subjects intuitively believe to be logically necessary and none that are felt to be contingent, i.e., factually true or false.[3] For formal simplicity the logical competence model may also be allowed to generate arbitrarily long and complex statements, most of which do not give rise to any intuitions at all. For simplicity also, the competence model need not be held accountable for any responses and judgments concerning logical truths that subjects would regret had they more comfort and leisure for reflection. Such lapses are the domain of the performance model, of which is demanded a description of the real-time mental processes whereby people actually produce the judgments described by the competence model as well as an explanation of human logical error. Only the performance model is required to reflect actual psychological mechanisms; the competence model may be far removed from the mental mechanisms the productions of which it describes. Therefore, whereas a finished performance model is perforce an accurate competence model, the converse relation does not necessarily hold, although it may. The terms "competence" and "performance" are used in this sense in this chapter.

It would be of great interest to psychologists should an already existing logical formalism be either an accurate competence model, or a performance model, or both. One such logical system can be examined in this regard: the standard "nonmodal" logic brought to near perfection in the twentieth century. This is essentially the logic discussed in introductory courses. Whereas this standard logic admits of revealing characterizations that are of great concern to philosophers and mathematicians, for present purposes this standard logic may be defined with respect to any reputable textbook in the field, such as those by Suppes (1957) or Quine (1952). A standard logical truth, then, is any statement provable by means of the methods given in such textbooks.

Standard logic may be treated as a performance model by determining whether the formal mechanism of any proof procedures, the results of which are coextensive with the set of standard logical theorems, mirrors the mental steps underlying the subjects' judgments of the necessity of those theorems. One test of whether a proof procedure can serve this function is whether there is a linear correlation between the number of steps in the formal derivation of a theorem and suitable measures of the difficulty that subjects experience in understanding that theorem. Only if such a

[3] Naturally, models of logical competence and performance must be assessed relative to specified populations of subjects. In what follows, middle-class children and adults constitute the target population.

linear relationship exists can each step in the logical derivation be regarded with justified confidence as corresponding to a mental step in the psychological derivation of that theorem.

In a series of experiments described in detail elsewhere (Osherson, 1974), I had an opportunity to examine this possibility by using a set of problems based on a restricted class of logical truths. These truths had the following form:

$$(p \rightarrow q) \rightarrow (r \rightarrow s),$$

where p, q, r, and s stand for declarative sentences built up of conjuncts, disjuncts, and negations, or for similar constructions of simple predicates.[4] Notice that this formula is a conditional, having as antecedent the conditional $p \rightarrow q$ and as consequent the conditional $r \rightarrow s$; each of these latter conditionals has an antecedent and consequent part as well. An example of this kind of formula is the following:

$$(A \vee B \rightarrow C) \rightarrow (-C \,\&\, -B \rightarrow -A).$$

If the logical connectives are interpreted in the usual way, this formula can be read "If *A* or *B* is true only if *C* is true, then not *C* and not *B* is true only if not *A* is true." Alternatively—without bothering to alter notation—the formula can be read "If everything that has properties *A* or *B* also has property *C*, then everything without property *C* and without property *B* is without property *A*." To be more concrete, the formula, in one condition of the experiment, can translate into the following task, concerning a fictitious set of jars and their contents:

Hint: All the red jars and all the large jars have tacks.
Question: Can you be sure that every jar that does not have tacks and is not large is not red?

The hint for this problem corresponds to the antecedent conditional of our illustrative formula; that is, it has the form, essentially, $A \vee B \rightarrow C$. The question part of the problem corresponds to the consequent conditional, $-C \,\&\, -B \rightarrow -A$. In the experiment the subject's task is to decide as quickly as he can whether the statement in the question follows from the statement in the hint. That is, given that the hint is true, can he be sure that the statement in the question is true? The correct answer in the illustration is affirmative; in some problems the correct answer is negative.

[4] The experiments were thus confined to formulas from propositional logic or, when one-place predicates were involved, to the associated logic of classes.

Twenty-eight of these problems were administered to 52 adults. A similar set of problems was administered to 104 children in Grades 4–7. No subject had appreciable training in logic. In assessing the results of the experiment the relative difficulty of each formula for the subjects should be noted. Difficulty was measured by latency (for the adult subjects only) and error rate (for both the children and adults). With such data any theory of how subjects attempt to solve the problems can be tested by assessing its ability to predict, up to linearity, the relative difficulty of the experimental formulas. The subjects' introspections about these problems were generally unintelligible, which precludes them as a source of evidence. Their solution strategies seemed, therefore, to be largely unconscious.

The question posed in this chapter is whether one of the proof procedures of standard logic—such a procedure being one way to define that logic or a significant subdomain of it—can serve as a description of what the subjects do to solve the problems mentally. Because the problems may be represented as formulas in propositional logic, there are a variety of proof procedures that take advantage of the "truth-functional" nature of this logic. One of the most familiar is the method of truth tables, which provides an exhaustive enumeration of all the ways constituent propositions in a formula can be true or false. Knowing this, it can be calculated whether any assignment of truth values to constituent propositions makes the entire formula false; if no such assignment exists then the formula is tautological, or logically true. The truth-table method recommends itself because it is finite and deterministic, thereby allowing unambiguous predictions about performance. In fact, one general restriction on the class of performance models for logical intuitions is that they be of this algorithmic nature. The truth table for our tautological illustrative formula looks like this:

$(A$	$\vee$	B	$\rightarrow$	$C)$	$\rightarrow$	$(-C$	&	$-B$	$\rightarrow$	$-A)$
T	T	T	T	T	T	FT	F	FT	T	FT
T	T	T	F	F	T	TF	F	FT	T	FT
T	T	F	T	T	T	FT	F	TF	T	FT
T	T	F	F	F	T	TF	T	TF	F	FT
F	T	T	T	T	T	FT	F	FT	T	TF
F	T	T	F	F	T	TF	F	FT	T	TF
F	F	F	T	T	T	FT	F	TF	T	TF
F	F	F	T	F	T	TF	T	TF	T	TF

Were the subjects in some sense using truth tables such as these to determine the answers to the formulas? If so, then it might be expected that the difficulty of a formula would be related to the size of the associated truth table; the more elements to scan in the body of the table, the longer it should have taken and the greater the likelihood of "misreading" one. In fact, however, the correlation between formula difficulty and truth-table size was generally not significant. Other algorithmic proof procedures that I have investigated, including various methods for reduction to normal disjunctive or conjunctive form and methods for finding falsifying truth-value assignments, are beset by the same difficulty. Generally, the number of steps in these procedures does not correlate significantly with formula difficulty.

There are at least three options open to us in dealing with these failures. First, a number of free parameters can be admitted into the algorithms in an effort to raise the correlations. For example, columns of the truth table headed by disjuncts can be given more "weight" than columns headed by conjuncts. Such a procedure is consistent with the well-documented finding that conjuncts are psychologically easier to process than are disjuncts (Bourne & O'Banion, 1971; Neimark & Slotnick, 1970). However, given the extremely poor performance of the unweighted versions of these models, this may be a mistake. Moreover, these procedures—as well as a variety of others that may be investigated—all harbor a fatal flaw even as definers of competence, which I shall come to shortly. Second, we might try to find a set of logically true axioms from which the experimental formulas may be deduced by means of a given set of inference rules (using, perhaps, the Whitehead and Russell axioms for propositional logic). Derivational length may then be used as the predictor of difficulty. However this approach is also inadvisable. Students of artificial intelligence (Newell, Shaw, & Simon, 1963; Nilsson, 1971) have discovered how difficult it is to find efficient algorithms for deriving theorems in this way, even given the enormous memorial capacity of computers. That adults, not to mention children, proceed in such fashion at the unconscious level is quite implausible. Finally, a so-called "natural deduction procedure" may be sought that will logically connect contingent premises with contingent conclusions. Such a theory of performance built around natural deduction will include a set of acceptable rules of inference (acceptable, that is, from the subject's point of view) and a set of explicit instructions determining the occasions for the use of each in a mental derivation.

Although the details cannot be recounted here, this last approach has been pursued with some success. Given the ordered set of rules proposed above, along with the conditions on their use, derivation length correlates well with formula difficulty. A simplified version of these rules is given below. Each rule is an instruction to rewrite the formula above the line as the formula below the line, if that rule appiles in a given derivation. The arabic numerals determine their order of application:

$$\frac{p \vee q}{-(-p \;\&\; -q)} \tag{1a}$$

$$\frac{p \;\&\; q}{-(-p \vee -q)} \tag{1b}$$

$$\frac{p \vee q \rightarrow r}{p \rightarrow r} \tag{2a}$$

$$\frac{p \rightarrow q \;\&\; r}{p \rightarrow q} \tag{2b}$$

$$\frac{p \rightarrow q}{-q \rightarrow -p} \tag{3}$$

$$\frac{p \rightarrow q}{p \vee r \rightarrow q \vee r} \tag{4a}$$

$$\frac{p \rightarrow q}{p \;\&\; r \rightarrow q \;\&\; r} \tag{4b}$$

$$\frac{p \rightarrow q}{p \rightarrow q \vee r} \tag{5a}$$

$$\frac{p \rightarrow q}{p \;\&\; r \rightarrow q} \tag{5b}$$

The set of operations works successively on the antecedent conditional of a problem (i.e., the "hint"), acting to convert it by stages into the consequent conditional of the problem (i.e., the statement in the "question"). The conditions for the use of each rule are designed to reduce the discrepancy between these two conditionals, in a sense made familiar by the work of Newell and Simon (1963). For example, Rule (5b) applies when the conditional representing the hint—or that conditional as transformed by previous operations—lacks a conjunct in its antecedent that is present in the antecedent of the conditional representing the question. The conditions governing application of the other rules are similar.

Our illustrative formula provides a sample derivation within the model. The rules justifying each step appear to the right:

Derivation of formula $(A \vee B \rightarrow C) \rightarrow (-C \;\&\; -B \rightarrow -A)$:

(i)	$A \vee B \rightarrow C$	antecedent conditional
(ii)	$A \rightarrow C$	(2a)
(iii)	$-C \rightarrow -A$	(3)
(iv)	$-C \;\&\; -B \rightarrow -A$	(5b)

Since in this derivation the final line matches the consequent conditional $-C \& -B \rightarrow -A$, the subject will answer that the statement in the problem's question has followed from the hint. Should the subject fail to achieve a match after running through his finite repertoire of inference rules, he will reply in the negative—all of this assuming, of course, that no *faux pas* has occurred during the mental derivation to lead the subject into error.

If latency and error rate are used as indices, the difficulty of a formula correlates around .6 with the number of lines in the derivation provided by the model for that formula. Moreover, if the operations of the model are differentially weighted in accord with such findings as the relative ease of conjunctive compared to disjunctive concepts (Bourne & O'Banion, 1971; Neimark & Slotnick, 1970), the correlation between formula difficulty and the weighted sum of the hypothesized operations rises to around .8 in three different experiments.

Now although the performance model discussed above receives some support from these experiments (by dint of the correlation between formula difficulty and derivation length), it is far from verified. Moreover, it does not provide derivations for all of the truths of propositional logic, nor even for all of the truths of the form $(p \rightarrow q) \rightarrow (r \rightarrow s)$ given before. Still less does it illuminate the subjects' thought processes when they are faced with problems involving complex predicates and quantifications. For the sake of argument, however, assume that something comparable to the process outlined above is taking place when subjects attempt to solve a problem. What implications are there for the question posed earlier, of whether an accurate performance model resembles any of the standard logical profit techniques that serve to characterize standard logic?

There are two aspects of the proposed performance model that are relevant in this regard. First, all the inference rules of the model are sanctioned by standard logic. Consonant with this feature of the model, some data from my studies indicate that subjects' errors result not from deviant inference rules—such as the illicit "conversion" of a conditional (see Taplin & Staudenmayer, 1973)—but from limitations on their processing capabilities, in terms of the mental "space" required for assembling individual rules into a derivation. Briefly, for the younger subjects each problem was administered more than once in different guises and at different times. The children's difficulty with particular formulas was generally reflected in chance performance or in admissions of ignorance; incorrect answers were seldom given systematically over repetitions of the same problem. Therefore, incorrect responses seemed to be due more to an overload than to an invalid logical rule. In this respect, then, the current performance candidate does resemble standard logic.

The second crucial aspect of the model, however, should help dispel the illusion that standard logic has much correspondence to either the performance or competence of human subjects. The so-called "paradoxes" of material implication cannot be derived from the model's rules; nor does the formula $p \rightarrow q$ allow the derivation of a formula with something other than a conditional as its main connective. Thus, the following formulas are not derivable in the performance model, although they are theorems of standard logic:

$(p \rightarrow q) \vee (q \rightarrow p)$	(Take any two statements, and at least one materially implies the other)
$-p \rightarrow (p \rightarrow q)$	(A false statement materially implies any statement)
$q \rightarrow (p \rightarrow q)$	(A true statement is materially implied by any statement)
$(p \rightarrow q) \leftrightarrow (-p \vee q)$	(Material implication is equivalent to a function built of disjunction and negation)
$(p \rightarrow q) \leftrightarrow -(p \& -q)$	(Material implication is equivalent to a function built of conjunction and negations)

These truths of standard logic are called "paradoxical" because they fail to correspond to our intuitions about how *if . . . then . . .* and *all . . . are . . .* constructions should behave. For example, the second paradox listed indirectly makes the following sentences true: "If $2 + 2 = 5$, then $2 + 2 = 4$," and "All winged horses are hot fudge sundaes."[5] Johnson-Laird and Tagart (1969) and Matalon (1962) have experimental evidence that adults who are logically unsophisticated do not understand such sentences in the standard logical way. It is therefore an important feature of the proposed model that it accounts for the subjects' performance on the formulas utilized in my experiments by means of a proof procedure that does not generate these intuitively suspect standard theorems. In fact, the unsuitability of the truth-table method, normal-form method, and similar techniques as psychological models probably hinges on the very fact that the standard interpretation of $p \rightarrow q$ is integral to them.

One tentative conclusion of these experiments, then, is that standard logical derivation techniques do not accurately mirror the mental derivations of the subjects, at least not for the kind of problems investigated.

[5] Some logicians argue that there is nothing paradoxical about these statements if $p \rightarrow q$ is understood simply as an abbreviation for $-p \vee q$ or for $-(p \& -q)$, which is generally how the conditional is defined in a formal system. It is true that in this case the paradoxes disappear. However, the problem is whether *if . . . then . . .* constructions in ordinary language behave in a manner consistent with these definitions; they seem not to.

And just as important, the use of standard logic as a competence model is discredited as well. For not only does that competence model label as "logically true" a class of formulas that human intuitions reject as implausible (viz., the paradoxes surrounding material implication), but the tentative performance model indicates that humans also have no need for these formulas, even as intervening or hypothetical steps in describing the mental construction of judgments about the implications that they do deem correct.

If not in standard logic, where can the correct competence model for our intuitions about logical necessity be found? As menitoned above, the errors the subjects commit seem to be due only to the difficulty of stringing together during a mental derivation the valid rules they possess. This suggests that buried within the performance model lies an intact competence model, namely, the set of Rules (1)–(5), together with their ordering and occurrence restrictions, apart from any "processing" limitations built into the performance model. As pointed out above, such a situation is not a necessary condition for an accurate competence model, and future investigation may well complicate matters. For this reason, in searching for a competence model it is prudent to keep an eye on the rapid developments in logic, especially concerning the modal and many-valued systems that have been devised. Many of these systems have been developed precisely with the idea of capturing our intuitions about implication in a superior fashion to that of standard logic (cf. Hughes & Cresswell, 1968).

It can be seen, then, that the problem of human logical intuitions is largely the problem of how people understand implication. More progress is likely to be made in solving this problem if we guard against the simplified belief that there is only one genuine notion of implication germane to human logic. How people understand and reason with *if . . . then . . .* and *all . . . are . . .* statements is surely very sensitive to the content that fills in the blanks of these statements, that is, to the subject matter being reasoned about. This is the burden of the intriguing work of Wason and Johnson-Laird, lucidly summarized in a recent monograph (Wason & Johnson-Laird, 1972). That implicative statements, similar in surface form, actually involve very different meanings can be illustrated with an example devised by Goodman (1965). Consider these two statements:

Everyone in this room is safe from freezing. (1)
Everyone in this room is English speaking (2)

Both seem to have the same logical structure; in standard notation,

$$(x)(Px \rightarrow Qx)$$

where the predicate P means "is in this room," and the predicate Q means either "is safe from freezing," or "is English speaking." To see how differently people reason with them, however, Goodman considers a certain Eskimo in the Arctic who is now freezing to death. According to our intuitions, were he in this room right now he would be safe from freezing, as Sentence 1 implies. In contrast, our intuitions tell us that he would not be English speaking; instead, Sentence 2 would cease to be a true generalization. Any adequate model of logical competence must distinguish such pairs of sentences in a rigorous and illuminating way, and an adequate performance model must shed some light on the processes whereby we are led from them to different conclusions. The difference between the two sentences is connected in some way to the "lawful" nature of the first generalization, as opposed to the "accidental" nature of the second. In this fashion the study of deduction and logical intuitions leads inevitably to the problems of induction and causal intuitions.

I conclude with an analogy that has guided my remarks on competence and performance models for logical thinking. Linguists are to psycholinguists as logicians are to "psychologicians." From our psychological vantage point we may construe the work of many linguists and logicians as models of competence. It is up to psycholinguists and psychologicians to uncover the mental processes that mediate the judgments captured by these competence models. In this way we may hope to carry out the psychological program initiated by George Boole.

REFERENCES

Boole, G. *An investigation of the laws of thought.* London: Walton & Maberley, 1854.

Bourne, L. E., Jr., & O'Banion, K. Conceptual rule learning and chronological age. *Developmental Psychology,* 1971, **5,** 525–534.

Goodman, N. *Fact, fiction, and forecast.* Indianapolis, Ind.: Bobbs-Merrill, 1965.

Henle, M. On the relation between logic and thinking. *Psychological Review,* 1962, **68,** 366–378.

Hughes, G. E., & Cresswell, M. J. *An introduction to modal logic.* London: Methuen, 1968.

Johnson-Laird, P., & Tagart, J. How implication is understood. *The American Journal of Psychology,* 1969, **82,** 367–373.

Lewis, C., & Langford, C. *Symbolic logic.* New York: Dover, 1959.

Matalon, B. Étude génétique de l'implication. In E. W. Beth *et al.* (Eds.), *Implication, formalisation et logique naturelle.* Paris: Presses Universitaires de France, 1962. Pp. 69–95.

Neimark, E., & Slotnick, N. Development of the understanding of logical connectives. *Journal of Educational Psychology,* 1970, **61,** 451–460.

Newell, A., Shaw, J., & Simon, H. A. Empirical explorations with the Logic Theory Machine: A case study in heuristics. In E. Feigenbaum & J. Feldman (Eds.), *Computers and thought.* New York: McGraw-Hill, 1963.

Newell, A., & Simon, H. A. GPS, a program that simulates hman thought. In E. Feigenbaum & J. Feldman (Eds.), *Computers and thought*. New York: McGraw-Hill, 1963.

Nilsson, N. J. *Problem-solving methods in artificial intelligence*. New York: McGraw-Hill, 1971.

Osherson, D. N. *Logical abilities in children*. Vol. 2. *Logical inference: Underlying operations*. Hillsdale, N.J.: Lawrence Erlbaum Associates, 1974.

Piaget, J. *Logic and psychology*. New York: Basic Books, 1955.

Quine, W. V. O. *Methods of logic*. London: Routledge & Kegan Paul, 1952.

Suppes, P. *Introduction to logic*. Princeton, N.J.: Van Nostrand, 1957.

Taplin, J. E., & Staudenmayer, H., Interpretation of abstract conditional sentences in deductive reasoning. *Journal of Verbal Learning and Verbal Behavior*, 1973, **12**, 530–542.

Wason, P., & Johnson-Laird, P. *Psychology of reasoning: Structure and content*. Cambridge, Mass.: Harvard University Press, 1972.

4

SYLLOGISTIC REASONING: LOGICAL DECISIONS FROM A COMPLEX DATA BASE

Russell Revlis
California State University, Fullerton

All men are mortals
Socrates is a man
Therefore:
Socrates is a mortal
*Socrates is a Greek

For more than 2000 years, students have been asked to decide whether Socrates is a mortal and whether it can be logically determined that he is also a Greek (given the information concerning his mortality). Such problems are called "categorical syllogisms" or "Aristotelian syllogisms." The solution to such problems requires that the reasoner discover whether the relation holding between the subject and predicate terms of the conclusion (e.g., *Socrates* and *mortals*) can be determined unambiguously from the known relation holding between each of these terms and a third one mentioned in the premises of the problem (e.g., *men*). Although the decision may seem transparent in the present problem, reasoners from every walk of life have shown themselves to be less than perfect logicians on these syllogisms (Sells, 1936, provides an analysis of errors for different occupations). A typical error on such problems is starred in the example above: although the proposition "Socrates is a Greek" may be historically true, it does not necessarily follow from the information provided in the premises. Indeed, some reasoners may accept this incorrect conclusion because they believe it is empirically true, rather than because it necessarily follows from the information provided. This kind of thinking is analogous to that of a juror, who finds it difficult to disregard inadmissible testimony and base his decisions only on the presented evidence.

Reasoning errors of this kind have given rise to a traditional (if not archaic) issue: are people who are untrained in formal logic logical? For example, in syllogistic reasoning, it is frequently noted that the content of the individual premises has an effect on the reasoner's assessment of the validity of the overall argument (e.g., Feather, 1965; Gordon, 1953; Henle & Michael, 1956; Janis & Frick, 1943; Janis & Terwilliger, 1962; Kaufman & Goldstein, 1967; Lefford, 1946; Morgan & Morton, 1944; Parrott, 1967, 1969; Wilkins, 1928; Wilson, 1965; Winthrop, 1946). For some researchers, these findings suggest that untrained reasoners are not strictly logical in their inferences and base their decisions primarily on personal knowledge and biases. In contrast, this chapter presents an alternative interpretation of these findings, namely that deductive errors on categorical syllogisms are only indirectly affected by the problem's content and that errors are attributable to the reasoner's misrepresentation of the problem's propositions—certainly not to insufficiencies in the reasoners' logical skills.

This notion of the "rational" reasoner is developed in five parts. The first section introduces a schematic model of formal decisions, which is offered as an organizational aid for a discussion of the literature on syllogistic reasoning. The second summarizes the major findings in terms of the schematic model. The third and fourth sections elaborate the model and its major predictions. The last section speculates on the relation between categorical and other forms of reasoning, in terms of both the underlying processes and the methods for describing the findings. Before considering the first section, the reader may find it useful to glance over the following description of the syllogism's structure—if only to see how certain critical terms are used in the text.

Preliminaries: The syllogism's structure. In its traditional form, the categorical syllogism consists of two propositions, called "premises," and a third proposition, which may logically follow from the premises, called the "conclusion," for example,

All M *are* P	(major premise)
Some S *are* M	(minor premise)
Therefore:	
1. *Some* S *are* P	(valid conclusion)
2. **Some* S *are not* P	(invalid conclusion)

Each proposition asserts a relation between two sets of terms. The Major Premise expresses a relation between the predicate of the conclusion (P)

and another term (M). The minor premise expresses a relation between the subject of the conclusion (S) and the other term (M). The reasoner's task is to judge what conclusion can be validly inferred from the premises. The syllogistic inference entails an analysis of the relations holding between each of two terms (S and P) and a third term (M). The purpose of making such an analysis is to determine the relation holding between the two basic terms, the subject and predicate of the conclusion. The formal rules for making this judgment are expressed in their traditional forms by Cohen and Nagel (1934) and by Peirce (1957).

In the foregoing example, conclusion 1 is a valid deduction from the two premises, whereas conclusion 2 is not. In part, this is a result of the special meaning of the term *Some*. In traditional logic, the word *Some* should be interpreted as "at least some (conventional meaning) and possibly all." Therefore, although the reasoner knows that at least some of the S are P, it is also possible that all of the S are P (either by their inclusion in the set M or by some other means). In this case, the reasoner cannot be certain that there are S which are not P; therefore, conclusion 2 is not a valid deduction—it does not necessarily follow from the information imparted by the premises. Clarification of the meaning of "some" is an important part of the instructions given to people in syllogistic reasoning experiments (cf. Frase, 1966, who explicitly manipulated these instructions).

The premises in each syllogism are selected from among four types of propositions, determined by the orthogonal pairings of two attributes: quantification (universal and particular) and polarity (affirmative and negative). These four propositions and their letter designates (*A*, *E*, *I*, *O*) are shown in Table 1.

Within each proposition, the terms may appear in two orders (e.g., S—M or M—S). Consequently, there are four possible orderings for each syllogism (2 orders of terms ×2 premises). These orderings are called "figures":

Fig. I	Fig. II	Fig. III	Fig. IV	
M–P	P–M	M–P	P–M	(major premise)
S–M	S–M	M–S	M–S	(minor premise)
S–P	S–P	S–P	S–P	(conclusion)

Because any of the four types of propositions may be the major premise and any of the four types may comprise the minor premise, there are 16

TABLE 1
Categorical Propositions

Type [a]	Features	Relation
A	Universal affirmative	*All* A *are* B
E	Universal negative	*No* A *are* B
I	Particular affirmative	*Some* A *are* B
O	Particular negative	*Some* A *are not* B

[a] For affirmative propositions (*A* and *I*), the letters represent the first two vowels in *affirmo*; whereas for the negative propositions (*E* and *O*), the letters are the two vowels in *nego*—the universal is assigned the first vowel in each word (Cohen & Nagel, 1934).

combinations of premise types, called "moods." Each of these 16 moods can appear in any of the four figures shown above. As a result, there are 64 possible syllogisms—only 19 of which have a conclusion that validly follows from their premises. The sample problem which introduced this discussion can therefore be characterized as having an *A*-type major premise and an *I*-type minor premise. It has an *AI* mood and is written in the first figure (therefore, *AI*-1). The conclusion that validly follows from its premises is an *I* proposition.

The psychological importance of the structural variables have undergone only a preliminary assessment; however, current findings tentatively indicate that: (*a*) the order of presentation of the premises is irrelevant to performance (Chapman & Chapman, 1959); (*b*) the problem's figure contributes only marginally to error rates (Frase, 1966, 1968; Pezzoli & Frase, 1968); and (*c*) quantification and polarity of the premises are important factors in deductive inference—syllogisms with *I* and *O* premises are more difficult to solve than those with *A* and *E* premises.

Two cautionary notes about the foregoing description of categorical syllogisms are in order. First, several subtle points of historical or philosophical interest have been obscured in the interest of presenting a consistent task domain. For example, the philosophically oriented reader will recognize that it is a moot point whether Aristotle distinguished four figures or discussed the major and minor premises (Lukasiewicz, 1951; Rescher, 1966). These and other historical issues are not considered here. The structural properties presented above have achieved substantial acceptance as characterizing features for categorical syllogisms; they are adhered to in the discussions that follow. Second, the structural description of the syllogism should not be construed by the reader as a complete specification of the total task environment in which the reasoner works (cf. Newell & Simon, 1972). Aspects of such a specification are presented in the appropriate sections below.

SCHEMATIC MODEL OF FORMAL REASONING

The available notions of how people reason with syllogisms reflect an emphasis on either the logical (and alogical) operations in reasoning or the representation of the syllogism's statements. Although any model must treat both aspects of the reasoning process, the distinction between states of knowledge (the reasoner's representation of the problem and its propositions) and operations on those states is a useful device for focusing on the major contributions of each piece of research. The model of reasoning introduced here is of the former type: it characterizes the reasoner as a rational information processor who applies formally correct operations to a flawed representation of the propositions. Of course, this notion is not new to categorical reasoning: it was suggested nearly five decades ago by Wilkins (1928) and more recently by Henle (1962) and others (Ceraso & Provitera, 1971; Chapman & Chapman, 1959; Henle & Michael, 1956; Wason & Johnson-Laird, 1972). This characterization has also been applied to conditional reasoning problems by Taplin (1971).

In a major statement of the "representation" position, Henle (1962) has suggested that there are four basic sources of errors in syllogistic reasoning: (*a*) misinterpretation (or restatement) of the propositions; (*b*) omission of a premise in memory; (*c*) addition of a premise in memory; and (*d*) a failure to accept the logical task (cf. Richter, 1957). Here, errors are viewed as resulting primarily from an incorrect encoding of the meaning of the proposition [(*a*) and (*b*), above] and from an inability to distinguish between the information given in the premises and that already stored in long-term memory (LTM) about the topic covered in the syllogism [(*c*) above]. The fourth factor (acceptance of the logical nature of the task) is a presupposed motivational condition in the discussion that follows. Therefore, the view taken here is that reasoners do not possess faulty inference mechanisms in any simple way: deductive errors are the result of the reasoner's applying logical operations to a faulty data base. "Data base" refers to the information kept in working memory for the purpose of solving the problem and includes information taken from LTM, which is either needed for comprehension of the premises or directly relevant to the manipulations required by the logical operations.

The following is a schematic model of categorical reasoning that embodies the "representation" view of the reasoner. The component processes and operations outlined are specified in more detail in a later section.

Form of the Model

The general form of the model is portrayed in Fig. 1, where *N* designates the *N*th conclusion on the list of alternatives and ranges from 1 to 5. The model consists of four processing stages: (*a*) an encoding stage, in which the individual premises are given a first reading and in which the processes necessary to establish the data base operate; (*b*) a composite stage, in which logical operations work to produce a single predicate, representing the information in the premises; (*c*) a conclusion-encoding stage, similar to the premise-encoding stage; and (*d*) a comparison stage, in which the composite information is compared with the contents of the conclusion. This last stage also includes a decision substage, in which the reasoner selects his response.

It is not coincidental that the form of the model corresponds to models used to account for reasoning with linear syllogisms (Clark, 1969) and for sentence comprehension and verification (Chase & Clark, 1972; Glucksberg, Trabasso, & Wald, 1973; Trabasso, Rollins, & Shaughnessy, 1971). Such models account for decisions by describing the representation of the information in the data base and the logical operations that the language user (*qua* reasoner) applies in those tasks.

There are at least three critical components of this model that must be specified if the model is to be taken seriously: (*a*) description of the encoding process; (*b*) the nature of the deduction operations (which work to produce the composite representation); and (*c*) the nature of the comparison process. It is the intention of the following discussion to touch upon

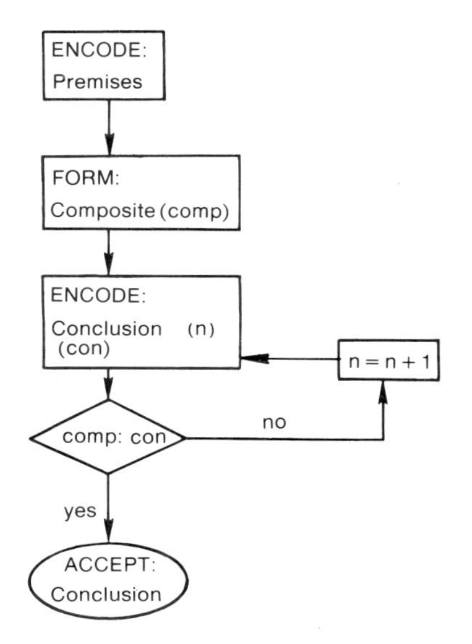

FIG. 1. Schematic model of syllogistic reasoning.

these three aspects of the model and to provide, wherever possible, existant data that support both the overall conception of the model and its specific components. This information is then called upon in a more elaborate presentation of the model.

MAJOR FINDINGS

Encoding

The processes necessary to establish the relevant data structures in formal reasoning tasks are probably the same as those entailed in any natural analysis of sentences. That is, the reasoner must apply both syntactic and semantic rules in order to comprehend and remember the information presented. From the point of view of the present model of formal reasoning, syntactic rules are important to the extent that they affect either memory load or the meaning of the propositions that the reasoner is asked to work with. That is, syntactic complexity may influence the course of reasoning by affecting (*a*) the time necessary to process a complex proposition, which may cause a loss of information from short-term memory (STM), while the propositions are being disambiguated, or (b) a general loss of syntactic features during the course of analyzing subsequent propositions. Therefore, negation (as a syntactic function), voicing, and word order may be critical factors for reasoning. Negation provides a useful example of how the systematic forgetting of syntactic features alters the information reasoned about. If the negative marker in *some* A *are not* B is lost from memory, the meaning of the proposition remembered may be glossed as *some* A *are* B—a considerable change in meaning. The psycholinguistic literature supports the possibility of forgetting negative features, although the explanations for the added complexity of negatives are often debated (for syntactic arguments, see Eifermann, 1961; Gough, 1966; Savin & Perchonock, 1965; semantic arguments are presented by Clark, 1970, 1973a, b; Greene, 1970a, b; among others).

Two implications of this work on negatives are that: (*a*) deductive errors should be greater for syllogisms with propositions that contain negative features than for those whose propositions contain only affirmative features; (*b*) when offered alternative conclusions for a syllogism, reasoners should make more errors on negative conclusions than on affirmative ones. These predictions were tested against the data of three representative studies: Begg and Denny (1969), Chapman and Chapman (1959), and Wilkins (1928). The findings are counter to the first prediction: Table 2 shows that for students in the three studies, negatives facilitate correct

TABLE 2

Invalid Syllogisms: Percent Error for Each Premise Pair: (Choice of Propositional Conclusion)[a]

Premise pair	Totally universal	Totally particular	Totally affirmative	Totally negative
Begg and Denny (1969):	AA = 81.8	II = 100.0	AA = 81.8	EE = 69.7
$N = 33$	EE = 69.7	00 = 81.8	II = 100.0	OO = 81.8
	AE = 89.4	I0 = 91.7	AI = 90.9	EO = 88.6
	80.3	91.2	90.9	80.0
Chapman and Chapman	AA = 91.3	II = 80.3	AA = 91.3	EE = 65.3
(1959):	EE = 65.3	00 = 70.0	II = 80.3	00 = 70.0
$N = 222$	AE = 92.3	I0 = 74.6	AI = 91.9	E0 = 65.7
	82.9	74.9	87.8	67.0
Wilkins (1928)[b]	AA = 36.9	II = 41.5	AA = 36.9	EE = 12.2
$N = 81$	EE = 12.2	00 = 27.2	II = 41.5	00 = 27.2
	AE = 39.5	I0 = —	AI = 36.9	E0 = —
	29.5	34.4	38.4	19.7

[a] Error rates are a percentage of the total number of possible responses on invalid syllogisms. An average was taken for each Mood–Figure combination and then averaged over Figures for the Moods of interest.

[b] Data were tabulated only for decisions which correspond to the kind available to the *Ss* in Chapman and Chapman (1959) and Begg and Denny (1969).

deductions rather than hinder them. In contrast, Tables 3 and 4 show that the studies support the second prediction: *reasoners are less likely to either accept an erroneous conclusion or reject a correct one when the conclusion is affirmative than when it is negative.*

Surface-structure syntactic rules affect the meaning of the propositions in addition to contributing to memory complexity. For example: *negation* performs a semantic as well as a syntactic function; the *ordering* of quantifiers in a sentence affect the reasoner's representation of those terms (Johnson-Laird, 1969a, b); voicing can influence the identification of actor and agent (Huttenlocher, Eisenberg, & Strauss, 1968; Johnson-Laird, 1968a, b; Tannenbaum & Williams, 1968; and many others). Of special interest to categorical reasoning is that in the standard syllogistic premises, the ordering of the subject and predicate terms corresponds to the passive sentence in normal discourse. For example, in the proposition *All* A *are* B, the potentially dominant, including class is mentioned last. In a sense, this violates normative subject—predicate topicality constraints (cf. Johnson-Laird, 1968a, b), although there are many occasions in which the locative is appropriately placed in the predicate (e.g., "The books are on the shelf"). Revlis and Moore (in preparation) have informally tested the importance of voice in solving syllogisms by asking 50 students to solve a

TABLE 3
Valid Syllogisms: Percent Errors of the Total Possible Errors for Particular Types of Conclusion [a]

	Valid conclusions[b] (failure to accept)		Invalid conclusions (failure to reject)	
	Universal	Particular	Universal	Particular
Affirmative	3.8	17.4	18.8	5.0[c]
Negative	21.4	35.0	33.7	30.6

[a] From Wilkins (1928).

[b] The problems included here were abstract, valid syllogisms with explicitly quantified propositions whose conclusions met the formal requirement stated earlier.

[c] Based on a single problem.

TABLE 4
Invalid Syllogisms: Proportion of Error of Each Type (Acceptance of Invalid Conclusions)[a]

		Universal	Particular	Total
Begg and Denny (1969)	Affirmative	7.3	13.1	20.4
	Negative	29.2	37.7	66.9
	Total:	36.5	50.8	87.3
Chapman and Chapman (1959)	Affirmative	7.7	21.9	29.6
	Negative	19.7	28.6	48.3
	Total:	27.4	50.5	77.9
Wilkins (1928)	Affirmative	15.9	37.5	—[b]
	Negative	38.5	38.3	—

[a] Error rates are a percentage of the total number of possible responses on invalid syllogisms. An average was taken for each Mood–Figure combination and then averaged over Figures for each Mood.

[b] Error types were not mutually exclusive. Consequently, summing error rates would be inappropriate for these data.

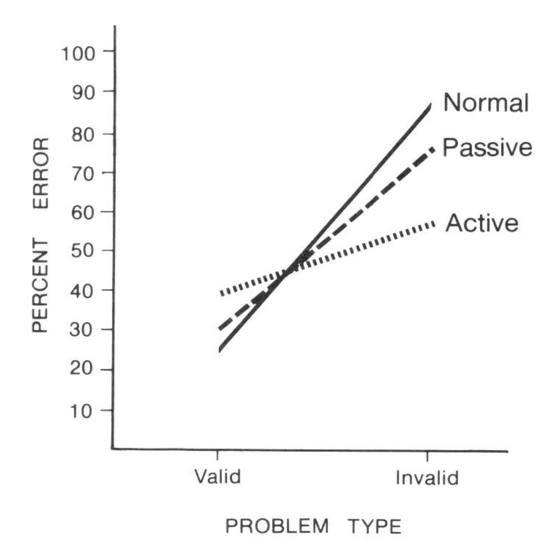

FIG. 2. The effect of voice on formal deductions. (——) Normal; (– – –) passive; (· · ·) active.

set of 64 syllogisms. Half of the students were given problems expressed in the passive form (*All* A *are included in* B) and the other students solved syllogisms expressed in an active form (B *includes all* A).[1] Half of the problems had a valid conclusion, half did not. An additional group of 25 students solved the same problems, but they were expressed in the traditional manner (*All* A *are* B).

The overall findings are presented in Fig. 2, which shows that there is a small but consistent improvement in reasoning on indeterminate syllogisms when the propositions are expressed in an active rather than a passive form. It is important that for these data, reasoning was improved as a result of clarification of the relational term (*is a* compared with *is included in*). These findings suggest the importance of syntactic–semantic factors in the establishment of a representation of the propositions.

One explanation of the observed effect of voicing is that word order may influence the expected size relation between the subject and predicate terms and, thereby, require additional processing to disambiguate the relation. That is, when reading *All* A *are* B, the reasoner may initially expect that the class B must be smaller than A. However, because B must be at least identical to A in size (or, alternatively, larger than A), the reasoner must alter his representation of the propositions to accord with the constraints of his logical operations: larger classes cannot be included in smaller ones. An alternative view of the process is expressed by Lippman (1972), who claims that the voicing in the premises may lead to expecta-

[1] My thanks to H. H. Clark for suggesting the relational terms used in this experiment.

tions of voicing in the conclusion (cf. Tannenbaum & Williams, 1968). However, Lippman does not specify how such voice-matching effects may lead to deductive errors. The foregoing suggests, therefore, that the encoding stage in deductive reasoning is affected by the syntactic and semantic functions performed by the surface structure of the premises.

In addition to the syntactic encoding factors just mentioned, the semantic component of the encoding process separately contributes to the organization of the data base by an analysis of (*a*) the quantificational terms (*all, no, some*)[2]; (*b*) the class terms: either letters, in the case of abstract propositions (e.g., A and B) or concrete terms, as in the case of problems dealing with *men, mortals,* and *Socrates;* (*c*) the relational terms (*is a* and *has a*).[3]

Quantifiers. The interpretation of quantifiers is critical to the reasoner's representation of the propositions. The ambiguity of the word *some* has already been mentioned. Its normative meaning (partitive: SOME = [few, not all]) is not the same as the logical one (distributive: SOME = [at least one, possibly all]). Error rates and time to make decisions are considerably reduced when this meaning is clarified (Frase, 1966). Although the quantifiers *all* and *no* differ on the feature of polarity, they are similar in that they are both universals—in contrast to *some,* which is a particular quantifier. A retabulation of some published data (Tables 2 and 3) reveals that universally quantified premises engender fewer errors than ones with particular quantifiers. Similarly, fewer universally quantified conclusions are erroneously accepted than are particularly quantified ones. Perhaps this ease of reasoning with universals is due to the alacrity with which the reasoner can construct a representation for universally quantified propositions. Figure 3 shows the Venn diagram representations for each of the quantified propositions. Clearly, the universal propositions have fewer possible alternative representations than do the particularly quantified propositions.

Error rates for quantified propositions cannot, however, be related in any simple way to the number of alternative "diagrams" available. If such were the case, then we would expect that the ratio of errors between one premise pair and another would correspond to the ratio of the number

[2] Other quantificational terms have occasionally been used (e.g., Henle, 1962). Some of these are *many, most,* and *few*. Although they represent a departure from the strict Aristotelian form, these quasi-quantifiers have brought to focus the importance of encoding processes for deductive reasoning.

[3] The property-assignment relation, expressed with *has a,* has appeared in the reasoning literature (e.g., Wilkins, 1928) without any precise analysis of whether the property relation has a different implication for deductions than the class-inclusion relation. Revlis (1974) and Revlis and Hayes (1972) have shown that very different processes attend the use of *is a* and *has a* in a hypothetical reasoning task.

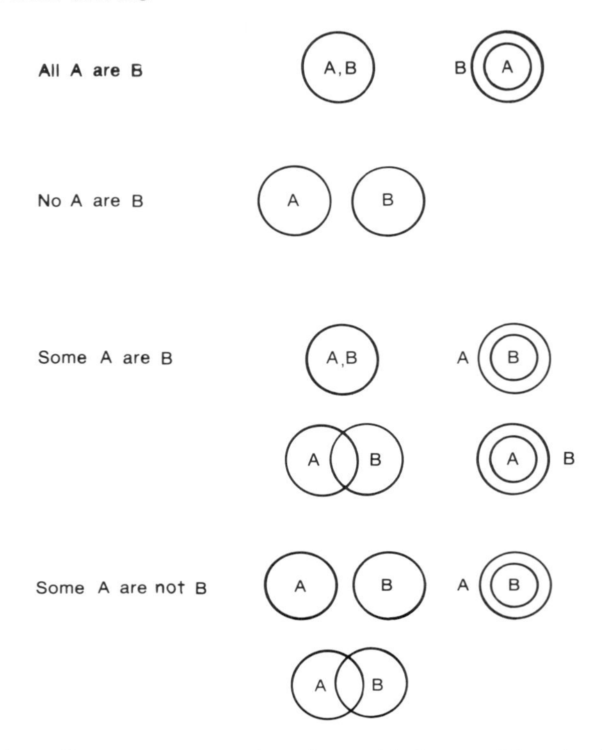

FIG. 3. Venn diagram representation of quantified propositions in their converted and unconverted forms.

of diagrams available for each pair. A casual inspection of the data shows that such a correspondence does not appear (in contrast, see discussions by Ceraso & Provitera, 1971; Erickson, 1974).

Although the precise basis for the differential complexity of quantified propositions cannot be answered conclusively at present, a strong possibility is that reasoners possess readily available, data-manipulation operations, which act on hierarchically ordered information. That is, when information can be represented in a hierarchical ordering (as with universally quantified propositions), the reasoner is able to apply well-learned schemes for retrieving relevant class relationships. Indeed, when students are presented with a hypothetical reasoning task that contains at least two paths to the solution, they select the path in which the information is hierarchically ordered and expressed in terms of universals rather than as particulars (Revlis, Lipkin, & Hayes, 1971; Revlis & Hayes, 1972; Revlis, 1974). This preference for reasoning with a hierarchically ordered data base may be related to the fact that reasoners will force information into an ordering described by general predicates, even when such predicates have not been provided, as Dawes (1964, 1966) has shown in paragraph memory studies (cf. Revlis, 1974). Such findings clearly point to the dual importance of both the representation of the problems and the nature of the operations which manipulate that representation.

Class terms. Psychologists have frequently claimed that whereas formal, syllogistic inference requires an analysis of only the form of the problems, the reasoner's decisions appear to result from an additional analysis of the syllogism's content—specifically, an analysis of the empirical (extra-experimental) truth value of the information contained either in the premises or in the conclusion. For example, personal knowledge is frequently claimed to exert an influence on categorical judgments (Feather, 1965; Gordon, 1953; Janis & Frick, 1943; Janis & Terwilliger, 1962; Kaufman & Goldstein, 1967; Lefford, 1946; Morgan & Morton, 1944; Parrott, 1967, 1969; Parrott & Johnson, 1968; Pezzoli & Frase, 1968; Thouless, 1959; Winthrop, 1946; but also see Henle, 1962; Henle & Michael, 1956). However, the availability of personal knowledge does not necessarily bias the reasoner's decisions nor lead to judgmental errors. Indeed, such information may be introduced as a natural extension of normal comprehension processes.

Wilkins (1928) examined the importance of personal knowledge and concreteness on the ability to solve syllogisms. She had students solve four different kinds of problems, two of which had concrete terms and two of which had abstract ones: (*a*) concrete–neutral (the relation between the class terms was unknown to the reasoner prior to the experiment), (*b*) concrete–subjective (the reasoner's personal knowledge contradicted the conclusions he had to read), (*c*) abstract–simple (letters represented class names), and (*d*) abstract–complex (long, scientific sounding words stood as the class names). The results show that concreteness and not personal knowledge *per se* was the major factor in the solution to such problems. Even when the propositions contradicted the reasoner's personal knowledge, he was correct more often with concrete material than when the problems described abstract categories. Concrete–neutral problems were the easiest to solve (fewest errors), with concrete–subjective only slightly more difficult. The most difficult problems were the abstract–complex problems, in which long names stood for the categories and personal knowledge was not entailed.

These findings of Wilkins and others (e.g., Whimbey & Ryan, 1969) suggest that memory critically influences reasoning performance. The reasoner must store the information given by the premises in order to form the composite representation. When the propositions describe familiar categories, the definitions for these terms are given in LTM and their familiarity facilitates recall. Even in those cases where relations expressed by the propositions are contrary to the reasoner's knowledge, the facilitating effect of available representations outweighes the potential effects of biased knowledge. In contrast, the abstract material may be more difficult to reason about than concrete material as a result of the relative unavailability of representations in LTM. In addition, memory processes may be implicated in differentiating among the abstract terms. That is, the long scientific names may induce greater memory load than the shorter terms because of the number of processing decisions necessary to store them (cf. the EPAM theory: Feigenbaum, 1963; Simon & Feigenbaum, 1964).

It is not the view here that reasoners make their judgments by directly appealing to their personal knowledge. Rather, reasoning errors may be a result of a failure to either retain the presented information or to properly discriminate between information given in the propositions and information added to the data base through LTM. That is, the knowledge provided by LTM may include real-world, pragmatic information as well as emotionally laden definitions for category terms; this logically "extraneous" information may be placed in working memory without an adequate tag as "supplemental information" (i.e., information not contained in the propositions of the syllogism). This may be analogous to similar effects shown in memory for complex prose (Barclay, 1973; Bransford, Barclay, & Franks, 1972; Bransford & Franks, 1971), where people store semantic units and loose the information concerning the original form or source of the semantic units.

Relational terms. The copula *is a* represents a critical term for deriving an interpretation of the syllogism's premises. Chapman and Chapman (1959) reported that reasoners tend to encode the copula as *is equivalent to* rather than the logical meaning *is included in* (the meaning of the term is debated even by philosophers; cf. Frege, 1892). Such a miscoding of the relational term distorts the meaning of both the universal affirmative and the particular negative propositions. Consequently, if reasoners do interpret the copula in just the way described, their inferences will be based on a restricted encoding and will result in errors on problems with *A*-type and *O*-type premises.

In the study described, Revlis and Moore asked students to solve syllogisms that were expressed with either *is a* or *is included in* as the relational terms. Two aspects of the study are of interest here. First, disambiguation of the copula significantly improves the performance of every syllogism. Second, the improvement is greatest for syllogisms that contain universal affirmatives or particular negatives. The interpretation of the copula is therefore an important aspect of the encoding of the syllogistic premises and has its greatest effect on just those problems for which the interpretation severely alters the initial representation of the propositions.

Conversion operation. The discussion of the encoding mechanism so far has been concerned with the strict interpretation of terms and the importance of memory for providing pragmatic, relational information. An encoding mechanism that includes the operations discussed above as well as more general ones, has been termed "illicit conversion" by the Chapmans (Chapman & Chapman, 1959). When the reasoner is told that *All* A *are* B, he may interpret this proposition to mean that the converse is also true; that is, *All* B *are* A. Notice that this is similar to the equivalence interpretation for the copula *is a.* In addition, when the reasoner is told that *Some* A are not B, he interprets this to mean that it is also the case that *Some* B *are not* A. Illicit conversion as a source of errors in syllogistic reasoning was noted by Wilkins (1928) as a form of interpretation that occurs in single-premise problems as well as in formal syllogisms.

The Chapmans suggest that conversion is based on two factors: first, on the experience of reality and second, on the ambiguity of the copula. With respect to the first factor, the converse of many particular negative (*O*) propositions are accepted empirically (although not logically): *Some plants are not green* may be converted to an equally true proposition (empirically) that *Some green things are not plants.* When a speaker asserts a particular negative (e.g., *Some plants are not green*), he is not normally in a position to assert the universal converse, *All green things are plants.* If a universal affirmative were appropriate, normal conventions of communication would require its use (cf. Grice, 1967). Clark (1973b) describes the importance of such conventions for the comprehension of sentences and suggests that the speaker provides as informative a message as possible (here, as universal a quantifier as possible) and asserts new information that builds on presupposed given knowledge possessed by the listener. When solving a series of syllogisms, it is difficult for the reasoner to bridge the gap between his general knowledge (as stored in LTM) and the necessary antecedent for comprehending the syllogistic premises. In such situations, the reasoner must add to his data base a proposition (or set of propositions) that can serve as the given antecedent for the new information. It is suggested here that the converse of many propositions (in the present example, the particular negative) provides the missing information to the data base. Clearly, pragmatic and communicative processes are implicated in the interpretation of these propositions. The second factor contributing to conversion, ambiguity of the copula, has been described in the discussion above concerning the encoding of the relational terms.

Recent linguistic discussions of conversational implications provide empirical support for the notion of conversion (Gordon & Lakoff, 1971; Horn, 1972; Lakoff, 1970). The linguists' arguments point to the necessity of employing both of the Chapmans' bases for conversion. Horn (1972), for example, views the "reality" explanation (cf. Clark's *given–new* distinction) as accounting mainly for conversion of particularly quantified propositions. This leaves the basis for universal conversion unspecified. One plausible explanation is that the copula *is a* is ambiguous. Combining these factors, conversion may be viewed as an important encoding operation that participates in the representation of every quantified proposition. That is, conversion may be the paramount source of misinterpretation and critical for the observed deductive errors.

The conversion operation is far reaching in its possible implications for deductive inference. If conversion operates in the encoding of the premises, then the reasoner makes his validity judgments based on a representation of a syllogism which is quite different from the syllogism objectively presented. By the conversion of each proposition in the problem, the entire syllogism is transformed into a different syllogistic figure. An example of how conversion operates is illustrated with the following:

All C *are* B
All A *are* B
———
Therefore:
no conclusion follows (1)

All B *are* C
All B *are* A
———
Therefore:
Some A *are* C (2)

In Syllogism 1 the relation between A and C cannot be completely determined from the information provided in the premises. If the reasoner correctly encodes the propositions and reasons logically on this problem, he must claim that no valid conclusion is possible. An alternative view is that while encoding the premises, the reasoner converts each one in turn and stores both the original and converted propositions in his data base (with the converted proposition given priority in the "stack" of meanings for the premises. In this case, the problem (under conversion operation) would appear to the reasoner as Syllogism 2. This converted syllogism does have a solution, *Some* A *are* C. Therefore, when the reasoner converts the propositions and applies correct logical operations, a new problem is produced with a conclusion that is inappropriate for the original syllogism.

Conversion may not only participate in the encoding of abstract propositions but may also operate in the interpretation of concrete ones. Indeed, conversion, along with pragmatic processes, offers a partial explanation for the facilitating effect of concrete material. When the reasoner encodes the information on concrete propositions, the converted meaning will not appear in his data base in just those cases where the meaning of a converted proposition does not make empirical sense. Just as we generate only semantically meaningful readings of sentences, so we may not generate pragmatically deviant sentences that result from the presence of a conversion operation. For example, if the reasoner is told that "All horses are animals," he will balk at the idea that it may be interpreted to mean that "All animals are horses"—a conversion that reasoners are quite willing to make when they are told that *All* A *are* B. Consequently, the representation of some concrete propositions may be more accurate than that of abstract propositions, because the latter prescribes a converted interpretation and the former does not. That is, conversion may be blocked on concrete propositions with the effect of reducing the erroneous conclusions derived.

The foregoing discussion argues that encoding processes entailed in the comprehension of normal English expressions are present at the encoding of the syllogism's premises and that, to some degree, such factors may affect the conclusions reached by the reasoner. Clearly, the interpretation of quantifiers and the relational copula affects the validity judgments. In addition, memory processes differentially affect decisions on concrete and abstract propositions, as well as the decisions on syllogisms with terms of different lengths.

Deduction

Stage 2 of the model requires the reasoner to deduce (and write in the form of a single proposition) a composite representation of the information he has encoded. Any mechanism offered to deal with deduction is necessarily based on psychological principles rather than strictly formal ones, since there is no predicate calculus (of moderately low order) available as a mechanical prototype of such inference. The psychological literature provides some useful hypotheses concerning deduction in the form of reasoning schemes. These schemes fall into two general categories: (*a*) those requiring the reasoner to inspect some form of pictorial representation of the terms and (*b*) those requiring an inferential chain of propositions.

The pictorial schemes have a long history (some are even fun to work with; see Carroll, 1897). They all suffer from the difficulty of having to specify the translation rule from premise to diagram (predicate calculus formulations are similarly stymied by the translation problem). Current work on pictorial solutions generally rely on Venn or Euler diagram representations. That is, the reasoner is said to first represent the propositions (by some unspecified process) as a diagram and then combine such diagrams, using simple rules, to derive a composite diagram. This kind of deduction model has been used most recently by Ceraso and Provitera (1971), Erickson (1974), and Pezzoli (1970) (cf. Neimark, this volume). The approach has the singular advantage of being able to specify the source of deductive errors based on (*a*) the mechanism for selecting diagrams for the individual premises, (*b*) the combinatorial rules for concatenating individual diagrams, and (*c*) the stop rules that determine when the reasoner decides to stop searching for, or checking diagrams for, possible deductions (analogous to Klahr & Wallace's (1970) MOTIVE). Showing diagrams to reasoners clearly facilitates performance (Henle & Michael, 1956) and reduces memory load (Whimbey & Ryan, 1969). It should not be claimed, however, that the Venn diagram form of deduction is offered as anything more than a notational scheme for the representation of the information that the reasoner includes in his data base (except in those cases where diagrams are explicitly part of the task environment).

The use of inferential chains has an equally long history (De Morgan, 1966; Frase, 1966; Pezzoli & Frase, 1968; see also a model logic approach in Rescher, 1969; cf. Johnson-Laird, this volume). The onymatic system of De Morgan and the modal logic approach of Rescher have not exercised an appreciable influence on the psychological literature. The work of Frase and his associates is based on a traditional, mediation-paradigm framework that has provided relevant data on the importance of the syllogism's structure for decisions and decision times. However, Frase's work has not had a major impact on current research. In part, this is because of the mediation framework's inability to account for differential performance as a function of quantification of the premises.

The more elaborate model presented in the next section makes no explicit claims as to how the composite representation is formed—except to argue that the output of Stage 2 is notationally equivalent to a single proposition and depends on the separate encoding of the syllogisms premises.

Comparison

The nature of the comparison process (Stage 4) is left unspecified here because it largely depends on the notational form employed to describe the representation of the propositions and the composite representation. The data presented in this chapter are normative and therefore do not require a precise specification of whether the comparison occurs in serial or parallel or whether it is self-terminating or exhaustive. The present formulation requires only that the outputs of Stage 2 and Stage 4 be compatible and that a conguency match between the two be possible. Consequences of assuming that propositions or images constitute the underlying representation of the premises are discussed by Chase and Clark (1972) among others.

A MODEL OF FORMAL REASONING

Several quite strong assumptions about the nature of the encoding of propositions inhere in this model. First, it is assumed that the reasoner always converts the premises on all syllogisms. Second, both the converted and original forms of the propositions are stored in the data base with the converted meaning at the "top" of a meaning stack. Third, both the composite representation and the conclusions provided are also subject to the conversion operation. This does not mean that conversion prevents retrieval of the initial proposition since that proposition holds the "bottom" position in the meaning stack (i.e., the first reading to enter the stack). This is one way in which the data base can be said to contain "historical markers" that permit the return to previous knowledge states. That is, the reasoner may reconsider the meaning of the propositions by a backup operation through the meaning stack.

A fourth assumption of the model is that there is a response bias working when the reasoner is faced with a nonpropositional conclusion, such as "None of the above is true." In all but a few studies, students were presented with a preponderant number of invalid (e.g., indeterminate) syllogisms—approximately 70%. This may enhance the likelihood of an invalid conclusion being accepted: the problem solvers clearly do not normally expect that most of the problems they encounter cannot be answered (Chapman & Chapman, 1959). Consequently, on difficult problems, the reasoner may suspect that a "None" conclusion is unlikely to occur so frequently (70%), he may therefore incorrectly accept a propositional conclusion. In addition, the instructions given to reasoners appear to direct them to accept a propositional conclusion, even when none is valid. For example, in one study (Begg & Denny, 1969), reasoners were instructed to put a question mark in the margin of the booklet if they could not find a conclusion that validly followed from the premises. Furthermore, the "None" conclusion is often placed as the last alternative to be considered, which may further reduce its acceptability as a viable alternative (in contrast, see Roberge, 1970).

Moore and Revlis (in preparation) tested the possibility that reasoners are biased against *none* responses and thereby make a propositional selection when it is inappropriate. Two groups of ten reasoners each were given

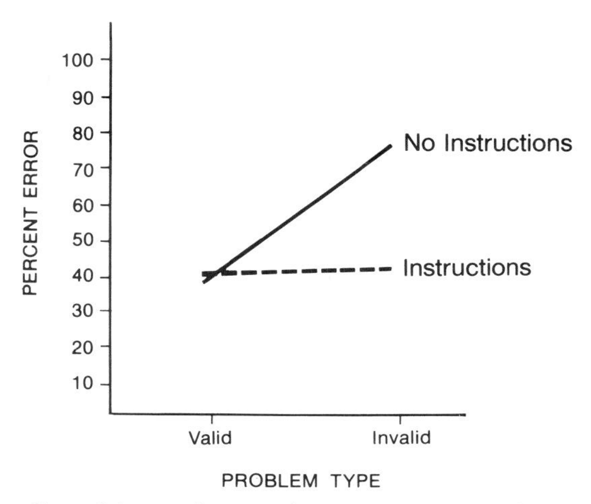

FIG. 4. The effect of instructions on the acceptance of an indeterminate solution. (——) No instructions; (– – –) instructions. (Moore & Revlis, in preparation.)

instructions concerning either the percentage of correct propositional conclusions or the percentage of "None" responses in their booklet of 12 problems. A third group was not given information on the percentage of each kind of response. A portion of the results are presented in Fig. 4. As expected, the performance of reasoners with information concerning the response frequencies is significantly better than for those with no such information provided. Of particular interest, however, is that the improvement in performance has been shown only for invalid syllogisms. That is, the error rates have been reduced on just those problems for which a *none* conclusion appears if the student is reasoning logically.

As the standard manipulations may therefore pressure students into accepting any propositional conclusion, the present model of formal reasoning presumes that the problem solvers do not wish to respond with a "None" conclusion and try to either work the problem again or make a guess from among the alternatives provided.

With the foregoing strong assumptions in mind, the following is an expanded restatement of the model of formal reasoning (see Fig. 5).

Stage 1. In the first stage, the reasoner reads the premises and stores a representation of the individual propositions. The encoding process entails a conversion operator as well as other operators that may be required for the establishment of the initial data structure. These other operators may include mechanisms for retrieving the "meaning" of the category terms from LTM. That is, the problem space in which the reasoner works the problem must not only consist of the temporary information created within

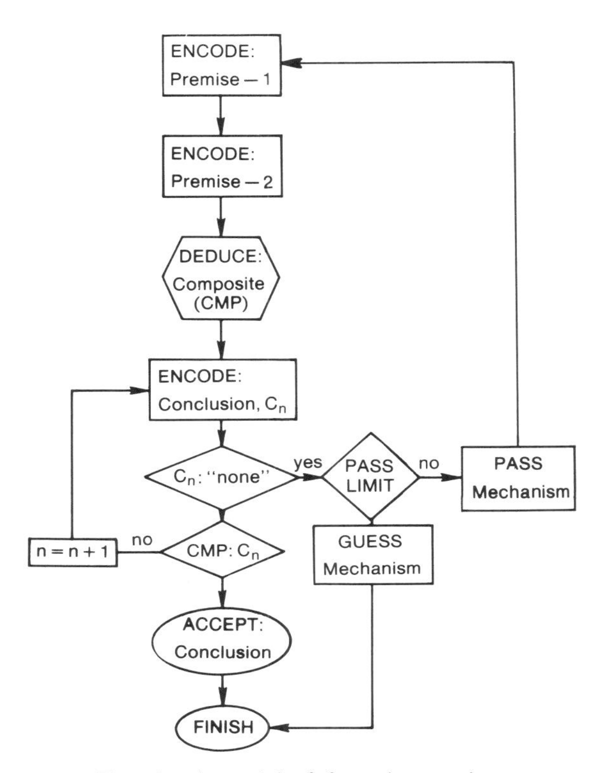

FIG. 5. A modal of formal reasoning.

the initial knowledge state but must also permit accessing of information that may be derived from additional symbol structures held in LTM or in external memory (in those cases where the reasoner is permitted to repeatedly scan the problem).[4]

Knowledge derived from LTM may include procedures that the reasoner has found useful in representing other knowledge states. These may include the availability of task-independent programs for dealing with highly used representations. For example, a frequently employed procedure is to represent information in a top-down ordering, from the most general predicates (cf. Kintsch's model of semantic memory, 1972; Revlis & Hayes' model

[4] This report borrows freely from the thorough analysis given to problem solving by Newell and Simon (1972). The reader familiar with that work will note the reliance, and burdensome references may be eliminated. One departure in terminology should be noted, however: "data base" here corresponds to Newell and Simon's notion of the total knowledge state available to a problem solver at any point during problem solution.

of hypothetical reasoning, 1972). In fact, the conversion encoding may be a consequence of one such task-independent procedure for representing information termed "overgeneralization" by Dawes (1964, 1966).

The mode of representing the encoded propositions may be a bracketed notation used in other forms of reasoning (e.g., Clark, 1969) or a predicate calculus format employed by Johnson-Laird (1970). Alternatively, we may use a pictorial form as described in the previous discussion. Any form selected must permit the encoding and decision processes described here.

Stage 2. In the second stage, the composite representation of the pair of premises results from an as yet unspecified deduction operation (either immediate or mediate deduction). The model specifies that the output of this stage is a single proposition relating the subject and predicate terms of the conclusion. This representation may be in the form of either a deep structure sentence (proposition) or a Venn diagram. Whatever the notational form, the composite representation must be organized as a meaning stack, as are the other propositions in the reasoning task, with a conversion reading at the top of the stack.

One way in which Stage 2 might proceed is to first select the "top" meaning from each premise stack and then to use these to generate a composite proposition. As part of the comprehension of this proposition, another meaning stack is created to which the reasoner has access. The notational basis for the representation is necessarily constrained by that given in Stage 1.

Stage 3. In this stage, the conclusion is presumed to be encoded with conversion and represented in a form amenable to a comparison with the composite proposition (output of Stage 2).

Stage 4. The reasoner compares the encoding of the conclusion with that of the composite proposition. If the two propositions are congruent, the reasoner accepts the conclusion as "valid." If the two are incongruent, the reasoner considers the next conclusion offered. For those problems in which none of the propositional conclusions match the reasoner's composite predicate (i.e., a *none* conclusion is the only one remaining for him), the reasoner makes a second pass through the propositions, restricting his interpretation of the syllogism's premises. That is, he either rereads the propositions or recovers them by selecting the next "meaning" in the meaning stack. In any case, subsequent representations of the premises do not contain the converted meaning. This is not to say that the reasoner has complete and purposive control over conversion interpretations. It may simply be the case that a more cautious reading reduces the range of possible interpretations, which quite incidentally eliminates the conversion transformation or, alternatively, the unconverted form of the proposition is simply selected for consideration without alteration of its meaning. If this additional pass through the reasoning process also results in a nonpropositional conclusion, the reasoner makes a guess from among the alternative conclusions. A discussion of this guessing process is reserved for a later section. It must suffice for the present that, at base, the guessing is carried out by a feature selection mechanism quite similar to the atmosphere hypothesis found in the syllogistic reasoning literature (Woodworth & Sells, 1935; Sells, 1936; Sells & Koob, 1937).

PREDICTIONS FROM THE MODEL

The model of formal reasoning assumes that a conversion operation participates in the encoding of quantified propositions. As a result of this operation, the reasoner's representation of the syllogism is equivalent to that for an unconverted syllogism, written in the same mood but in a different figure. That is, the reasoner makes his initial deductions from a different syllogism than the one provided by the experimenter. The model, therefore, makes the following general predictions. First, the reasoner's accuracy is maximum (he makes fewest errors) on those syllogisms in which conversion of the premises leaves the logically required conclusion unchanged (these syllogisms are called SAMES because their conclusion is identical to the conclusion for the objectively presented problem).

Second, the reasoner's accuracy is minimal (he makes maximum errors) on those syllogisms the conclusion of which has been altered by the presence of a conversion operation. That is, on those syllogisms for which conversion transforms the problem so that a different conclusion is logically demanded, the reasoner's decisions are scored as "incorrect" (these problems are called DIFFERENTS).

Third, the reasoner makes fewer errors on valid syllogisms than on invalid ones because overall, the response bias results in more errors for invalid syllogisms than for valid ones.

The general predictions of the model are clearly supported by existant data in the published literature. Error rates for a sample of the studies are given in Fig. 6. Although the functions do not have the same slopes or intersections, the trends are clear: when conversion does not alter the logically required conclusion (SAMES), error rates are low; when conversion alters the conclusion (DIFFERENTS), error rates are high. In addition, valid syllogisms are easier to solve than invalid ones.

Although the model of formal reasoning is supported by these previous studies, a replication is fruitful for at least three reasons: (*a*) to determine whether the conversion findings are an artifact of the sample of problems used in the previous studies, (*b*) to have more detailed data than the present literature makes available, and (*c*) to have a baseline for further

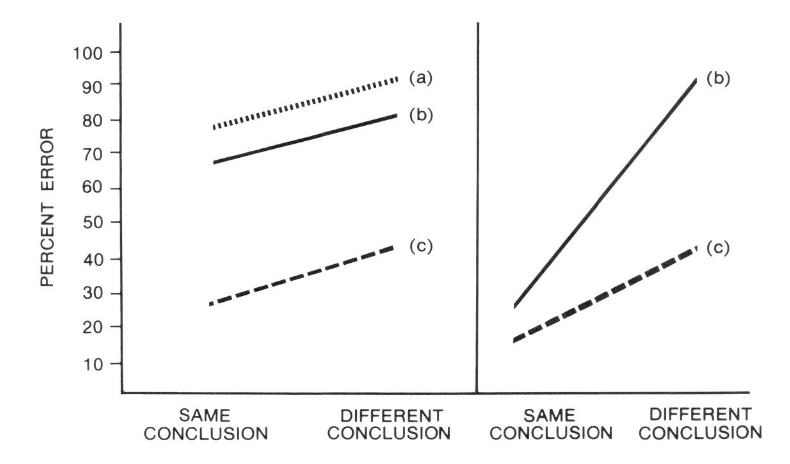

FIG. 6. The effect of conversion on decisions for valid and invalid syllogisms: Historical summary. (· · ·) Chapman and Chapman (1959); (——) Morgan and Morton (1944); (– – –) Wilkins (1928).

experiments on a different sample of students. Therefore, 50 students at California State University, Fullerton were given a booklet of 64 problems (including many problems found in previous experiments). Half of the problems had a propositional conclusion logically demanded and half did not. Although the pool of problems used did not exhaust the number of possible syllogisms, they were selected to insure at least a broad range of different moods and figures.

There were 18 unique valids and 21 unique invalids. The valid syllogisms were: *AA*-1, *AA*-3, *AA*-4, *AI*-1, *AI*-3, *IA*-3, *IA*-4, *AE*-2, *AE*-4, *EA*-1, *EA*-2, *EA*-4, *AO*-2, *OA*-3, *EI*-1, *EI*-2, *EI*-3, *EI*-4. The invalid syllogisms were: *AA*-2, *AI*-2, *AI*-4, *IA*-1, *IA*-2, *AE*-1, *AE*-3, *AO*-1, *OA*-1, *II*-1, *II*-2, *IO*-1, *IO*-2, *OI*-1, *OI*-2, *IE*-1, *IE*-2, *EE*-1, *EE*-2, *OO*-1, *OO*-2. The ordering of the problems within the booklets was randomized with the restriction that runs of more than three instances of a single problem or problem type (valid or invalid) were not permitted.

Each reasoning problem consisted of two premises and five alternative conclusions: *All* A *are* C, *No* A *are* C, *Some* A *are* C, and *Some* A *are not* C, and *None of the above is proved.* Although the letters were changed on each problem, the order of the conclusions remained the same on each problem (i.e., *A, E, I, O,* and *none*).

Students were given two different time periods in which to solve the syllogisms: half of them were permitted 15 sec per problem and half were given 30 sec. Although this may seem a brief amount of time, in those studies for which a maximum time has been specified for a set of problems, 20 sec per problem is a reasonable time estimate.

Results

The overall results are presented in Fig. 7, which shows that the model is successful in predicting the decisions on abstract syllogisms. Syllogisms that, on the initial pass, have different conclusions in the converted form show higher error rates than those the conclusions of which are unaffected by conversion [$F(1, 48) = 32.9$, $p < .001$]. This holds equally well for syllogisms with a valid propositional conclusion [$F(1, 48) = 23.3$, $p < .001$] and for those with no valid conclusion [$F(1, 48) = 14.5$, $p < .001$. In addition, the reasoners are correct more often on syllogisms with a valid conclusion than on those with no valid conclusion [$F(1, 48) = 902$, $p < .001$].

Although the data support the three general predictions of the model, firm support cannot be claimed without consideration of derived predictions. The following is a more detailed examination of the model. It considers (*a*) valid and invalid syllogisms separately and (*b*) the predictive accuracy of the model (i.e., the ability of the model to specify the precise decisions the reasoner reaches on each syllogism).

Invalid syllogisms. On the initial pass through the problem, the representation of the propositions entails a conversion operation. When

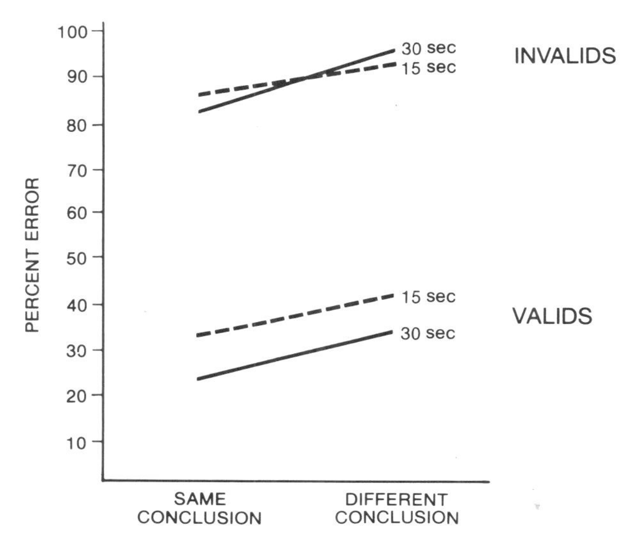

FIG. 7. Conversion effect for valid and invalid syllogisms. (– – –) Wilkins (1928). (——) 30 sec; (– – –) 15 sec.

conversion results in a syllogism with a propositional conclusion, the reasoner accepts this conclusion in a manner described previously. When the converted syllogism does not have a propositional conclusion (i.e., only the nonpropositional *none* is appropriate), the reasoner makes a second pass through the premises. This additional pass involves either (*a*) considering the next proposition at the top of the meaning stack in the data base or (*b*) a rerepresentation of the premises with a restricted interpretation (i.e., without conversion). For invalid syllogisms, this will again result in a nonpropositional conclusion that is logically correct but contrary to the reasoner's response biases. In this case, the reasoner either makes another pass (which may entail another selection from the meaning stack) or guesses from among the possible conclusions (there are always five alternatives to select from). As a result of the guess, a correct *none* response should occur on approximately 20% of the problems; an incorrect propositional conclusion should occur on the remaining problems. Therefore, the conversion decisions, along with the guess responses, will produce an overall conversion function for invalid syllogisms.

These predictions are supported by the data: (*a*) the reasoners are correct 15.5% of the time on problems requiring a guessed response (compared with 20% as predicted) and (*b*) the model correctly predicts the precise conclusion that the reasoner reaches on 64% of the remaining invalid syllogisms—those for which, as a consequence of converting, the reasoner selects a propositional conclusion.

Two aspects of these findings should be noted. First, the predictive accuracy of the model is not perfect. Of the 36% of decisions unaccounted for, the reasoner makes a logically correct decision on 45% of these problems. The model of formal reasoning, therefore, predicts approximately 70% of the erroneous decisions made on invalid syllogisms. Second, the reasoners do not appear to be making a "fair" guess from among the alternatives. For those syllogisms in which the reasoner is said to guess from among the conclusions, all the alternatives are not equally likely to be guessed. An explanation for this finding must await a discussion of the PASS and GUESS mechanisms; however, in anticipation of that discussion: (*a*) the GUESS mechanism is initiated by finding a "None" conclusion after repeated passes through the problem: (*b*) the basis for the guess is a feature-matching process rather than a fair-guess procedure.

Valid syllogisms. The model distinguishes among three types of valid syllogisms: (*a*) those in which conversion results in the same conclusion as the presented problem (SAMES), (*b*) those in which conversion produces a syllogism with a different propositional conclusion (DIFFERENTS), and (*c*) those in which conversion results in a nonpropositional conclusion (NONES). For SAMES and DIFFERENTS, the reasoner makes a single pass through the problem and finds a propositional conclusion that matches his composite representation. For NONES, the reasoner's bias against such decisions initiates additional passes through the problem without converting the premises. On these subsequent passes, the reasoner will logically accept the appropriate conclusion.

There are three major predictions made for valid syllogisms. First, SAMES and NONES should have the same observed error rates: because the reasoner makes the correct deductions on both problems (on NONES, this occurs on the second or subsequent passes through the syllogism), the observed error rates for both types of syllogisms should approximate zero. Second, both SAMES and NONES should have lower error rates than DIFFERENTS. Since for the latter syllogisms the reasoner readily accepts an incorrect propositional conclusion, the observed error rate for DIFFERENTS should approximate 100%. Third, the error rates for DIFFERENTS should be equivalent to that observed for those invalid syllogisms in which conversion results in a propositional conclusion, because the reasoning process is the same for both types of problems.

The predictions are largely confirmed by the data. There is an overall difference in observed error rates for the three types of valid syllogisms [$F(2, 96) = 302.2$, $p < .001$]. SAME and NONE problems do not differ in their error rates (27.2 and 28.4%, respectively) and both are significantly lower in error than the DIFFERENT problems (88%). DIFFERENT problems are equal in their error rates to those invalid syllogisms that have a propositional conclusion as a result of conversion (88.0 and 93.5%, respectively).[5]

PASS Mechanism

The reasoner is assumed to be capable of reevaluating his knowledge state—his representation of the premises. This may be accomplished by either an actual rereading of the premises or by a trace-back procedure, which transforms the present knowledge state to a previous one. This trace back may be accomplished by selecting the proposition at the top of the meaning stack for each premise—it has been assumed throughout that the top-to-bottom order of the stack corresponds to the historical order in which semantic readings of the premises were generated (from recent to earliest).

[5] In its strong form, the model predicts that the reasoner makes no errors on SAMES and NONES and always makes errors on DIFFERENTS. The observed deviations from these strong predictions may be attributable to (*a*) random processing errors, equally distributed to all stages or (*b*) insufficiencies in the model's specification. However important these deviations are, they are not critical for the general scope of the model.

In the model of formal reasoning, the PASS parameter is a composite of the factors of time and the number of passes a subject is willing to make through the problem. Time is important because of the reasoner's processing parameters, whereas the number of passes is determined by both his motivation and the number of propositions in his meaning stack. In the brief trials given in this experiment (15–30 sec in duration), the reasoner probably can make no more than one or two passes and still respond in the required time interval. In none of the data reported here was the time interval a major factor in the decisions. Because the number of passes the reasoner can make is determined by the time taken to make a single pass, further research on the nature of this processing parameter is of obvious importance to the present model.

GUESS Mechanism

Although the "None" response is selected at approximately chance level, the reasoner does not appear to make a fair guess from among the four remaining alternatives. The guesses from among the propositional conclusions are decidedly biased: the reasoner bases his selection on a feature match between the premises and the conclusions. The GUESS mechanism accounts for the "guess" of a propositional conclusion by means of a four-stage procedure [this feature-matching mechanism is functionally equivalent to the atmosphere hypothesis suggested by Woodworth and Sells (1935) and restated by Begg and Denny (1969)].

Stage 1: Premise representation. In the first stage, the reasoner accesses from his data base a single representation of each premise in the syllogism. This representation is either formed anew or is simply the proposition at the top of the meaning stack. It is based on the extraction of two features from the premises: quantity [±universal] and polarity [±affirmative]. These features are presumed to be based on a superficial analysis of the premises and may be the earliest "meanings" glossed.

Stage 2: Composite representation. The composite representation consists of a predicate composed of the attributes and their values given in Stage 1. The composite representation is formed in two steps and is guided by two rules:

1. If the two premises have the same sign on an attribute, the composite sign for the two premises (for that attribute) is the sign of any single premise for that attribute.
2. If the signs differ for an attribute, the sign of the composite representation for that attribute is minus (i.e., particular or negative).

In the first step of this stage, the reasoner compares the values for the first attribute [±universal]. Rule 1 is applied unless there is a mismatch on the attribute values, in which case Rule 2 is applied. The second step proceeds in an identical manner as the first, for the attribute [±affirmative].

Stage 3: Representation of the conclusion. As each conclusion is considered, the problem solver extracts the relevant features of the proposition and represents the proposition using the operations in Stage 1.

Stage 4: Comparison. In this stage, the composite representation is compared with that of the conclusion. If the composite representation and the conclusion are congruent, the reasoner responds by accepting the conclusion. If the two representations are incongruent, the reasoner reads the next conclusion. The procedures used in the experiments reported in this chapter guarantee that the reasoner always finds a match before exhausting the list of alternatives (see Fig. 8).

The predictions of this guessing mechanism were compared with the decisions made by each reasoner on each of the SAME invalid problems. The feature-matching procedure accounted for 67.4% of the decisions in which a propositional conclusion was selected (chance = 25%). Although this predictive accuracy is not optimal, it does suggest that the atmosphere hypothesis, when framed as a feature-matching mechanism, can reasonably account for the decisions of the problem solvers when their logical inferences fail to result in a propositional conclusion.

One prediction from this model is that when the reasoner is given information concerning the proportion of times a "None" response is appropriate in the set of problems, the bias mechanism is invoked on a smaller percentage of the problems (if at all). In the Moore and Revlis experiment described above, the reasoner was provided such information. A major finding of that experiment was that informing the reasoner about the objective frequency of a "None" conclusion significantly improved the performance on only those invalid syllogisms for which the GUESS mechanism would be invoked. No change was shown on the other invalid syllogisms or on any of the valid syllogisms. Clearly, response biases operate in the reasoner's decisions and, with few exceptions (e.g., Henle & Michael, 1956), the instructions given to the reasoners are often not adequate to dispel such biases. In these cases, the reasoner's decisions are frequently categorized as irrational or alogical.

Concrete Syllogisms

The present model claims that a conversion operation participates in the derivation of a semantic reading for quantified propositions. However, when the propositions describe a relation between classes for which the reasoner has real-world knowledge stored in LTM, conversion interpretations will be "blocked" in those instances for which conversion results in

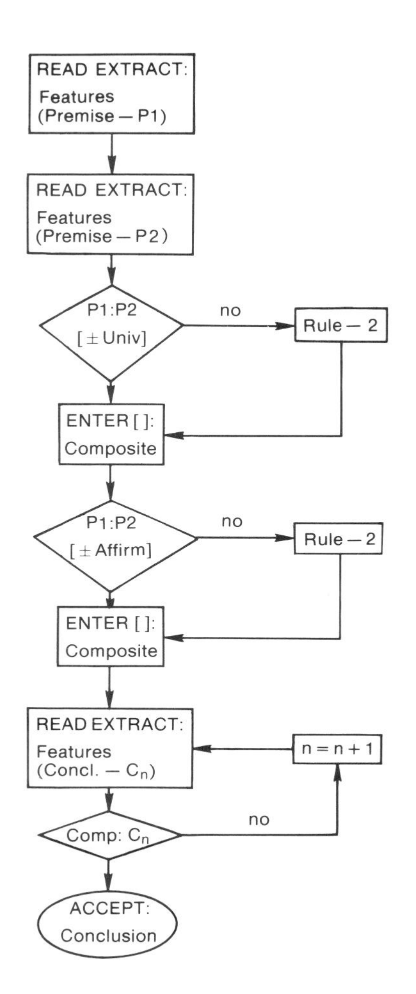

FIG. 8. The guessing mechanism: a feature-selection procedure.

a semantically (i.e., pragmatically) deviant relation. This is not to say that the reasoner necessarily controls his use of the conversion operator; instead, his semantic processor derives a pragmatically appropriate reading from the premises—it remains possible that the "deviant" interpretation may be recovered, with some difficulty.

Predictions. The model makes the following predictions with respect to reasoning with concrete relations. First, when the reasoner is given syllogisms in which conversion does not result in a "deviant" underlying meaning, he should exhibit the same conversion function that characterizes the abstract problems (on both valid and invalid syllogisms). In addition, when conversion errors occur, they should be of comparable frequency to that shown for abstract syllogisms, because the reasoning processes are the same. Second, when conversion results in a "deviant" reading, conversion should be blocked and the reasoner's decisions should not show a conversion function. Error rates for these problems should be lower than those for the converted, abstract syllogisms.

To test the assertion that conversion operates on concrete syllogisms as it does on abstract ones, two groups of students ($n = 30$) were given booklets of 12 reasoning problems. These booklets contained propositions that were designed to either enhance conversion (C group) or ones that were designed to block conversion (B group). Half of the problems in each booklet were valid syllogisms, half were invalid syllogisms. Half of the problems were SAMES and half were DIFFERENTS.

The problems for the C group consisted of propositions for which the conversion interpretation was reasonable, if not actually implied:

C1. All history books are among the books on this corner of the shelf.
C2. Some history books are not among the books on this floor of the library.
B1. All history books are among the books on this floor of the library.
B2. Some history books are not among the books on this corner of the shelf.

For the C group problems, the universal affirmatives would be interpreted very nearly as identity relations (C1), as there are few if any elements of the predicate class that would not also be elements of the intersection of the subject and predicate classes. For the particular negatives, there were many elements of the predicate class that were not also elements of the intersection of the subject and predicate classes (C2).

In contrast, the B group was shown problems so constructed that the universal affirmatives would not be interpreted as an identity relation because there were many possible elements in the predicate class that were not necessarily elements of the intersection of the subject and predicate classes (B1). In addition, the particular negatives were intended to be interpreted as an inclusion relation: there were many possible elements of the predicate class that would be included in the intersection of the subject and predicate classes (B2).

Notice that the different interpretations of the premises are a result of manipulating the relative number of elements in the predicate class that are excluded from the intersection with the subject class. In the traditional terminology of set theory, where S stands for the elements in the subject class, the manipulations in this experiment vary the size of the S' set, the number of elements not in the subject class.

These materials were constructed to test the assumption that conversion operated in the interpretation of concrete, quantified propositions. It was necessary, therefore, for conversion interpretations to be implicitly given in the premises, rather than to be explicitly stated for the reasoner. That is, were it to be specified to the reasoner that although *All* A *are* B, it is not necessarily the case that *All* B *are* A, it would not be possible to test the strong assumption that conversion normally operated when encoding concrete propositions. In contrast, a procedure explicating possible interpretations of sentences was used by Ceraso and Provitera (1971), who showed that by disambiguating the relationship between the subject and predicate terms (i.e., by blocking a conversion interpretation), reasoning errors were reduced—although their analysis was quite different from the one presented here.

The results for valid and invalid syllogisms are given in Fig. 9, which shows that for the C group, there is a definite conversion function: errors are largest on just those problems for which conversion produces a syllogism with a different conclusion than the one objectively presented [$F(1, 29) = 43.6$, $p < .001$]. Although overall, the valid syllogisms have fewer errors than the invalid ones [$F(1, 29) = 13.1$, $p = .001$], there is no interaction between the validity of the problem and the effect of conversion operations.

The B group also showed a slight effect of conversion [$F(1, 29) = 4.4$, $p < .05$]. However, as predicted, there was no difference in error rates

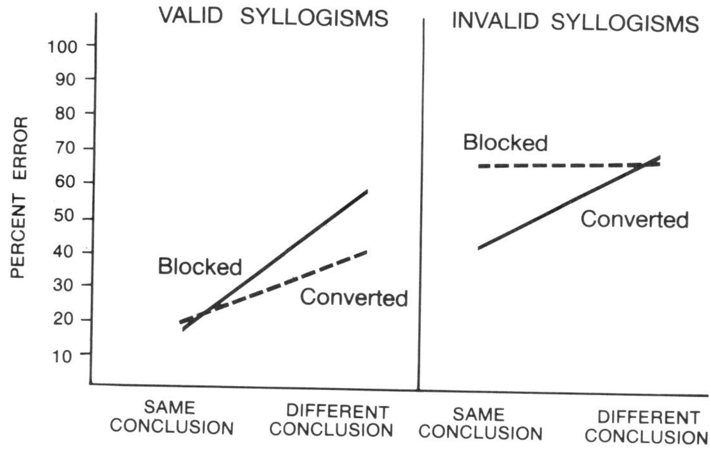

FIG. 9. The effect of implicit, pragmatic factors on the conversion of valid and invalid syllogisms. (——) Converted; (– – –) blocked.

between SAMES and DIFFERENTS on the invalid syllogisms. As in the C group, valid syllogisms were easier for the reasoners to solve than were invalid syllogisms [$F(1, 29) = 38.8$, $p < .001$].

The critical test of the model is found in a comparison of the two groups, which shows that: (*a*) there is no overall difference between them in their error rates but (*b*) there is a significant interaction between the groups and the two types of problems (SAMES and DIFFERENTS); the effect of conversion is greater for the C group than for the B group [$F(1, 58) = 10$, $p < .01$]. That is, there is a difference between the two groups on just those problems in which conversion is claimed to have an effect.

Because the set sizes on these problems were implicit in the propositions, it is possible that making the set sizes more explicit would alter the conversion function to a greater extent than in the implicit propositions. Therefore, four additional groups of students ($n = 30$) were given modified forms of the two kinds of problem booklets described above: numbers were added indicating the sizes of the classes mentioned in the major premise, e.g., *All history books* (#) *are among the books on this corner of the shelf* (#). There were two sets of numbers; in the first set, the size of the predicate class was large in comparison to the number of elements in the intersection of the subject and predicate classes (the size of the predicate class was always nine times that of the subject class). In the second set, the size of the predicate class was small relative to the intersection of the classes (the predicate class was larger than the subject class by one or two elements). Some number pairs from these two sets contributed to a conversion interpretation (C) and others blocked it (B). The two kinds of number pairs were orthogonally paired with the two kinds of problems, resulting in four treatment groups: (*a*) C–C, (*b*) C–B, (*c*) B–C, and (*d*) B–B.

An overall analysis of variance failed to show a significant effect across the four groups. However, there was an effect that was precisely pertinent to the present model. The reasoners showed more errors on C–C problems than they did on B–B problems [$F(1, 58) = 7.7$, $p < .01$]. Figure 10 shows that this difference was largely due to an interesting interaction between validity and conversion (SAME versus DIFFERENTS) [$F(1, 58) = 25.3$, $p < .001$]. For valid syllogisms, both the C–C and B–B problems induced a conversion encoding (SAME versus DIFFERENTS—C–C: $F(1, 29) = 72.5$, $p < .001$; B–B: $F(1, 29) = 8.1$, $p < .01$). However the effect of conversion was greater for the C–C problems than for the B–B ones [$F(1, 58) = 7.0$, $p = .01$]. That is, for valid syllogisms, these two types of problems differed on precisely those cases in which the model of formal reasoning predicted that set size would effect the encoding of the propositions.

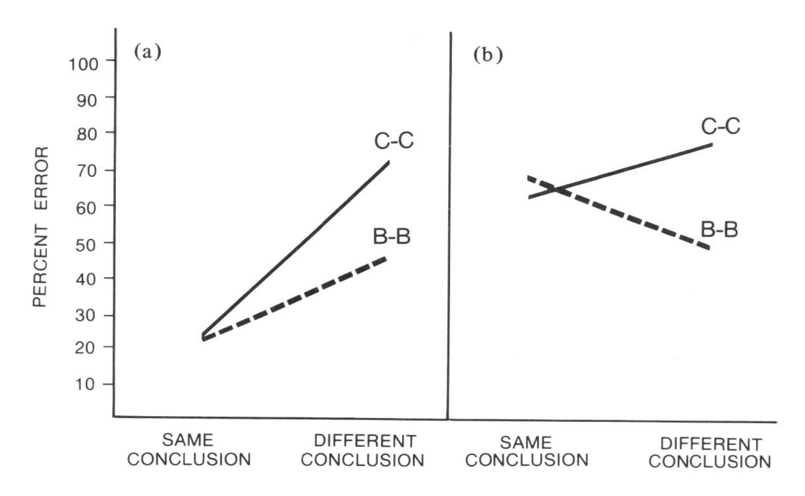

FIG. 10. The effect of explicit blocking of conversion interpretation: (a) valid and (b) invalid syllogisms. (——) C–C; (– – –) B–B.

For invalid syllogisms, the interaction between the two groups is more dramatic: the B–B problems show a decline in errors on those problems for which conversion blocking should have its effect [$F(1, 29) = 5.3$, $p < .05$]. For the C–C problems, moreover, there is the predicted effect of conversion: SAME problems are easier to solve than DIFFERENT problems [$F(1, 29) = 5.1$, $p < .05$]. This differential effect of encoding results in an interaction between the two groups [$F(1, 58) = 9.7$, $p < .01$].

Comparison of the reasoners' performance on the present, concrete syllogisms with that shown for the abstract problems mentioned above shows that the C group has a poorer performance than reasoners on the abstact, valid problems, whereas the B group shows a better performance. These differences occur primarily on those problems in which the logically required conclusion is altered by a conversion operation (i.e., DIFFERENTS).

This model of formal reasoning offers an explanation for the well-known facilitating effect of concrete propositions in deductive reasoning. When the reasoner's data base contains information that blocks a conversion interpretation, his performance improves on just those problems on which conversion would normally have its effect—his decisions can be considered more "rational" than when he is asked to reason with abstract classes (for which conversion occurs). When conversion is not blocked for concrete problems, the reasoner makes as many deductive errors on those problems as he does on abstract ones.

This interaction between concreteness of the material and conversion is not only seen in the present experiment, which was specifically designed to illustrate it, but is also present in the data of Wilkins (1928). She showed a major effect of concreteness; however, a retabulation of Wilkins' data indicates that for valid syllogisms: (*a*) on abstract problems, SAMES were easier to solve than DIFFERENTS (16 and 43.4% errors, respectively), (*b*) on concrete problems, there was little difference between SAMES and DIFFERENTS (17.4 and 10.4%, respectively), and (*c*) on those problems on which conversion should have no effect (SAMES), there is no difference between abstract and concrete syllogisms (16.0 compared with 17.4%, respectively). That is, the major effect of concreteness is largely accounted for by the differential blocking of the conversion operation at encoding.

Summary

The data summarized on these pages argue that the disparate findings of the syllogistic reasoning literature may be explained by a single model that attributes deductive errors to a miscoding of the problems' premises. The model of formal reasoning claims that a conversion operation participates in the establishment of a representation of the syllogism in the reasoner's data base. This data base is complex and contains logical operators (for deductions) as well as a host of linguistic and pragmatic information accessed from LTM.

Two aspects of the model are in critical need of development. First, the syntactic and semantic processes shown to be important for categorical reasoning need to be determined and formally specified within the model. Second, the deduction operations in the second stage of the model—formation of a composite representation—also need to be specified. That is, if the knowledge state embodying the reasoner's understanding of the premises is a consequence of combinatorial operations on "diagrams" or deep structure propositions, then those operations (and the data structures to which they are applied) also must be actualized within the model.

Although the model of formal reasoning needs further elaboration, its present formulation has several desirable attributes. First, it accounts for differences in reasoning on valid and invalid syllogisms. Second, it properly distinguishes among the problems within each category (SAMES, NONES, and DIFFERENTS). Third, it specifies the conditions under which knowledge of the categories reasoned about affects the deductions. In addition, the model is sufficiently explicit that it permits reasonable tests of its assumptions and, thereby, offers a guide to the study of deductive inference.

SPECULATIONS ON CONDITIONAL REASONING

The specification of the model of formal reasoning suggests commonalities between categorical reasoning and conditional reasoning in terms of both the encoding operations and the guessing mechanisms that these forms of reasoning entail. For example, reasoning errors on both kinds of tasks may be attributed to the encoding of the premises. When asked to make inferences from conditional propositions of the form *if P then Q*, reasoners tend to miscode these propositions and take them to mean that both *P implies Q and Q implies P* (e.g., Geis & Zwicky, 1971; Staudenmayer, this volume). This biconditional interpretation of the propositions has been offered as an explanation for the decisions made in conditional reasoning experiments—specifically for the data of Wason and Johnson-Laird (e.g., Johnson-Laird & Wason, 1970; Wason, 1968; Wason & Johnson-Laird, 1969). The major proponent of this analysis is Taplin (Taplin, 1971; Taplin & Staudenmayer, 1973; Taplin, Staudenmayer, & Taddonio, 1974). As in categorical reasoning, a guessing mechanism has also been implicated in conditional reasoning (Evans, 1972a, b, 1973; Evans & Lynch, 1973; Johnson-Laird, this volume). Evans claims that the reasoner's decisions appear to be based on a feature-matching process, which may be an analog of the mechanism described here for categorical reasoning.

The conversion and biconditional encodings exhibit sufficient superficial similarities to warrant the conjecture that they may have similar underlying mechanisms. First, both forms of reasoning appear to entail operations that derive an underlying reading in which the subject and predicate terms may be reversed without altering the meaning of the derived encoding: (*a*) *all* A *are* B is taken to mean that it is also the case that *all* B *are* A, (*b*) *P implies Q* is taken to mean that it is also the case that *Q implies P*.

Second, universally quantified categorical propositions may be expressed as a conditional. That is, *all* A *are* B may be glossed as *if there is an* A, *it is a* B (although only in a narrow sense can *if P then Q* be treated as a categorical). Notice that when the universal is given a conversion interpretation, its conditional analog is given a biconditional reading.

Third, both operations are affected by the information stored in the data base. The reasoner uses this information to construct the knowledge states on which he applies his inference operations. That is, both conversion and the biconditional interpretations are affected by LTM, pragmatic information. Such information has been shown here to influence decisions on categorical syllogisms by blocking (or permitting) a conversion operation from participating in the encoding stage. So too, researchers have shown that when the conditional reasoning problems are phrased in terms of real-world parameters, the kind and frequency of errors decline (Johnson-Laird, Legrenzi, & Legrenzi, 1972; Wason & Shapiro, 1971).

Fourth, the guessing mechanism described by Evans is particularly interesting in the parallel it offers between categorical and conditional reasoning. Specifically, Evans claims that when the meaning of the propositions may be obscure (or ambiguous), the reasoner tends to accept a conclusion that matches the conditional propositions in terms of two features: (*a*) subject or predicate terms and (*b*) polarity of the terms. This mechanism is similar to the one introduced in this chapter in that (*a*) they both view the guessing mechanism as interacting with comprehension of the material (see Evans, 1972a) and (*b*) the incidence of guessing appears most pronounced in situations where the reasoner is faced with a propositional conclusion (which is invalid) or an indeterminate response (e.g., "None of the above is true" compared with "Indeterminate value"); this is also shown in Evans (1972a, Experiment I).

Finally, a "pass" mechanism may be entailed in both kinds of reasoning. The number of passes through a problem that the reasoner is willing to make can effect the decision he reaches. For categorical reasoning, not finding a propositional conclusion causes the reasoner to select the next proposition in the meaning stack (or, consider an alternative Venn diagram); where he stops determines his decision (a slightly different view is offered by Ceraso & Provitera, 1971). So too, in conditional reasoning, an "incomplete analysis" of the alternatives leads to the premature acceptance of an inappropriate conclusion.

These commonalities suggest that differences in cateorical and conditional reasoning may only be apparent and may not correspond to structural properties of the reasoner's problem space when he solves these syllogisms. Certainly, such commonalities are worth exploring. Perhaps a single model can yet account for the deductions in both forms of inference.

ACKNOWLEDGMENTS

I wish to express my appreciation to H. Clark, R. Falmagne, N. Revlis, H. Staudenmeyer, and S. Woll for their comments on earlier drafts of this chapter.

REFERENCES

Barclay, J. The role of comprehension in remembering sentences. *Cognitive Psychology,* 1973, **4,** 229–254.

Begg, I., & Denny, J. Empirical reconciliation of atmosphere and conversion interpretations of syllogistic reasoning. *Journal of Experimental Psychology,* 1969, **81,** 351–354.

Bransford, J., Barclay, J., & Franks, J. Sentence memory: A constructive versus interpretative approach. *Cognitive Psychology,* 1972, **3,** 193–209.

Bransford, J., & Franks, J. The abstraction of linguistic ideas. *Cognitive Psychology,* 1971, **2,** 331–350.

Carroll, L. *Symbolic logic.* London: Macmillan, 1897.

Ceraso, J., & Provitera, A. Sources of error in syllogistic reasoning. *Cognitive Psychology,* 1971, **2,** 400–410.

Chapman, L. J., & Chapman, J. P. Atmosphere effect re-examined. *Journal of Experimental Psychology,* 1959, **58,** 220–226.

Chase, W. G., & Clark, H. H. Mental operations in the comparison of sentences and pictures. In L. Gregg (Ed.), *Cognition in learning and memory.* New York: Wiley, 1972.

Clark, H. H. Linguistic processes in deductive reasoning. *Psychological Review,* 1969, **76,** 387–404.

Clark, H. H. Comprehending comparatives. In G. Flores d'Arcais & W. J. M. Levelt (Eds.), *Advances in psycholinguistics.* Amsterdam: North-Holland Publ., 1970.

Clark, H. H. Semantics and comprehension. In T. A. Sebeok (Ed.) *Current trends in linguistics,* Vol. 12. The Hague: Mouton, 1973. (a)

Clark, H. H. Comprehension and the given-new contract. Paper presented at the Conference on the Role of Grammar in Interdisciplinary Linguistic Research, Bielefeld, Germany, 1973. (b)

Cohen, M. R., & Nagel, E. *An introduction to logic.* New York: Harcourt, 1934.

Dawes, R. Cognitive distortion. *Psychological Reports,* 1964, **14,** 443–459.

Dawes, R. Memory and distortion of meaningful written material. *British Journal of Psychology,* 1966, **57,** 77–86.

De Morgan, A. On the syllogism and on various points of the Onymatic System. In P. Heath (Ed.), *On the syllogism and other logical writings.* New Haven: Yale, 1966. (Originally published 1863.)

Eifermann, R. Negation: A linguistic variable. *Acta Psychologica,* 1961, **18,** 258–273.

Erickson, J. R. A set analysis theory of behavior in formal syllogistic reasoning tasks. *Loyola symposium on cognition,* II. Hillsdale, New Jersey: Lawrence Erlbaum Assoc., 1974.

Evans, J. St. B. T. Reasoning with negatives. *British Journal of Psychology,* 1972, **63**, 213–219. (a)

Evans, J. St. B. T. Interpretation and 'matching bias' in a reasoning task. *Quarterly Journal of Experimental Psychology,* 1972, **24,** 193–199. (b)

Evans, J. St. B. T. On the problems of interpreting reasoning data: Logical and psychological approaches. *Cognition,* 1973, **1,** 373–384.

Evans, J. St. B. T., & Lynch, J. S. Matching bias in the selection task. *British Journal of Psychology,* 1973, **64,** 391–397.

Feather, N. T. Acceptance and rejection of arguments in relation to attitude strength, critical ability, and intolerance of inconsistency. *Journal of Abnormal & Social Psychology,* 1965, **69,** 127–136.

Feigenbaum, E. A. The simulation of verbal learning behavior. In E. A. Feigenbaum & J. Feldman (Eds.), *Computers and thought.* New York: McGraw-Hill, 1963.

Frase, L. T. Validity judgments of syllogisms in relation to two sets of terms. *Journal of Educational Psychology,* 1966, **57,** 239–244.

Frase, L. T. Associative factors in syllogistic reasoning. *Journal of Experimental Psychology,* 1968, **76,** 407–412.

Frege, G. On concept and object. *Vierteljahrsschrift fur wissenschaftliche Philosophie,* 1892, **16,** 192–305. In P. Geach & M. Black (Eds.), *Translations from the philosophical writings of Gottlob Frege.* Oxford: Blackwell, 1970.

Geis, J. L., & Zwicky, A. M. On invited inferences. *Linguistic Inquiry,* 1971, **2,** 561–566.

Glucksberg, S., Trabasso, T., & Wald, J. Linguistic structures and mental operations. *Cognitive Psychology,* 1973, **5,** 338–370.

Gordon, D., & Lakoff, G. Conversational postulates. Seventh Regional Meeting of the Chicago Linguistic Society, University of Chicago, Chicago, 1971.

Gordon, R. Attitudes toward Russia on logical reasoning. *Journal of Social Psychology,* 1953, **37,** 103–111.

Gough, P. B. The verification of sentences: The effects of delay on behavior. *Journal of Verbal Learning & Verbal Behavior,* 1966, **5**, 492–496.

Greene, J. M. The semantic function of negatives and passives. *British Journal of Psychology,* 1970, **61,** 17–22. (a)

Greene, J. M. Syntactic form and semantic function. *Quarterly Journal of Experimental Psychology,* 1970, **22,** 14–27. (b)

Grice, H. P. *The logic of conversation: William James lectures.* Cambridge, Massachusetts: Harvard University Press, 1967.

Henle, M. On the relation between logic and thinking. *Psychological Review,* 1962, **69,** 366–378.

Henle, M., & Michael, M. The influence of attitudes on syllogistic reasoning. *Journal of Social Psychology,* 1956, **44,** 115–127.

Horn, L. R. On the semantic properties of logical operators in English. Unpublished doctoral dissertation. Department of Linguistics. University of California, Los Angeles, 1972.

Huttenlocher, J. Eisenberg, K., & Strauss, S. Comprehension: Relations between perceived actor and logical subject. *Journal of Verbal Learning & Verbal Behavior,* 1968, **7,** 527–530.

Janis, I., & Frick, F. The relationship between attitudes toward conclusions and errors in judging logical validity of syllogisms. *Journal of Experimental Psychology,* 1943, **33,** 73–77.

Janis, I., & Terwilliger, R. An experimental study of psychological resistances to fear arousing communications. *Journal of Abnormal & Social Psychology,* 1962, **65,** 403–410.

Johnson-Laird, P. N. Interpretation of the passive voice. *Quarterly Journal of Experimental Psychology,* 1968, **20,** 69–73. (a)

Johnson-Laird, P. N. The choice of the passive voice in a communicative task. *British Journal of Psychology,* 1968, **59,** 7–15. (b)

Johnson-Laird, P. N. Reasoning with ambiguous sentences. *British Journal of Psychology,* 1969, **60,** 17–23. (a)

Johnson-Laird, P. N. On understanding logically complex sentences. *Quarterly Journal of Experimental Psychology,* 1969, **21,** 1–13. (b)

Johnson-Laird, P. N. The interpretation of quantified sentences. In G. B. Flores d'Arcais & W. J. M. Levelt (Eds.), *Advances in psycholinguistics.* Amsterdam: North-Holland Publ., 1970.

Johnson-Laird, P. N., Legrenzi, P., & Legrenzi, M. S. Reasoning and a sense of reality. *British Journal of Psychology,* 1972, **63,** 395–400.

Johnson-Laird, P. N., & Wason, P. C. A theoretical analysis of insight into a reasoning task. *Cognitive Psychology,* 1970, **1,** 134–138.

Kaufman, H., & Goldstein, S. The effects of emotional value of conclusions upon distortions in syllogistic reasoning. *Psychonomic Science,* 1967, **7,** 367–368.

Kintsch, W. Notes on the structure of semantic memory. In E. Tulving & W. Donaldson (Eds.), *Organization and memory.* New York: Academic Press, 1972.

Klahr, D., & Wallace, J. G. An information processing analysis of some Piagetian experimental tasks. *Cognitive Psychology,* 1970, **1,** 358–387.

Lakoff, G. Linguistics and natural logic. *Synthese,* 1970, **22,** 151–271.

Lefford, A. The influence of emotional subject matter on logical reasoning. *Journal of General Psychology,* 1946, **34,** 127–151.
Lippman, M. Z. The influence of grammatical transform in a syllogistic reasoning task. *Journal of Verbal Learning & Verbal Behavior,* 1972, **11,** 424–430.
Lukasiewicz, J. *Aristotle's syllogistic.* London and New York: Oxford University Press, 1951.
Moore, W., & Revlis, R. Feature-matching in syllogistic reasoning. In preparation.
Morgan, J. J., & Morton, J. T. The distortion of syllogistic reasoning produced by personal convictions. *Journal of Social Psychology,* 1944, **20,** 39–59.
Newell, A., & Simon, H. A. *Human problem solving.* Englewoods Cliffs, New Jersey: Prentice-Hall, 1972.
Parrott, G. L. The effects of premise content on accuracy and solution time in syllogistic reasoning. Unpublished Masters thesis. Michigan State University, 1967.
Parrott, G. L. The effects of instructions, transfer, and content on reasoning time. Unpublished Doctoral dissertation. Michigan State University, 1969.
Parrott, G. L., & Johnson, D. M. Effect of premise content on accuracy and solution time in syllogistic reasoning. Paper presented at the Midwestern Psychological Association, 1968.
Peirce, C. S. The syllogism. In J. M. Baldwin (Ed.), *Dictionary of philosophy and psychology,* Vol. 2. Gloucester: Peter Smith, 1957.
Pezzoli, J. A. Syllogistic inference: A problem-solving task. Unpublished Doctoral dissertation. University of Massachusetts, 1970.
Pezzoli, J. A., & Frase, L. T. Mediated facilitation of syllogistic reasoning. *Journal of Experimental Psychology,* 1968, **78,** 228–232.
Rescher, N. *Galen and the syllogism.* Pittsburgh: University of Pittsburgh Press, 1966.
Rescher, N. *Essays in philosophical analysis.* Pittsburgh: University of Pittsburgh Press, 1969.
Revlis, R. Prevarication: Reasoning from false assumptions. *Memory & Cognition,* 1974, **2,** 87–95.
Revlis, R., & Hayes, J. R. The primacy of generalities in hypothetical reasoning. *Cognitive Psychology,* 1972, **3,** 268–290.
Revlis, R., Lipkin, S. G., & Hayes, J. R. The importance of universal quantifiers in a hypothetical reasoning task. *Journal of Verbal Learning & Verbal Behavior,* 1971, **10,** 86–91.
Revlis, R., & Moore, W. A conversion model of syllogistic reasoning. In preparation.
Richter, M. The theoretical interpretation of errors in syllogistic reasoning. *Journal of Psychology,* 1957, **43,** 341–344.
Roberge, J. J. A reexamination of the interpretations of errors in formal syllogistic reasoning. *Psychonomic Science,* 1970, **19,** 331–333.
Savin, H., & Perchonock, E. Grammatical structure and the immediate recall of English sentences. *Journal of Verbal Learning & Verbal Behavior,* 1965, **4,** 348–353.
Sells, S. B. The atmosphere effect: An experimental study of reasoning. *Archives of Psychology,* 1936, **29,** 3–72.
Sells, S. B., & Koob, H. F. A classroom demonstration of "atmosphere effect" in reasoning. *Journal of Educational Psychology,* 1937, **28,** 514–518.
Simon, H. A., & Feigenbaum, E. A. An information processing theory of some effects of similarity, familiarization, and meaningfulness in verbal learning. *Journal of Verbal Learning & Verbal Behavior,* 1964, **3,** 385–396.

Tannenbaum, P., & Williams, F. Generation of active and passive sentences as a function of subject or object of focus. *Journal of Verbal Learning & Verbal Behavior,* 1968, **7,** 246–250.

Taplin, J. E. Reasoning with conditional sentences. *Journal of Verbal Learning & Verbal Behavior,* 1971, **10,** 218–225.

Taplin, J. E., & Staudenmayer, H. Interpretation of abstract conditional sentences in deductive reasoning. *Journal of Verbal Learning & Verbal Behavior,* 1973, **12,** 530–542.

Taplin, J. E., Staudenmayer, H., & Taddonio, J. A. Developmental changes in conditional reasoning: Linguistic or logical? *Journal of Experimental Child Psychology,* 1974, **17,** 360–373.

Thouless, R. Effect of prejudice on reasoning. *British Journal of Psychology,* 1959, **50,** 289–293.

Trabasso, T., Rollins, H., & Shaughnessy, E. Storage and verification stages in processing concepts. *Cognitve Psychology,* 1971, **2,** 239–289.

Wason, P. C. Reasoning about a rule. *Quarterly Journal of Experimental Psychology,* 1968, **20,** 273–281.

Wason, P. C., & Johnson-Laird, P. N. Proving a disjunctive rule. *Quarterly Journal of Experimental Psychology,* 1969, **21,** 14–20.

Wason, P. C., & Johnson-Laird, P. N. *Psychology of reasoning: Structure and content.* London: Batsford, 1972.

Wason, P. C., & Shapiro, D. Natural and contrived experience in a reasoning problem. *Quarterly Journal of Experimental Psychology,* 1971, **23,** 63–71.

Whimbey, A., & Ryan, S. Role of short-term memory and training in solving reasoning problems mentally. *Journal of Educational Psychology,* 1969, **60,** 361–364.

Wilkins, M. C. The effect of changed material on ability to do formal syllogistic reasoning. *Archives of Psychology,* 1928, **102,** 83 pp.

Wilson, W. R. The effect of competition on the speed and accuracy of syllogistic reasoning. *Journal of Social Psychology,* 1965, **65,** 27–32.

Winthrop, H. Semantic factors in the measurement of personality integration. *Journal of Social Psychology,* 1946, **24,** 149–175.

Woodworth, R. S., & Sells, S. B. An atmosphere effect in formal syllogistic reasoning. *Journal of Experimental Psychology,* 1935, **18,** 451–460.

5

DEVELOPMENT OF THE COMPREHENSION OF LOGICAL QUANTIFIERS

Edith D. Neimark
Robin H. Chapman
Douglass College, Rutgers, The State University

There has been an increase in the use of formal logical models for the psychological study of logical reasoning and its development. The motivation for a number of studies has been to either prove or disprove Piaget's contentions that the ability to reason logically with formal propositions is attained during the stage of formal operations, which develops during adolescence. However, crucial tests of this assumption are not so readily attained, and there are reasons to question whether they are even worth seeking at this stage of our understanding of the development of thought. Certainly there is no trick to devising situations so simple that even preoperational children can turn in a creditable performance, or tasks so difficult that even college-educated adults fail miserably on them. A number of instances of both extremes are already available (e.g., Hill, 1960, for the former and Wason & Johnson-Laird, 1972, for the latter). In interpreting such dramatic findings one is confronted with the thorny problem of separating underlying competence from observed performance (Flavell & Wohlwill, 1969). Flavell and Wohlwill maintain that valid inference of competence necessitates the demonstration that a subject performs consistently on various tasks differing in form and content. Such a demonstration requires the use of several versions of a given task along with analysis for individual consistency in responding to them. Unfortunately, most studies do not provide relevant data to meet this requirement, although there are some praiseworthy exceptions e.g., (Taplin & Staudenmayer, 1973; Taplin, Staudenmayer, & Taddonio, 1974).

Given that the experimental design satisfies the requirement of demonstrating consistency, assessment of a subject's logical competence requires, in addition, that the task be designed to enable identification of specific sources of error. For example, in reasoning from given premises a subject may reach an erroneous conclusion for a number of reasons: (*a*) he has not mastered the logical operations required (i.e., lacks the competence in question); (*b*) he lacks accessory skills for storing and processing the relevant information (as this problem is irrelevant to questions of competence, it is best dealt with by eliminating demands on memory, through providing mnemonic aids, etc.); (*c*) his interpretation of a key term, or terms, does not coincide with the logician's interpretation of them; or (*d*) some combinations of these possible causal factors obtain. The third possibility is more properly a question of semantics rather than operational competence and is best answered by direct assessment of the subject's understanding of the term. Logical connectives (e.g., "and," "or," "if–then") comprise one class of crucial terms concerning which there is a good deal of developmental evidence showing differential difficulty (Nitta & Nagano, 1966; Peel, 1967; Neimark & Slotnick, 1970; Neimark, 1970; Paris, 1973; Suppes & Feldman, 1971; Youniss & Furth, 1964, 1967; Furth, Youniss, & Ross, 1970; Hatano, 1973). Another obvious class of key logical terms is the class of logical quantifiers, which has received little experimental scrutiny. Existing evidence employs only adult subjects (Johnson-Laird, 1970) and a context of syllogistic reasoning (Ceraso & Provitera, 1971). The study presented in this chapter attempts to provide detailed developmental evidence concerning the comprehension of the quantifiers "all" and "some" as embodied in the four proposition forms of classical logic taken singly as well as in all possible combinations of proposition pairs.

THE EXPERIMENTAL TASK

A mimeographed test consisting of 24 numbered statements describing set relations in classical propositional form was employed. There were six numbered response alternatives available, the first five of which corresponded to pictured relations among sets A and B in Venn diagram form (see Fig. 1): (1) A and B are identical, (2) A is a subset of B; (3) B is a subset of A; (4) A and B are partially overlapping sets; and (5) A and B are mutually exclusive sets. The sixth alternative was the statement "incompatible" which was explained in the instructions as meaning "impossible," i.e., the described relation cannot exist. The subject was instructed to read each statement carefully and to circle the number corresponding to

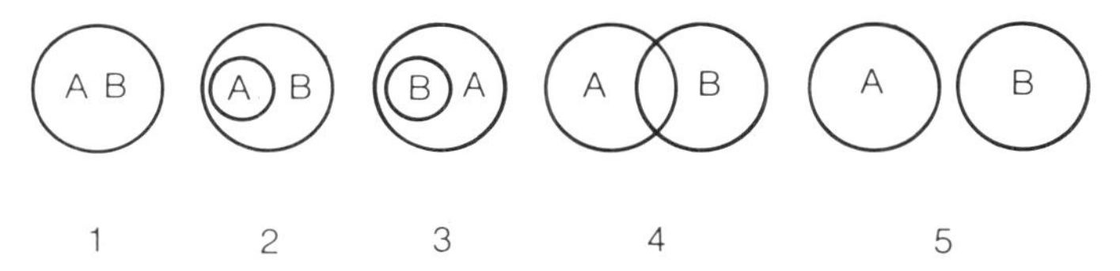

FIG. 1. The five Venn Diagram alternatives picturing possible relations among sets A and B.

each of the alternatives described by that statement. It was emphasized that more than one alternative might be appropriate and that a correct answer required circling of all the appropriate alternatives.

The first eight statements included two possible orders of the four basic propositional forms: *A, all* A *are* B (or *all* B *are* A); *E, no* A *are* B; *I, some* A *are* B; *O, Some* A *are not* B. These items provide evidence concerning interpretation of the quantifiers "all" and "some" and their negation, "no" and "some are not" along with evidence (on a group rather than an individual basis) as to the consistency of interpretation. The remaining 16 statements were compounds of the four basic propositions: Statements 9–12 were homogeneous compounds, e.g., *A·A, all* A *are* B *and all* B *are* A, whereas Statements 13–24 were heterogeneous compounds (two versions of each of the six possible compounds), e.g., *I·O, some* B *are* A *and some* A *are not* B. Analysis of an individual's error in the compounds in relation to his response to each simple component provides evidence as to whether the error is a logical consequent of interpretation of its components or whether there is, in addition, difficulty in dealing with their intersection. The 24 statements and the responses prescribed by logical convention are given in the appendix at the end of the chapter.

The test was group administered, by the first author, to mathematics classes at the middle and high schools of Highland Park, New Jersey, and to college students enrolled in a class in thinking at Douglass College during a regular class period. In the winter of 1971, 123 public school students were tested: 20, 23, 20, 21, 23, and 16 in Grades 7–12, respectively, and 13 college girls. The following year the experiment was replicated with 42 eighth graders, 27 tenth graders, 29 twelfth graders, and 28 college students.

Because none of several comparisons for sex differences have revealed any, sex differences are not discussed further here. Differences between replicates also were not statistically significant. In the discussion of results that follows, all analyses have been performed for each replicate separately; reported differences obtain in both replications.

INTERPRETATION OF QUANTIFIERS IN SIMPLE PROPOSITIONS

Comparison of group frequencies for each pair of propositions reveals such close consistency as to warrant pooling of items for all analyses. Group mean percent of responses corresponding to logical convention (as shown in the Appendix) for each of the four simple propositions is shown as a function of grade level in Fig. 2. Improvement with age is statistically significant (as demonstrated by a χ^2 test of independence with six degrees of freedom for each of the eight propositions). The most striking effect, however, is the marked difference[1] in conformity to logical convention shown for universal propositions, *A* and *E,* as contrasted with particular propositions, *I* and *O*. If comprehension is inferred on a group basis with respect to an arbitrary criterion of 50% or more of the group, then it is clear that even the youngest group interprets universal propositions in accord with logical convention, whereas particular propositions are not so interpreted even by college students. Moreover, the negative form of the universal, "no," is significantly more likely to be interpreted according to logical convention than its positive counterpart, "all," whereas for particular propositions there is no significant difference between positive, "some," and negative, "some are not," forms. Finally, it should be noted that the observed pattern of differential difficulty is independent of age within the age ranges employed (i.e., none of the interactions with age is statistically significant).

Analysis of Errors

Although errors in interpretation of universal propositions are very infrequent, there is a consistency to the errors which do occur. With respect to "no," in the case of a few of the younger children, Alternative 6 is chosen; they are, in effect, correct in spirit. Most of the other errors consist in circling the nonoverlapping sets (Alternative 5) plus one other alternative in which one set—usually the second named—is a subset of the other set. In the interpretation of "all," for which logical convention requires circling two alternatives (set identity and the first set a subset of the second), the only error of older subjects (Grade 12 and college) is circling one or the other of these alternatives but not both. This error occurs among younger children along with two other errors, both of which are suggestive of memory failure for the original statement: (*a*) they circle the alternatives that are correct for the reversed form of the proposition: i.e., treat

[1] All differences that are discussed as meaningful, unless otherwise noted, are statistically significant at or beyond the .05 level of significance; the reader is spared detailed reporting of the *F, t,* or χ^2 in question.

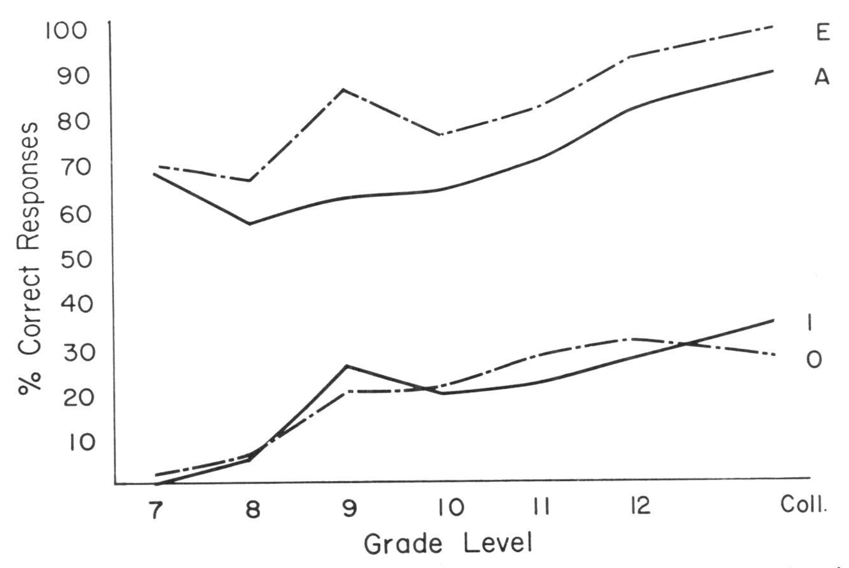

FIG. 2. Group mean percent correct responses on simple propositions as a function of grade level.

All A *are* B as *All* B *are* A; or (*b*) they circle both alternatives in which one set is a subset of the other in addition to the set-equivalence alternative.

With respect to the particular propositions, most subjects appear to interpret the quantifier "some" more narrowly than logicians do—the younger the subject the narrower the interpretation. Although the younger groups show a greater variety of responses, it is generally the case that a few specific responses account for the majority of all "errors." The most frequent responses for all groups are plotted in terms of percent of total errors, as a function of grade, in Fig. 3 for each order of the *I* proposition, *Some* A *are* B and *Some* B *are* A, and for each version of the *O* proposition, *Some* A *are not* B and *Some* B *are not* A.

The most common response of seventh graders to both *I* and *O* propositions is to select Alternative 4, partial overlap, exclusively. In other words, *Some* A *are* B cannot mean that *All* A *are* B either by set equivalence or by A being a subset of B. Instead, the statement is interpreted as, in effect, the intersect of two compounds: *Some* A *are* B *and some are not* and *Some* B *are* A *and some are not* or as *Some but not all* A *are* B and *Some but not all* B *are* A. This very narrow interpretation declines with age and accounts for a negligible proportion of all errors among the older subjects. At all

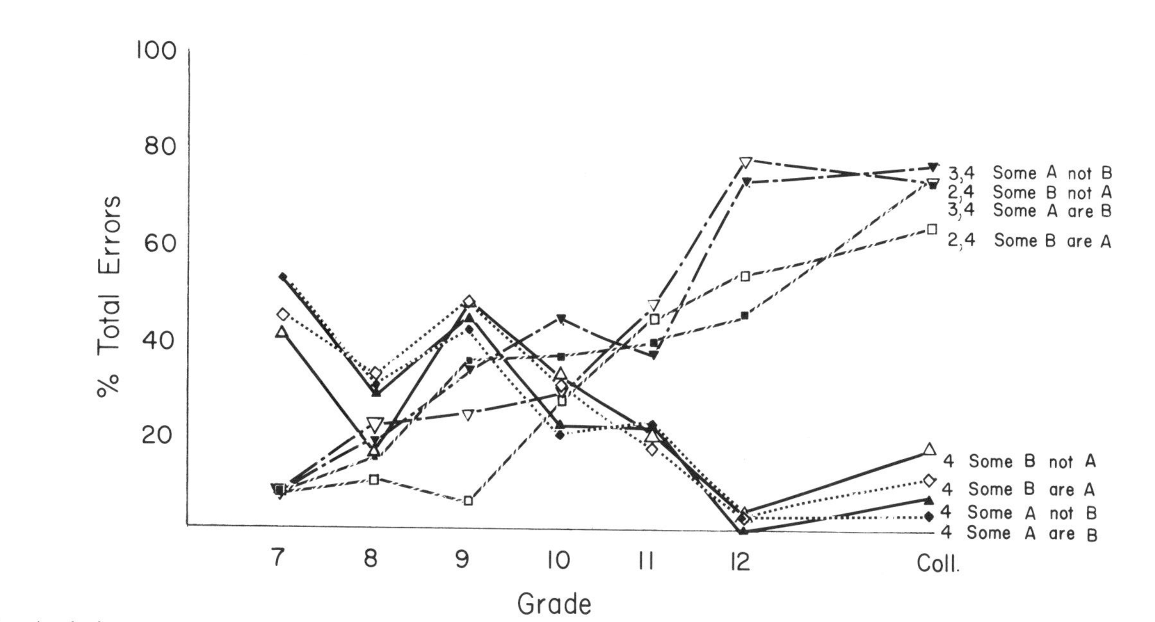

FIG. 3. Analysis of responses on *I* and *O* propositions, in terms of percent of total error, as a function of grade level. The numbers in the legend refer to response alternatives in Fig. 1. (▼) 3,4, *Some* A *are not* B; (▽) 2,4, *Some* B *are not* A; (■) 3,4, *Some* A *are* B; (□) 2,4, *Some* B *are* A; (△) 4, *Some* B *are not* A; (◇) 4, *Some* B *are* A; (▲) 4, *Some* A *are not* B; (◆) 4, *Some* A *are* B.

ages error frequencies are directly comparable for the two forms of each particular proposition.

As exclusive choice of Alternative 4 declines, choice of Alternative 4 plus a second alternative showing one set as a subset of the other increases: e.g., choice of Alternatives 3 and 4 for *Some* A *are* B or of Alternatives 2 and 4 for *Some* B *are* A. Among the younger children there is some evidence of the same apparent reading or memory confusion that was noted earlier for interpretation of "all": e.g., although choice of Alternatives 3 and 4 is the most common response to *Some* A *are* B from the eleventh grade on and choice of Alternatives 2 and 4 is the most common response to *Some* B *are* A from the tenth grade on, there is a suggestion of interchange of responses to these two statements at earlier ages.

The first alternative, equivalence of A and B, is infrequently included in interpretation of *some*—nor is it ever selected exclusively—whereas Alternative 5, A and B mutually exclusive, is more commonly selected—frequently as the exclusive alternative—in interpretation of "some are not." In other words, although *no* is included in interpreting *some are not, all* is almost never included in interpreting *some are,* despite the fact that both inclusions are in accord with logical convention. In fact, in posttest discussions with a class it was common for children to argue vehemently that "some" cannot ever mean "all" (implying that if one intended "all" he should say so). This assymetry in the interpretation of *I* and *O* propositions is certainly in the spirit of restricted interpretation at younger ages.

Discussion

The evidence is remarkably clear: (*a*) universal propositions, embodying the quantifiers "all" and "no," are interpreted in accord with logical convention, whereas particular propositions, embodying the quantifier "some," are not; (*b*) the negative universal is "easier" than the positive, whereas for particular propositions there is no difference; (*c*) freqency of conventional interpretation increases with age for all propositions, with no Age × Proposition Form interaction; and (*d*) *some* is interpreted too narrowly, at first exclusively as partial overlap of two sets, later with broadening to include one set as a proper subset of the other; set equivalence is the last possibility to be included. These findings can be accounted for in terms of a number of factors that are not totally independent, either in theory or in empirical indices.

Response bias is quite likely a relevant factor, although it cannot be the only one operating. That is, if it is assumed that the subject has a preference for selecting a single alternative in response to each item, then a higher probability can be expected of (*a*) being "correct" on those items, such as *E* propositions, for which logical convention dictates a single alternative and (*b*) being incorrect on those items, such as particular propositions, for which it does not. Although of 262 subjects in the present study only two (one girl in Grade 9 and one in Grade 10) do, in fact, confine themselves to a single alternative for all 24 items, there is a good deal of evidence in this and other studies suggesting an inverse correlation between probability of correct response and number of alternatives required. For example, Nitta and Nagano (1966), using pictures of flags as set elements, required subjects to circle the applicable elements in one instruction condition or to cross out the inappropriate alternatives in another. Performance for statements involving the connective "or" improved under the second condition, which requires crossing out fewer alternatives than must be circled in the first. Even this evidence is ambiguous, however, for it involves interchange of "and" (which is correctly interpreted at all ages) and "or" (which is attained during late adolescence; Neimark, 1970). A comparable test for the present material would be to have subjects cross out alternatives that do not apply instead of circling those that do. Although this condition has not been run, we doubt very much that it would lead to a reversal of results with *E* propositions (which would require all but one alternative to be crossed out) leading to more "errors" than *I* propositions (which would require only two alternatives to be crossed out). Furthermore, an explanation solely in terms of response bias would not account for details of performance on compound statements (to be discussed in the next section).

The most convincing argument against a response bias explanation, however, is that it begs a more interesting question: why should response bias, if it operates, decline systematically with age? Studies of conditional reasoning (Taplin *et al.,* 1974) and of interpretation of logical connectives (Neimark, 1970) show a consistent broadening with age of response-class inclusion. Furthermore, there is fairly good correspondence across studies with respect to the age at which transitions to fully inclusive interpretations (i.e., in accord with accepted convention) are attained by most subjects. That magic age is the period of late adolescence, at 15–17 years, which corresponds to the age for equilibration of formal operations. We believe that this independent evidence of consistent age trends is not a coincidence—nor even a consequence of age-related improvement of memory span and information processing skills (a factor that has been shown to contribute to poor performance of younger children in the present study) but is, instead, an indication of the pervasive general change in the way in which experienced instances are dealt with cognitively. The concrete operational child thinks in terms of specific instances and their context, whereas the formal operational thinker deals with propositions instead of with the instances from which they derive. Moreover, another defining aspect of formal operations is that the thinker has a complete combinatorial system for generating all possible combinations of propositions; he starts from the realm of all possible combinations rather than from specific encountered instances. According to Piaget (Inhelder & Piaget, 1958) this fundamental restructing of thought begins in early adolescence and reaches stability, if ever, around college age.

INTERPRETATION OF COMPOUND PROPOSITIONS

Homogeneous Compounds

In principle, response to compound propositions requires only intersecting of simple components. Since the operation of intersection, that is, dealing with the connective "and," should be within the ability of all subjects in the age range employed in the present study, it should pose no additional difficulties beyond the additional demands on memory and/or some hypothetical processing space. In other words, performance on compound propositions should be predictable from performance on their simple components. Moreover, to the extent that dealing simultaneously with two propositions to attain a conclusion is a prerequisite for reasoning, then the results for this part of the task should shed some light on possible sources of error in syllogistic reasoning that do not derive from defects of reasoning operations per se.

There are four possible homogeneous compounds: $A \cdot A$, $E \cdot E$, $I \cdot I$, $O \cdot O$ (e.g., *All* A *are* B *and all* B *are* A), which comprise items 9–12. For the $I \cdot I$ and $E \cdot E$ compounds the response required by logical convention is identical with the response required for the individual component; for the other two compounds the number of required alternatives is reduced (which, according to a literal response bias explanation, should lead to improved performance). Group mean percent of responses in accord with logical convention for the four homogeneous compounds are plotted as a function of grade level in Figure 4; its general similarity with Figure 2 is readily apparent. Analysis of "correct" responses to compounds reveals: (*a*) universal compounds are more frequently "correct" than particular compounds; (*b*) negative compounds are easier than positive; but (*c*) the greater accuracy on negative form holds only for the universal compound, $E \cdot E$; (*d*) there is differential improvement with age, i.e., there is significant improvement with age for all compounds except $I \cdot I$.

With the exception of the absence of an age effect for the $I \cdot I$ compound, these findings exactly parallel the findings for responses to the simple component propositions. Direct comparison of response to homogeneous compound with response to simple components by means of analysis of

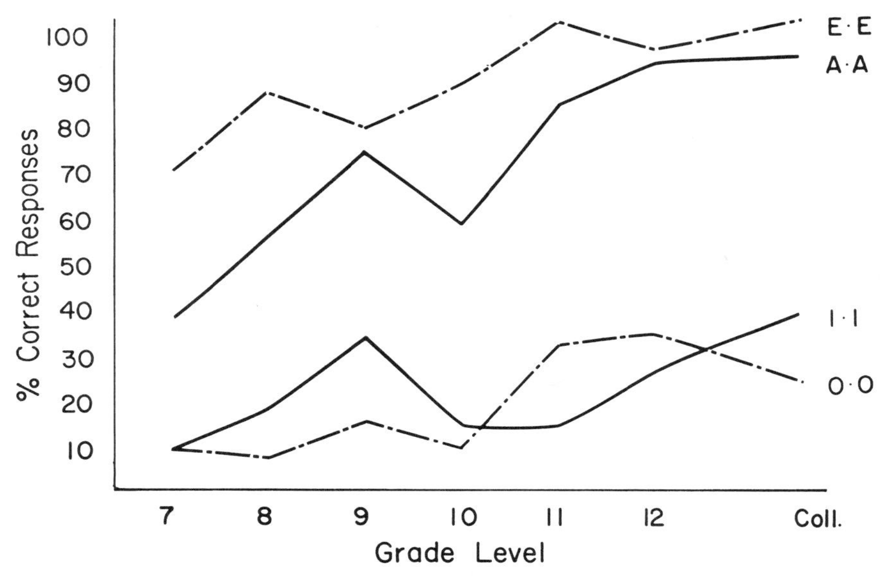

FIG. 4. Group mean percent correct responses on homogeneous compounds as a function of grade level.

variance fails to yield any significant difference between compound and component either as a main effect or in interaction with other variables. A homogeneous compound statement is thus shown to be no more difficult than response to its simple components; the additional mental operation of intersection poses no additional difficulties.

Analysis of errors on homogeneous compounds yields about what is expected from analysis of simple components. The major surprise is in response to $A \cdot A$ by the youngest groups, in which the most frequent error is choice of Alternatives 1, 2, and 3. This suggests that subjects form a union rather than an intersect of the two components. This error in interpretation of the connective has been reported elsewhere (Neimark & Slotnick, 1970; Hatano, 1973). For both particular premise compounds, $I \cdot I$ and $O \cdot O$, the most common response at all ages is exclusive choice of Alternative 4, partial overlap of sets A and B. Given the pattern of response to components (Figure 3) this reflects a correct intersection of narrowly interpreted components and is precisely what is expected.

Heterogeneous Compounds

Group mean percent of responses in accord with logical convention for each of the heterogeneous compounds is summarized as a function of grade level in Figure 5. Once again, because there is consistency in the two orders

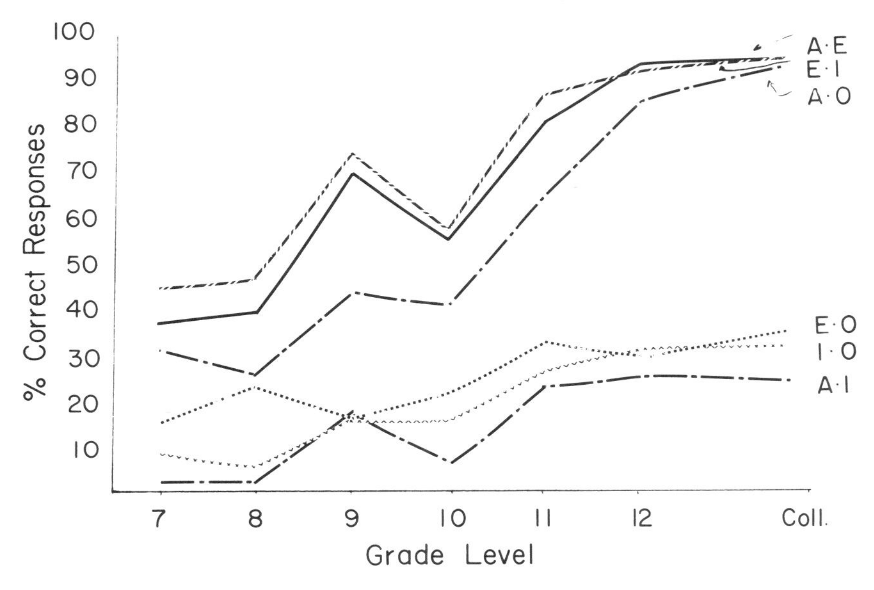

FIG. 5. Group mean percent of correct responses on heterogeneous compounds as a function of grade level.

of each compound, orders have been pooled. Heterogeneous compounds fall into two clear categories: compounds of $A \cdot E$, $E \cdot I$, and $A \cdot O$, to which the majority of older subjects respond in accord with convention, and compounds of $E \cdot O$, $I \cdot O$, and $A \cdot I$, to which a small minority of subjects respond in accord with convention at all ages. Differences between the two categories are statistically significant. Moreover, increase in conventional responding with age is statistically significant for all compounds save $E \cdot O$.

Analysis of the nature of the "errors," once again, suggests that they are lawfully determined. Although errors for the three easier compounds are very infrequent among older subjects, the response patterns for younger subjects are quite similar to them. For $E \cdot I$ and $A \cdot E$ compounds (which are logically incompatible and require the statement "incompatible," Alternative 6, as a response) the most common "error" is to chose the alternative in which one set is a proper subset of the other. This "error" suggests that the subject is responding with respect to one component, the I or A proposition, of the compound. In the case of the $A \cdot E$ compound, a few of the youngest groups appear to be forming (correctly) the union rather than the intersect of the two universal components. However, for the $A \cdot O$ compound, where the "correct" choice is one set as a proper subset of the other (i.e., Alternatives 2 or 3, depending on the order of component propositions) the most common response is to call the statement incompatible (Alternative 6). Although this may seem inconsistent in relation to response to the other two "easy" compounds, it is probably a logical consequence of the popular restricted interpretation of *O* propositions. When *some are not* is exclusively interpreted in terms of partially overlapping sets, there is no intersect with *all* (which includes set identity and one set as a proper subset of the other—the latter being the one common alternative). Here too, a few of the younger subjects appeared to be responding in terms of one component or the other, or with union rather than intersect (for this particular compound it is impossible to differentiate the two possible sources of error).

Table 1 summarizes the proportion of all errors accounted for by the single most common response (expressed in terms of the number of the response alternative) for each of the three "difficult" compounds. It is clear that response consistency increases with age, although there is fair consistency even among the younger children. For compounds of $A \cdot I$ and $I \cdot A$ the second most frequent response was choice of Alternative 6, "incompatible," which shows no systematic change with age but accounts for between 12 and 34% of responses at all grades except college. Once again, this response most likely results from a restricted interpretation of I propositions, in which case it is the logically correct response. Similarly, the response to $E \cdot O$ compounds parallels the response to $A \cdot O$ (and $A \cdot I$) compounds in being attributable to a restricted interpretation of the particular

TABLE 1
Probability of the Most Frequent Error for Three Difficult Heterogeneous Compounds as a Function of Grade Level along with Number of Subjects and Total Number of Errors for the Items

		Grade level						
Compound	Response	7	8	9	10	11	12	College
A·I, I·A	*p* (3)	.23	.24	.25	.43	.55	.75	.84
	Total all errors	49	127	36	89	40	67	63
E·O, O·E	*p* (6)	.45	.54	.68	.69	.87	.90	.90
	Total all errors	42	101	37	76	31	64	54
O·I, I·O	*p* (4)	.48	.28	.57	.56	.60	.76	.84
	Total all errors	46	123	37	80	34	62	56
	Number of subjects	25	65	22	48	23	45	41

premise component. However, the much greater difficulty of $E \cdot O$ compounds relative to $A \cdot O$ compounds at first glance appears surprising. Presumably, the greater relative difficulty is to be explained not in terms of the double negative but in terms of the fact that for $A \cdot O$ a restricted interpretation of an O proposition still includes one alternative (one set a proper subset of the other) in common with an A proposition and that alternative is the response prescribed by logical convention. For the $E \cdot O$ compound, in contrast, a restricted interpretation of the O proposition generally excludes the one alternative in common with E (mutually exclusive sets). This same principle also accounts for both of the common incorrect responses to $A \cdot I$ compounds, where Alternative 6 would be logically correct for the most restricted interpretation of an I proposition, whereas Alternative 3 would be the correct response for a less restricted interpretation. Moreover, the frequency of choice of Alternative 3 should increase with age concomitant with increase in a less restricitve interpretation of "some." This is exactly what does happen.

Finally, the response to a compound of two particular propositions is an obvious result of intersecting the most restricted interpretation of each of the components. It will be recalled (see Figure 3) that both O and I propositions are frequently interpreted solely as the partial overlap of two sets (Alternative 4); if either, or both, component is so interpreted, then their intersect is clearly that same alternative. In fact, as noted above, the most restrictive interpretation of O or I propositions is indistinguishable from the conventional response to an intersect of two compounds, $O \cdot I$ and $I \cdot O$.

Error Analysis for Individual Subjects

The foregoing analysis of "errors" on compound propositions has attempted to show through an analysis of group data that the response to proposition compounds is directly predictable on the basis of response to component propositions; i.e., that seeming errors are in fact logical consequences of the subject's interpretation of logical quantifiers. They are not errors of logic but tributes to logical reasoning from language conventions not in accord with the conventions of formal logic. A more compelling case for this conclusion derives from an analysis of the response of individual subjects to compound propositions in relation to their response to simple components. The results of this analysis are summarized in Table 2.

For this analysis, an interpretive error was defined as a response to a compound proposition which was not in accord with logical convention but was a correct intersect of the individual's response to each of the component propositions. Then, for each individual, the number of interpretive errors was divided by total number of "errors" to compounds to get a

TABLE 2
Group Mean and Standard Deviation for Percent of Interpretive Errors at Each Grade Level

Grade level	N	Mean	Standard deviation
College	36	62.9	39.3
Twelve	40	59.1	37.2
Eleven	22	52.8	34.1
Ten	49	45.1	34.6
Nine	22	39.6	34.0
Eight	60	32.1	27.7
Seven	22	37.4	29.1

percent of interpretive errors. The residual error percent for each subject contains all other errors from a variety of sources (e.g., giving union in place of intersect, responding to only one component, etc.), which were not broken down into finer detail.

The resulting measure is not a very sensitive one since, obviously, the sensitivity of the measure depends on the error total in the denominator; with only one error, the percent of interpretive errors can only equal zero or 100%. This factor undoubtedly results in a spurious inflation of variability, especially among older groups. Although the percent of interpretive errors appears to increase systematically with increasing age, age effects are not statistically significant, even with a covariance control for total number of errors. Nevertheless, it is clear that a sizable proportion of responses to compounds are directly predictable from response to individual components, especially among the older groups who are less prone to errors of intersection. The analysis of individual performance therefore supports the conclusions of the preceding analysis of group data.

Syllogistic Reasoning

Ceraso and Provitera (1971) presented two groups of college students with 13 premise pairs, for each of which the subject was to choose the best conclusion from among four possible alternatives: an *A, E,* or *O* proposition or "can't say." One group worked with traditional sentence-type syllogisms, whereas the second group received Venn diagram (see Figure 1) depictions of one possible form of the relation between two sets (i.e., only a specific one of the possible interpretations of the quantifiers *all, some,* or *no*). Subjects given the modified syllogisms with Venn diagrams made many fewer erroneous conclusions than did subjects given the traditional syllogisms. Moreover, subjects given the traditional syllogisms tended to respond as though they had received the modified counterpart. On the basis of these findings, Ceraso and Provitera concluded that one major source of error in syllogistic reasoning was the subject's tendency to misinterpret syllogistic premises in order to refer to simpler class relations.

The present study provides direct support of their conclusion by showing that (*a*) subjects interpret quantifiers not in accord with logical convention but in a more restricted fashion and (*b*) that errors which arise in combining propositions (in the absence of a middle term) are largely predictable from responses to the propositions individually. Ceraso and Provitera identified a second source of error in syllogistic reasoning that they identified with the logical structure of the syllogism: the more alternatives generated by a set of premises, the more difficult the syllogism. This conclusion is also supported by the findings of the present study—and of a number of other studies, as well—that the more alternatives required for a "correct" response, the lower the probability of that response.

SUMMARY AND CONCLUSIONS

It has been suggested that errors of reasoning may be the result of at least two independent factors: one associated with deficiencies in the operations themselves and a second, more properly linguistic, factor associated with the individual's interpretation of such key terms as connectives and quantifiers. Interpretation of logical quantifiers "all" and "some" has been investigated by presenting groups of subjects in Grades 7 through college with two orders of each of the four basic propositions of classical logic, along with all possible combinations of pairs of the four propositions, and requiring that all set relations, corresponding to Venn diagram illustrations, described by each statement be identified. Interpretation of "all" and "no" are generally in accord with logical convention at all ages studied, whereas "some" and "some are not" are interpreted in a more restricted fashion. The degree to which interpretation of quantifiers corresponds with logical convention increases systematically over the age range studied. Moreover, the nature of response to compound propositions is largely predictable from response to the individual components. It is suggested that the same Piagetian principles which describe the development of operational factors also govern the development of linguistic factors as reflected in the interpretation of logical quantifiers: that use of a term in its conventional general sense is associated with the development of formal operational thought.

APPENDIX

The 24 Statements and Alternatives to be Circled for Each (see Figure 1)

	Statement	Alternative to circle					
1.	*All* A *are* B	1	2				
2.	*Some* B *are* A	1	2	3	4		
3.	*No* A *are* B					5	
4.	*Some* B *are not* A		2		4	5	
5.	*Some* A *are* B	1	2	3	4		
6.	*All* B *are* A	1		3			
7.	*Some* A *are not* B			3	4	5	
8.	*No* B *are* A					5	
9.	*Some* A *are not* B *and some* B *are not* A				4	5	
10.	*No* A *are* B *and no* B *are* A					5	
11.	*Some* A *are* B *and some* B *are* A	1	2	3	4		
12.	*All* A *are* B *and all* B *are* A	1					
13.	*All* B *are* A *and some* A *are* B	1		3			
14.	*Some* A *are* B *and all* B *are* A	1		3			
15.	*Some* A *are not* B *and all* B *are* A			3			
16.	*All* A *are* B *and some* B *are not* A		2				
17.	*No* A *are* B *and some* B *are not* A					5	
18.	*Some* A *are not* B *and some* B *are* A			3	4		
19.	*All* A *are* B *and no* B *are* A						6
20.	*No* A *are* B *and all* B *are* A						6
21.	*No* A *are* B *and some* B *are* A						6
22.	*Some* A *are* B *and no* B *are* A						6
23.	*Some* A *are* B *and some* B *are not* A		2		4		
24.	*Some* A *are not* B *and no* B *are* A					5	

ACKNOWLEDGMENTS

This research was supported under Grant No. HD 01725 from NICHHD. We are grateful to John Sprout and the teachers of Highland Park High School and to Dr. Edward Leppert and the teachers of Highland Park Middle School for their cooperation in the collection of the data.

REFERENCES

Ceraso, J., & Provitera, A. Sources of error in syllogistic reasoning. *Cognitive Psychology,* 1971, **2,** 400–410.

Flavell, J. H., & Wohlwill, J. F. Formal and functional aspects of cognitive development. In D. Elkind & J. H. Flavell (Eds.), *Studies in cognitive development.* London and New York: Oxford University Press, 1969.

Furth, H. G., Youniss, J., & Ross, B. M. Children's utilization of logical symbols. *Developmental Psychology,* 1970, **3,** 36–57.

Hatano, G. Understanding and use of logical connectives. Paper presented at a meeting of the Society for Research in Child Development, Philadelphia, 1973.

Hill, S. A study of logical abilities of children. Unpublished doctoral dissertation, Stanford University, 1960.

Inhelder, B., & Piaget, J. *The growth of logical thinking from childhood to adolescence.* New York: Basic Books, 1958.

Johnson-Laird, P. N. The interpretation of quantified sentences. In G. B. Flores d'Arcais & W. J. M. Levelt (Eds.), *Advances in psycholinguistics.* Amsterdam: North-Holland Publ., 1970.

Neimark, E. D. Development of comprehension of logical connectives: Understanding of "or." *Psychonomic Science,* 1970, **21,** 217–219.

Neimark, E. D., & Slotnick, N. S. Development of the understanding of logical connectives. *Journal of Educational Psychology,* 1970, **61,** 451–460.

Nitta, N., & Nagano, S. Basic logical operations and their verbal expressions. *Research Bulletin of the National Institute for Educational Research,* 1966, No. 7.

Paris, S. G. Comprehension of language connectives and propositional logical relationships. *Journal of Experimental Child Psychology,* 1973, **16,** 278–291.

Peel, E. A. A method for investigating children's understanding of certain logical connectives used in binary propositional thinking. *British Journal of Mathematical & Statistical Psychology,* 1967, **20,** 81–92.

Suppes, P., & Feldman, S. Young children's comprehension of logical connectives. *Journal of Experimental Child Psychology,* 1971, **12,** 304–317.

Taplin, J. E., & Staudenmayer, H. Interpretation of abstract conditional sentences in deductive reasoning. *Journal of Verbal Learning & Verbal Behavior,* 1973, **12,** 530–542.

Taplin, J. E., Staudenmayer, H., & Taddonio, J. L. Developmental changes in conditional reasoning: Linguistic or logical? *Journal of Experimental Child Psychology,* 1974, **17,** 360–373.

Wason, P. C., & Johnson-Laird, P. N. *Psychology of Reasoning.* Cambridge: Harvard University Press, 1972.

Youniss, J., & Furth, H. G. Attainment and transfer of logical connectives in children. *Journal of Educational Psychology,* 1964, **55,** 357–361.

Youniss, J., & Furth, H. G. The role of language and experience on the use of logical symbols. *British Journal of Psychology,* 1967, **58,** 435–443.

6

RECALL OF CLASSICAL SYLLOGISMS: A CROSS-CULTURAL INVESTIGATION OF ERROR ON LOGICAL PROBLEMS

Sylvia Scribner
The Rockefeller University

These exploratory studies of logical reasoning among members of a West African tribal society face in two directions. As part of a long-term research program investigating the role of cultural factors in cognitive development,[1] they attempt to bring modern evidence to bear on the old controversy as to whether traditional people "think differently from us." (Is "logic" related to "culture"?) At the same time, their investigative techniques and findings are closely related to new lines of research and theorizing about logical thinking and the course of its development—work that seeks to identify the component processes involved in inferential reasoning within one culture (what is "logic"?).

To preserve both these interests—the historical, cross-cultural and the contemporary, theoretical—we will adopt the following course. We will first describe the background of the research and immediate questions motivating it, and present the principal findings and their implications. We will then discuss recent studies in the United States, using similar experimental techniques, to reexamine the cross-cultural data in relation to theoretical issues of the psychology of thinking posed by these studies.

[1]This research was supported by Office of Education Grant 0-71-1695 and Carnegie Corporation Grant 5-2917-230, both to Michael Cole and National Institute of Medical Sciences Grant GM 16735. We want to thank Dr. Akki Kulah and Messrs. Paul Ricks, Kiemu Kollie and Edward Yakpazuo for their assistance in research among the Kpelle; and Dr. Ethan Gologor and Messrs. Budu Sherman and Abraham Paasawe for help in work among the Vai. An earlier version of this paper was presented at Eastern Psychological Association, May 1973.

BACKGROUND

In the early nineteenth century, Western scholars inspired by reports of the strange beliefs and customs of colonial people began debating whether the *manner* of thinking of these people, as well as its *content,* was qualitatively different from their own.[2] In the twentieth century, after publication of the works of the French sociologist, Levy-Bruhl, this debate took the more specific form of querying whether the "logic" of primitive peoples conformed to Western logic. From his analysis of the literature, Levy-Bruhl concluded that it did not. He characterized primitive mentality as "prelogical," by which he meant that "it does not bind itself down as our thought does, to avoiding contradictions" (Levy-Bruhl, 1966, p. 63).

Similar views have been expressed within psychology. For example, the developmental psychologist Heinz Werner (1961) maintained that logical processes in members of primitive cultures differ from those of normal adults in Western societies: "It is one of the most important tasks of developmental psychology to show that the advanced form of thinking characteristic of Western civilization is only one form among many, and that more primitive forms are not so much lacking in logic as based on logic of a different kind [p. 15]."

In a more contemporary framework, the question of possible differences in logic arises with respect to the universality of Piaget's stages of logical operations. Piaget himself (1972) recently suggested that under some cultural conditions the "final stage" of formal propositional thinking may not appear.

Anthropologists have turned powerful critical arguments, buttressed by a mass of historical and observational evidence, against this view of two logics, but experimental research methods of psychology have rarely been brought to bear on this problem. The earliest investigation was conducted by the Soviet psychologist Luria and his colleagues (Luria, 1971) among peasant families in Central Asia. Their experimental material consisted of various types of classical syllogisms, a task long employed by psychologists to investigate the rules of reasoning (Woodworth & Sells, 1935). Similarly, Cole (Cole, Gay, Glick, & Sharp, 1971) employed a variety of verbal logic problems in both naturalistic and experimental settings to study inferential processes among the Kpelle in West Africa. In both investigations, adults with some minimal education solved the majority of problems correctly, whereas those lacking formal schooling (Cole *et al.,* 1971) or literacy (Luria, 1971) had no better than a chance solution rate. Explanations

[2] The terminology used in the works cited does not reflect modern usage, but for simplicity's sake the authors' original terms have been retained in the exposition of their views. The reader should supply quotation marks for the term "primitive."

traditional Kpelle farmers gave Cole for their answers were strikingly similar to those given Luria by the geographically and culturally distant Siberians. Both frequently justified their answers by appealing to fact or common knowledge:. "Because that's the way things are—I know it myself" (Luria, 1971, p. 270).

The following excerpt from an interview with a nonliterate Kpelle farmer illustrates the force of this empiric approach.

The problem has just been read by the experimenter. It is:

> All Kpelle men are rice farmers. Mr. Smith (this is a Western name) is not a rice farmer. Is he a Kpelle man?

The subject replies:

> *S:* I don't know the man in person. I have not laid eyes on the man himself.
> *E:* Just think about the statement.
> *S:* If I know him in person, I can answer that question, but since I do not know him in person I cannot answer that question.
> *E:* Try and answer from your Kpelle sense.
> *S:* If you know a person, if a question comes up about him you are able to answer. But if you do not know the person, if a question comes up about him, it's hard for you to answer it. (Scribner, this study).

This Kpelle man clearly fails to grasp the nature of the task as one involving logical implication in the sense in which Cohen and Nagle (1962) define it—inference determined solely by the structural relations between the stated propositions, independent of their factual status.

Both Luria and Cole identified this empirical bias as an important determinant of the poor problem performance of nonliterate traditional people, but they left unexplained the mechanisms by which such bias might operate to affect performance. A study by Henle (1962) suggested possible mechanisms. She gave American graduate students short written narratives that contained arguments in syllogistic form drawing conclusions about problems of everyday life. Students were required to evaluate the logical adequacy of the conclusions and to write out their judgments and the grounds for them. In her analysis of the written protocols, she identified a number of processes leading to erroneous judgments. These included omission of entire premises, modification of premises, and importation of new evidence. Henle (1962) concluded that "Where error occurs, it need not involve faulty reasoning but may be a function of the individual's understanding of the task or materials presented to him [p. 273]."

Whether or not one agrees with Henle's conclusion, the implication of her analysis is that it cannot be taken for granted that a logic task embedded in a verbal syllogism will elicit a process of inferential reasoning confined to the terms of the problem presented by the experimenter. Before drawing conclusions about the subject's reasoning processes, then, the investigator must determine what problem the subject is actually attempting to solve. This approach is rendered more specific by Evans (1972), who urges that experimental investigations of syllogistic reasoning should distinguish between two different task components: the first, the subject's encoding and interpretation of the sentences constituting the logical premises of the problem, and the second consisting of the operations the subject performs on the encoded information to reach a conclusion. Falmagne (this volume) similarly analyzes the operations involved in logical reasoning tasks in terms of stages—one or more stages in which linguistic information is encoded into a mental representation and a stage in which inferences are drawn from this representation.

This analysis of task components suggests one possible source of "error" for traditional people. Encoding and interpretative requirements of syllogisms may present special difficulty to them and, accordingly, differences in solution rates between traditional and schooled populations may reflect differences in the way these populations represent the problem rather than differences in their inferential operational processes.

To investigate this hypothesis among nonliterate people, the studies reported here used a recall procedure as an initial attempt to secure data on problem representation that could be analyzed independently of problem solution data. The notion of using problem recall as an indicator of subject's encoding and interpretation of the problem was suggested by an observation of Luria's that farmers who had difficulty in solving his problems also had difficulty in repeating them.

STUDY I

Research was conducted in central Liberia among the Kpelle with whom Cole *et al.* had conducted earlier investigations. The Kpelle are a subsistence rice-farming people who preserve many old tribal ways of life while adapting to the new (for ethnographic descriptions, see Gibbs, 1965; Cole *et al.,* 1971). The subjects were 36 nonliterate men and women farmers living in an isolated village off the road and an equal number of young adults attending a junior high school in the vicinity. To relate findings to other studies on logical reasoning, comparable problems were presented to young New York City adults whose education level ranged from completion of high school to completion of college. An effort was made to screen out students who had taken courses in formal logic but this did not insure that they were without prior instruction in rules of inference.

Experimental material was modeled after that used by Hill (1961) and consisted of three eight-problem lists, one of classical syllogisms and the other two of sentential logic problems. Twelve subjects in each population were randomly assigned to each list. The present analysis deals only with data on classical syllogisms.

The problems represented four figures of the syllogism (*AA, AE, IA, OA*) each one appearing in two content versions (Table 1). In one content version, the two premises express factually true propositions leading to a conclusion not only logically correct but also factually true. For example, the logically required conclusion on Problem 1, "Yes, the store is in town," is in accord with the social fact that stores in Kpelleland are located in towns. In the other content version, at least one premise asserts a factually false proposition (in Problem 4, for example, the premise that "All women

TABLE 1
Classical Syllogisms, Study I (Kpelle)

1.	All stores in Kpelleland are in a town. Mr. Ukatu has a store in Kpelleland. Is it in a town?
2.	All houses in Kpelleland are made of iron. My friend's house is in Kpelleland. Is it made of iron?
3.	All Kpelle men are rice farmers. Mr. Smith is not a rice farmer. Is he a Kpelle man?
4.	All women who live in this town are married. Lorpu is not married. Does she live in this town?
5.	Some people we know are not in school. All the people we know are in Liberia. Are all people in Liberia in school?
6.	Some animals we know do not have Kpelle names. All animals we know are in Kpelleland. Do all animals in Kpelleland have Kpelle names?
7.	Some kwi (Western) people are wealthy. All wealthy people are powerful. Are some kwi people powerful?
8.	Some Kpelle chiefs are children. All children are single. Are some Kpelle chiefs single?

TABLE 2
Steps in Experimental Procedure

1.	*E* reads problem.
2.	*S* answers "yes" or "no."
3.	*S* states reason for his answer.
4.	*S* repeats problem: Repetition # 1.
5.	*E* rereads problem slowly.
6.	*S* repeats problem: Repetition # 2.

who live in this town are married"), leading to a logically valid conclusion that is either factually false or ambiguous. Factual truth and falsity are only approximate judgments. Extensive pilot testing made it clear that for individual subjects there was considerable variation in evocation of "exceptions to the rule" (knowledge of a particular store on the road just outside of town, for example).

Instructions and experimental procedures were designed to make the task as meaningful as possible to the Kpelle. Problems were described as word games and the individual was told he could answer them by simply listening to the words and, as a colloquial Kpelle expression puts it, "taking them to be true." Instructions emphasized, "You don't need to know anything to answer these word games. All you have to do to find the answer is to listen carefully to the words and think about them." Each session began with a practice problem that the experimenter read aloud and answered. He then explained that he found the answer by putting the words together.

The experimental procedure is outlined in Table 2. For each experimental problem, the procedure consisted of the following steps: the experimenter read the problem and the subject gave a "Yes" or "No" answer followed by the reason for his answer. He was then instructed to repeat the problem exactly as it had been read to him. Following this, the experimenter read the problem again and secured another subject repetition. The experimenters were two Kpelle men, one a high school graduate and the other a doctoral student in anthropology. Both were local residents of the area with extensive experience in experimental investigations of this kind. All sessions were conducted in Kpelle and were taperecorded. They were later transcribed into English by one of the experimenters and, as a check for accuracy, a sample was also transcribed by a Kpelle college student with training in translation.

The necessity of translation from one language to another presents serious difficulties in an analysis depending wholly on linguistic responses as data. They caution against making a more fine-grained analysis of recall errors than the data warrant. As will be seen, however, recall protocols of the Kpelle subjects share a number of features with those of American subjects and a great deal of commonality with protocols secured in a subsequent study with the Vai tribe, another language group in Liberia. As far as basic phenomena are concerned, therefore, we can be confident that we are not dealing merely with artifacts of translation or unique properties of the Kpelle language.

Results on Problem Solution and Explanation

Before the recall data are analyzed, and as a means of placing this study in relation to previous research, the summary outcome on problem solution, will be reported.

Kpelle villagers answered 53% of the problems correctly (a chance solution rate), Kpelle students 80%, and American students 90%. Results among the Kpelle are in line with the Cole and Luria studies and indicate that present findings are not specific to the materials and procedures used in this study. Performance of American high school and college students, as expected, is above the 86% solution rate of third grade pupils whom Hill (1961) tested on similar problems.

Reasons given to support answers to the problems were classified into three categories. The first, theoretic, includes those statements explicitly relating the conclusion to the information contained in the premises of the problem as given by the experimenter; the second, empiric, includes statements justifying the conclusion on the basis of what the subject knows or believes to be true; the third, irrelevant, covers idiosyncratic and arbitrary answers as well as "don't know" responses. The respective percentages are shown in Table 3 for the three groups of subjects.

Villagers almost always justified their answers on the basis of belief or fact, whether or not their answers were correct or incorrect. There is a

TABLE 3
Reasons Justifying Answers to Problems, Study I (Kpelle)

	Percent justifications		
	Theoretic	Empiric	Arbitrary
Kpelle villagers	22.3	68.1	9.6
Kpelle students	75.0	21.9	3.1
American students	82.3	3.1	14.6

dramatic shift from empiric to theoretic explanations among Kpelle students and empiric reasons all but disappear from protocols of American students, although some give idiosyncratic replies.

Recall Accuracy

For evidence on how problem information was handled by the various subject groups, transcripts of problem repetitions were analyzed with respect to two questions: how much of the original problem content was retained in recall reproductions (a quantitative analysis of retention of meaning, or recall accuracy) and the nature of changes introduced into the material (a qualitative analysis of recall error).

As a measure of recall accuracy, protocols were scored for the extent to which recall repetitions preserved the meaning of each of the several parts of the syllogism—the two premises and the question. Changes in the material, such as word substitutions, transpositions, and paraphrases, that did not affect propositional meaning were ignored. "Recall accuracy," therefore, refers to semantic, not verbatim, reproduction. Comparative results are reported in Table 4.[3]

Columns 1 and 5 in Table 4 report the proportion of problems correctly repeated in their entirety for each of the experimental groups. In each group, some problem repetitions fall into this category, indicating that the recall demands of the task have been understood by individuals in all the populations being compared. As expected, every group improved on the second recall, since it occurred immediately after the experimenter reread the problem and it was the second time the subject heard it. Even on this recall, however, a great deal of information was lost. Villagers' reproductions were highly fragmentary. Thirty-seven percent failed to preserve the meaning of either premise; 42% preserved the meaning of one premise; only 25% reproduced the sense of all the information contained in the original problem. This appears as striking confirmation of Luria's observation. However, an unexpected finding is that villagers were not unique in faulty recall. Fully one-half of Kpelle students and nearly one-third of American students failed to reproduce all the information in the two premises that would have been essential to problem solution.

Recall accuracy was analyzed with respect to two characteristics of the problem material—their logical structure and the factual truth or falsity of their content. The response measure used in this analysis was the proportion of problems correctly repeated in their entirety on the second

[3] Table 4 is given in percentages because experimenters occasionally failed to secure first or second repetitions on some problems. Out of a possible total of 192 repetitions, the corpus available for analysis consisted of 179 among Kpelle villagers, 183 among Kpelle students, and 180 among American students.

TABLE 4
Proportion of Problems Totally or Partially Recalled, Study I (Kpelle)

	First recall				Second recall			
	(1) Total	(2) Both[a] premises	(3) One premise	(4) No premise	(5) Total	(6) Both[a] premises	(7) One premise	(8) No premise
Kpelle villagers (N = 87)	11.5	16.1	28.7	55.2	18.4	24.1	39.1	36.8
Kpelle students (N = 93)	28.9	34.4	31.2	34.4	35.5	48.4	31.2	20.4
American students (N = 90)	47.9	55.3	28.7	16.0	63.2	69.5	26.3	4.2

[a] This is a total count of problems in which both premises were correctly reproduced and therefore overlaps with Column 1.

recall—that is, repetitions given immediately after rehearing the problem that preserved the meaning of both premises and the question of the syllogism.

To investigate the effect of problem structure, the problem list was divided into two sets, one set containing problems with only universal propositions (the "universal set") and the second containing problems with both universal and particular propositions (the "particular set").

As shown in Table 5, every group recalled the universal set more fully and accurately. Kpelle villagers reproduced 45% of the universal problems in their entirety as compared to only 2% of the particular; Kpelle students reproduced 64% of the universal and 8% of the particular; American students reproduced 79% of the universal and 46% of the particular.

Although the pattern of error is consistent across groups, impairment of recall performance on the "particular set" is extreme for both schooled and traditional Kpelle. The explanation is not obvious. The Kpelle language has specific lexical terms for *all* (every one of) and *some* (a few of) and no problems are encountered in translation of these terms from English into Kpelle or retranslation into English. This does not rule out the possibility that these terms introduce linguistic difficulties for the Kpelle of a different nature than those involved in English and this requires further investigation. However, the qualitative analysis of errors involving

TABLE 5
Effect of Quantifiers on Recall Accuracy, Study I (Kpelle)

	Percent problems completely recalled, 2nd recall		
	Kpelle villagers	Kpelle students	American students
Universal Set			
Problem 1	36.3	81.8	100.0
2	0.0	50.0	100.0
3	50.0	64.0	72.7
4	50.0	64.0	41.6
Total	45.4	64.4	78.7
Particular Set			
Problem 5	0.0	8.3	16.6
6	0.0	8.3	41.6
7	0.0	8.3	58.3
8	9.1	8.3	66.6
Total	2.3	8.3	45.8

the quantifiers *some* and *all* (see Discussion, below) and findings in the second study reported in this chapter suggest that extralinguistic factors are also in operation.

In contrast, division of the problem lists into sets of factual truth or falsity showed no difference in recall accuracy for any group related to this aspect of problem content. Villagers had complete reproductions of six of the factually true and six of the factually false problems; Kpelle students reproduced 15 of the true and 18 of the false; Rockefeller University students reproduced 30 of the true and 29 of the false. This result, however, cannot be taken as a determinative demonstration of lack of content influence. In this study, factuality was not varied independently of problem structure and its effects might well have been masked by the overwhelming quantifier effect.

The relationship of recall accuracy to correct solution rate is of special relevance to the problem of identifying components of the syllogistic task that may contribute to differential performance of tribal villagers and school-educated individuals. A comparison of group averages shows that recall accuracy parallels solution accuracy: groups more successful in giving correct answers to the problems as they were presented are also more accurate in recalling them. Because both American students and Kpelle students had such a high proportion of correct answers, no meaningful within-group comparative analyses could be made for these subjects. For the villagers, recall accuracy was assessed independently for problems with "right" and "wrong" answers, using as a response measure the number of problems in which the meaning of both premises was retained in the second recall. Of the 48 problems answered correctly, 11 recalls reproduced both premises; of the 40 problems answered incorrectly, 11 recalls reproduced both premises.

It would be desirable to use the recall data to throw light on the logicality of the reasoning processes involved in the task and not merely on the attainment of some experimentally defined performance criterion. This would require that subjects' answers be related to their own representations of the problem. Unfortunately, this could not be done in the present study. The nature of the transformations made in the material, as presented below, was such that in the great majority of cases it was not possible to derive a logically valid inference. This was especially true with respect to the fragmentary villagers' reproductions.

Analysis of Errors in Recall

Measures of recall accuracy confirm the fact that the experimental problems undergo transformations in the course of subjects' operations with them. What is the nature of these changes and are they the same or different for the various experimental groups?

To introduce the discussion of problem transformation during recall, a complete transcript of one Kpelle villager's efforts at problem repetition is presented here:

Problem: Some kwi (Western) people are wealthy.
All wealthy people are powerful.
Are some kwi people powerful?

Subject's answer and reason: Yes . . . it is because some kwi are wealthy and they have power.
Subject's first repeat: Some kwi in this town are wealthy. They have power.
Experimenter: What question did I ask you?
Subject: Do some kwi have power?
(Experimenter reads the problem again.)
Subject's second repeat: Some kwi are wealthy. They have power. Do many wealthy men have power?

This example illustrates some common and interrelated errors. Considering the second repetition only, observe that the question, "Are some kwi people powerful?" has been transformed into a piece of evidence—"They have power." What was given as evidence—"All wealthy people are powerful"—has been turned into a question—"Do many wealthy people have power?" The term *many* has been substituted for the universal quantifier *all.* Although such examples are rare among Kpelle and American students, there are individual cases of similarly radical problem transformation within these groups.

We will now turn to a more systematic consideration of errors drawing on illustrative material from subjects' second recalls, supported where appropriate by qualitative data. A definitive or exhaustive classification of errors has not been attempted in this preliminary experiment. The major purpose has been to determine what kinds of evidence recall protocols may contribute to an understanding of information-processing difficulties in verbal syllogisms.

Omission of a premise. A principal form of error among the Kpelle was the complete omission, not merely distortion, of a premise. The premise overwhelmingly dropped was the second or minor premise; it disappeared from 40% of villagers' reproductions and 20% of Kpelle students'. American adults, in contrast, were rarely caught dropping a premise in its entirety. Here are typical illustrations of otherwise accurate villagers' reproductions in which the minor premise is not present in any form.

All the stores in Kpelleland are in a town.
Then is Mr. Ukatu's store in a town?

Omitted: the proposition that Mr. Ukatu's store is in Kpelleland.

> Some of the people we know are not in school.
> Then are all the people in Liberia in school?

Omitted: the proposition that all the people we know are in Liberia.

Dropping of or nonstatement of premises has been observed to be characteristic of reasoning on problems in everyday life. Cohen and Nagle (1962) point out that practical reasoning often proceeds on the basis of incompletely stated premises; implicit knowledge is combined with explicit statement to provide the basis for a conclusion. Henle (1962) has found that students sometimes drop entire premises when they are reconstructing their chain of reasoning, even though they are working from written texts. The data presented here indicate that this phenomenon may also occur when the individual's assigned task is not that of carrying forward an argument or reaching a solution but merely repeating a syllogism that he has heard.

Displacement of terms. Numerous reproduction errors involve displacement of subjects or predicates from one premise to another, destroying the implicative relations between them. These occur, with differing frequencies, among all populations and can be illustrated by transformations in problems presented to American students. The problem is this:

> All children who were born in this country are citizens.
> Achebe is not a citizen.
> Was he born in this country?

Several American students reproduced this problem as follows:

> All children who were born in this country are citizens.
> Achebe was not born in this country.
> Is he a citizen?

A second illustration is the problem:

> Some oil men are wealthy.
> All wealthy men are powerful.
> Are some oil men powerful?

This was reproduced by several students as:

> Some oil men are wealthy.
> All oil men are powerful.
> Are some oil men wealthy?

Changes in quantifiers. The largest class of errors involved the quantifier and appeared in the protocols of all populations, including American students, most frequently in villagers' reproductions.

A problem by problem analysis of villagers' errors with quantifiers showed that all errors occurred on problems containing both terms. In those problems in which *all* appeared in the first premise and no quantifier was used in the second, *all* was correctly reproduced in every repetition that included the first premise. In the four problems in which the term *all* appeared in the second premise and *some* in the first, there were errors involving *all* in 38% of the second premise repetitions and errors involving *some* in 41% of first premise repetitions.

There were many examples in which *all* or *some* substituted for each other or switched locations in the syllogism. Here is one version in which *all* has been replaced by *some* in the second premise, destroying the possibility of a valid conclusion: "Some Kpelle chiefs are children. *Some* children are single. Then are some Kpelle chiefs single?" Another reproduction of the same problem transposes the *all* of the second premise and the *some* of the question: "Some Kpelle chiefs are children. Some children are single. Then are all Kpelle chiefs single?"

Confusability of quantifiers is shown directly in recall protocols that present both terms in the same proposition. Kpelle villagers often give propositions in this form: *"all* the children, *some* are single." A New York adult recalled a problem in this fashion: "Some cardinals are religious. All religious people are married. Are all relig—are all cardinals married? Are some cardinals married?"

Recall errors involving the quantifier *some* are especially interesting because this quantifier has been consistently identified as a prime source of difficulty in other performance tasks using syllogistic material. Wilkins (1928), in her classical study of syllogistic reasoning among college men, attributed the greatest number of invalid conclusions to the ambiguity of the word *some*. In logic, it means at least some, whereas in ordinary usage, it often carries the implication *not all*. Wason and Johnson-Laird (1972), using a matching task to study subject's interpretations of single propositions, also found there was a tendency to interpret statements of the type "Some X are *not* Y" as implying "Some X *are* Y." Our recall protocols show frequent examples of denials and affirmations of this kind appearing in sequence. Here are two recalls of the problem containing the proposition "Some people we know are not in school":

Some people we know are going to school.
Some people we know are not going to school.
Then are they all in school?

All the people here in Liberia, some are going to school.
There are some who are not going to school.
Are those people going to school?

Conversion to the factual. Villagers recall protocols showed a variety of ways in which the hypothetical or theoretical status of the problem statements was transformed into a factual basis. Educated subjects, both African and American, did not show this bias. Problem questions were sometimes converted into statements of fact and incorporated into the problem. When retained as questions, they were frequently recalled as queries of fact or belief. Here are some examples from the protocols: "Do you *think* he can be a bachelor?" "All the people in Liberia, do you *believe* they are in school?" "Do you *know* some Westerners have power?" "Why is it Mr. Smith *cannot* make rice farm?" "Is Mr Ukatu's store in the town or in the bush?" "Does Lorpu have a husband or doesn't she have a husband?"

Although other examples can be cited, this analysis clearly demonstrates that subjects engaged in the task of repeating syllogisms make errors similar in kind to those made by subjects engaged in the task of evaluating single propositions or drawing conclusions from syllogisms.

Certain features of the experimental procedure, however, limit the extent to which such recall errors can be attributed to the encoding components of the task. Although the second recall was elicited immediately after a new presentation of the problem, it occurred at a point in the procedure when the subject had already produced an answer, a reason, and an initial repeat. In this context, the recall task may have reflected distortions introduced into the material by prior cognitive operations. A followup study attempted to get some measure of this effect by varying the point in the procedure at which the subject was asked to recall the problem.

STUDY II

This study was conducted among members of the Vai tribe living in small villages in Grand Cape Mount County, Liberia. Like the Kpelle, most Vai earn their living by subsistence farming. Their social and cultural life also shares certain common characteristics with the Kpelle and neighboring tribes and their language belongs to the same Mende language family. (A description of the Vai people is available in *Area Handbook for Liberia,* 1972).

All subjects were nonliterate adult men and women engaged in traditional occupations and speaking no English. With the aid of Vai informants, four syllogistic problems were prepared and presented in random order to all subjects under varying instructions. The four experimental groups, each with 12 subjects, were given different combinations of recall and solution tasks. In Group 1, subjects followed the procedure of the first study—answering each problem after it was read, stating the reason for their answer, and then, on the experimenter's request, repeating the problem. In Group 2, subjects first repeated the problem and then answered it and explained their answers. Group 3 subjects repeated the problem after hearing it but were not asked to provide an answer. Group 4 subjects were given an opportunity to hear and repeat each part of the problem, one sentence at a time. They were included in the study as a control to insure that features of individual sentences were not a major source of recall error.

Considering the control condition first, it was found that subjects repeating one sentence at a time almost perfectly preserved the meaning of the premises (91% correct repetitions) and the question (75%). In contrast, under all conditions requiring repetition of the complete syllogisms, recall was faulty and fragmentary (Table 6). On all measures except the 100% accuracy rate (Column 1), recall in Group 1 was inferior to that in Groups 2 and 3. This outcome might be expected on two grounds—first, recall in Group 1 was delayed rather than immediate and, second, the process of problem solution intervened between presentation and recall.

It is impossible to measure the effect of problem solution unconfounded by the recall delay factor but a comparison of Groups 2 and 3 gives some measure of the effect of instructions to answer on recall accuracy. Subjects engaged in the task as one only requiring recall (Group 3) have substantially more completely accurate recalls than those oriented to problem solution (Group 2), but this is offset by the fact that they also have more recalls that are completely incorrect. Results are therefore, inconclusive

TABLE 6
Proportion of Problems Totally or Partially Recalled, as a Function of Time of Recall, Study II (Vai)

		Percent problems			
			Partial		
	Time of recall	Total, both premises and question	Both[a] premises	One premise	No premise
Group 1:	Recall after answering	22.9	27.1	35.4	37.5
Group 2:	Recall before answering	20.8	37.5	47.9	14.5
Group 3:	Recall only	34.1	43.2	27.3	29.5

[a]This is a total count of problems in which both premises were correctly reproduced and therefore overlaps with the first column.

with respect to whether or not a solution set is an independent contributor to recall error. However, a solution set is clearly not a necessary condition for recall error to occur. Subjects whose only task is to listen to the syllogism under instruction to remember it retain its full meaning in no more than one-third of their recalls. Analysis of the recall protocols shows distortions in material similar to those found in other conditions and in the Kpelle study. It is accordingly clear that Study 1 findings on recall error do not depend on the condition that recall followed problem solution.

DISCUSSION

The introduction of a recall procedure in the syllogistic reasoning task was initially motivated by an interest in locating sources of error in performance of traditional people on such tasks and in bringing new evidence to bear on the question of "two logics." It had been anticipated that this procedure would permit a comparison of subjects' answers with their own constructions of the problems as represented in their problem repetitions. The fragmentary nature of problem repetitions and the destruction of the implicative relationship between propositions in the great majority of these repetitions makes it impossible to draw any inferences about the logicality of villagers' reasoning processes from data obtained in these studies.

This very fact, however, substantiates the hypothesis that the syllogistic task imposes encoding and representational difficulties for unschooled tribal people not ordinarily encompassed in the category of deductive processes. It emphasizes that investigators have no warrant for drawing conclusions about logical processes from solution data alone.

A significant finding from the point of view of cross-cultural comparisons was that encoding difficulties were not confined to Kpelle villagers. Not only did the Kpelle and American student groups show considerable "forgetting" but they introduced changes in the material paralleling in most respects the transformations made by the villagers. There were many commonalities in error patterns: effect of problem structure on recall accuracy, confusion of quantifiers, displacement of terms, and omission of entire or partial premises. Such commonality in classes of error suggests commonality in some underlying operational processes.

The difference in the magnitude of error between villagers and student groups remains striking, however, and requires further investigation. One clue to the discrepancy may be found in the single class of error unique to unschooled villagers—the importation of such truth statements as *think, believe,* and *know* into the syllogisms. Their reformulation of the problem from a hypothetical to a factual one, even when they are endeavoring to repeat it exactly, taken together with the empiric nature of their justifications for their answers, suggests that the formal reasoning problems of the type used in these experiments are "heard" and apprehended quite differently by traditional people and those exposed to formal schooling. The "empiric bias" appears to enter as soon as the subject becomes engaged with the material. Why this may be so and whether formal problems can be devised that are meaningful in a nonempiric sense to tribal people are challenging questions for future research.

Considered from the point of view of their theoretical implications for the psychology of thinking, the findings are most interesting in the correspondence they demonstrate between the nature of errors made in recall and errors other investigators have identified in tasks requiring inferential reasoning. Most compelling is the fact that retention of meaning is markedly affected by introduction of the quantifier *some,* which is known to be a prime source of difficulty in other performance tasks using syllogistic material. An explanation for the quantifier effect on recall is not immediately obvious. Problems 7 and 8, which not a single villager recalled correctly (i.e., gave a paraphrase preserving the meaning of the problem), were among the shortest on the list. They posed no greater overall memory burden than Problems 1–4, for example, yet the latter were recalled more accurately.

Neimark and Chapman (this volume) present direct evidence of the difficulties subjects encounter in representing the relationships stated in "particular" propositions. They required subjects ranging in age from 12 to 20 years to match logical propositions of the type "*All* A *are* B, *Some* A *are* B," and the like, to Venn diagrams exhibiting all possible set inclusion relationships. They found a dramatic difference between response accuracy to the universal propositions and to the particular propositions, with only a minority even of college students interpreting *some* and *some are not* correctly. Errors on compound propositions ("*All* A *are* B and *All* B *are* A," for example) paralleled those on single propositions and were not significantly greater in amount, leading the investigators to conclude that the major source of error on compounds arose from restrictive interpretations of the quantifiers in the simple propositions. They point out that the compound propositions they used did not provide an analog of the processes underlying syllogistic reasoning because they contained no middle term; however, they suggested that their data supported analyses of errors in syllogistic reasoning that attributed them to inaccurate interpretations of individual premises (Ceraso & Provitera, 1971).

The findings presented here, however, suggest that error in recall was largely a result of the combination of quantifiers in two premises rather than the effect of the single term *some* in individual propositions. In Study II, subjects required to repeat a syllogism containing a universal and a particular proposition one sentence at a time gave almost perfect reproductions, only three errors occurring in repetitions of the premises.[4] This result dismisses the possibility that the difficulties in recalling "particular" problems might be due to specific linguistic factors related to the term *some*.

Neimark and Chapman have directly tapped difficulties involved in representation of set inclusion relationships expressed in logical propositions. Similarities in errors revealed by their matching task and the recall task in the present study furnish some basis for considering these as converging operations from which inferences can be drawn about the mental organization or representation of logical propositions. They suggest, as a specific hypothesis for future testing, that integration and representation of information in syllogistic problems may be crucial to both recall and solution performance.

Barclay's (1973) assimilation theory of sentence memory provides a useful framework within which this hypothesis may be tested. He holds that, with the exception of the special case in which individuals are required to memorize the literal wording of sentences, memory for connected sentences is an active, constructive process that cannot be understood in terms of linguistic analysis of individual sentences. The constructive process of comprehension consists in relating the information given in the single sentences, and assimilating it to existing knowledge (both lexical and nonlexical) and to task demands. The outcome of this constructive process is a semantic representation (comprehension), which in turn serves as a memory representation. The process of retrieval, then, consists of reconstructing the information from this representation. Barclay's outstanding experimental finding is that American college students, given a set of sentences describing some ordered array, "recall" certain sentences describing relationships among the items that have not been included in the set of sentences given by the experimenter but constitute correct inferences from that set. Similarly, subjects recognize as "old" new sentences describing true relationships in the array.

Paris and Carter (1973) found the same false recognition for new sentences semantically consistent with old sentences among second and fifth grade children. They presented three-sentence stories comprised of two premise sentences and a filler sentence (for example, "The bird is inside the cage, the cage is under the table, the bird is yellow"). On a later recognition test, both younger and older children consistently responded that they had previously heard the true inference statement, "The bird is under the table," when, in fact, they had not. In a related study, Kevin (1971, referred to in Barclay, 1973) read subjects partial syllogisms lacking con-

[4] These errors did involve substitution or omission of the quantifier, however, and it might be that the single-sentence immediate recall task used was unsuited to an investigation of this question because it produced too little total error to permit differential analysis of error.

clusions. False recognitions were more frequent for valid than invalid conclusions, suggesting that subjects' memory representations "contained" the conclusion. Paris and Carter concluded from these findings that subjects' semantic representations for connected sentences embodied more information than was available from the linguistic inputs alone.

One implication from this work is that the converse proposition may also hold true: if subjects fail to achieve an integrated representation, either because they do not synthesize information in the individual sentences or do not assimilate it to existing knowledge, their memory representations may embody less information than is predicted by an analysis of the linguistic inputs alone. This implication is a matter for empirical confirmation.

A second implication goes to the adequacy of the conceptual framework within which the present studies have been conducted. The research proceeded from the assumption, suggested by temporal stage models of logical reasoning, that inference operations occur *after* information has been encoded and formalized in some representation—the deduction, as it were, being "read off" from the relationships expressed in the representation. Such a model makes a separation between the processes involved in understanding premises and those involved in reaching conclusions. The import of the work reported on memory for sentences is that understanding related sentences involves logical operations of inference and integration. Without identifying such inferential processes with those involved in reaching conclusions or answering questions, it nevertheless seems useful to approach future investigations of the syllogistic reasoning task on the assumption that thinking may be involved in memory representation as much as memory representation is involved in thinking.

REFERENCES

Area Handbook for Liberia. Washington, D.C.: The American University, 1972.

Barclay, J. R. The role of comprehension in remembering sentences. *Cognitive Psychology,* 1973, **4,** 229–254.

Ceraso, J., & Provitera, A. Sources of error in syllogistic reasoning. *Cognitive Psychology,* 1971, **2,** 400–410.

Cohen, M. R., & Nagel, E. *An introduction to logic.* New York: Harcourt, Brace & World, 1962.

Cole, M., Gay, J., Glick, J. A., & Sharp, D. W. *The cultural context of learning and thinking.* New York: Basic Books, 1971.

Evans, J. St. B. T. On the problems of interpreting reasoning data. *Cognition,* 1972, **1,** 373–384.

Gibbs, J. L., Jr. *Peoples of Africa.* New York: Holt, Rinehart & Winston, Inc., 1965.

Henle, M. On the relation between logic and thinking. *Psychological Review,* 1962, **69,** 366–378.

Hill, S. A study of the logical abilities of children. Unpublished doctoral dissertation. Stanford University, 1961.

Kevin, R. C. The generative nature of memory for inferences. Unpublished master's thesis, University of Texas at Austin, 1971. (Cited in Barclay, J. R., 1973).

Levy-Bruhl, L. *How natives think* (1910). New York: Washington Square Press, 1966.

Luria, A. R. Towards the problem of the historical nature of psychological processes. *International Journal of Psychology,* 1971, **6,** 259–272.

Paris, S. G., & Carter, A. Y. Semantic and constructive aspects of sentence memory in children. *Developmental Psychology,* 1973, **9,** 109–113.

Piaget, J. Intellectual evolution from adlescence to adulthood. *Human Development,* 1972, **15,** 1–12.

Wallace, A. F. C. *Culture and personality.* (2nd. ed.) New York: Random House, 1970.

Wason, P. C., & Johnson-Laird, P. N. *Psychology of reasoning: Structure and content.* Cambridge, Massachusetts: Harvard University Press, 1972.

Werner, H. *Comparative psychology of mental development.* New York: Science Editions. 1961. (first published 1948.)

Wilkins, M. C. The effect of changed material on ability to do formal syllogistic reasoning. *Archives of Psychology* No. 102, 1928, 1–79.

Woodworth, R. S., & Sells, S. B. An atmosphere effect in formal syllogistic reasoning. *Journal of Experimental Psychology,* 1935, **18,** 451–460.

7

DEDUCTIVE PROCESSES IN CHILDREN

Rachel Joffe Falmagne
Clark University

As contended in the introduction to this volume, the area of logical development encompasses two families of studies of unequal size and of partially different import: the Piagetian tradition, in which the child is studied as a scientist, and the study of the child as a logician. In the latter group of studies, the option is taken to enclose the child in an arbitrary universe in which the premises are explicitly specified and express arbitrary relations between the referents, and officially the deductions do not involve any external factual knowledge. This applies to the work of Hill (1961), Matalon (1962), and Shapiro and O'Brien (1970) on deductions in sentential and quantifier logic, and of Le Bonniec (1970), dealing with modal logic, as well as to the studies presented here. It also applies to recent studies on children's comprehension of logical connectives (Neimark, 1970; Neimark & Slotnick, 1970; Paris, 1973; Suppes & Feldman, 1971; Youniss & Furth, 1964), which do not deal with deductions but are related to this topic in an obvious way.

The studies reported here pertain to the second tradition and take the most radical option with respect to the arbitrariness of the premises (in contrast to Hill's work and one of Matalon's studies, which involve premises with a familiar content) by giving the subject partial information about some aspects of a geometrical material and requesting him or her to perform deductions about related or other aspects of this material.

Strategically, interest in the logic of the child (or the adult) can materialize into various sorts of questions of unequal generality. One approach is to attempt to characterize the logical knowledge that the child brings to bear on the problem and thereby to aim at a structural model of the natural logic at a given age and its development. Piaget's enterprise in the context of "scientific" rather than "verbal" situations is of this type. An alternative approach is to aim at a microanalysis of the process by which deductions are made. This is the approach taken in this chapter, which represents an attempt to outline a process model for the situations considered. The design of the experiments and the analysis of latency and error data are set up according to this perspective in order to unfold various aspects of the deduction process operating in real time. Because of the complexity of the process and the novelty of the situation, the analysis concentrates on general aspects of the process, namely the mode of representation of the information, the evidence for alternative representations, and a plausible mechanism generating errors. More specific hypotheses about details of the process are offered at a few places on a speculative basis, to illustrate the theoretical potential of the approach. The ambition of this chapter is limited to establishing the few inferences mentioned above, illustrating the application of the now widespread process models approach to this new task domain, and, it is hoped, suggesting further developments.

The structural approach and the process approach, although they involve different kinds of data analysis and theorizing, are bound to be related since the ingredients of the process generating responses are derived in part from the logical competence of the child. Therefore, developmental concerns, although not central to the studies reported here, are, nevertheless, present in the general approach. It seems strategically more efficient, however, to postpone the study of developmental changes until refined relevant aspects of the deduction process have been if not unequivocally identified, at least suggested by the data. Implications of the present results for developmental research are outlined in the final discussion, and their relation to some Piagetian findings is discussed, with the necessary qualifications about the comparability of the two approaches.

PARADIGM AND THEORETICAL FRAMEWORK

In the three experiments to be reported, the child is first presented and familiarized with a set of geometrical figures (e.g., circles, squares, triangles) that can be large or small and of various colors. This is the reference set to which the premises and propositions exclusively apply. After the child manipulates this material for a few minutes, the experimenter takes it away and, out of the child's view, puts a few items in a box. The premise is then given; it consists of partial information about the content of the box, of the form: "In this box I only put circles; I am not telling you which ones, but they are all circles. We will open the box later on so you can check that this is true." (Experimenter shakes the box to make it obvious that it is not empty.)

The child is then given verbally a list of propositions and is asked, for each of them, to judge whether it is true "(It is true"), false ("You are lying") or undecidable ("Nobody could tell"), given the premise. Latencies of responses are recorded. The details of procedure are given in the next section.

There are potentially several modes in which the child can operate to evaluate the truth value of a proposition in the present situation.

1. A first type of evaluation process consists in building a mental representation of the premise in terms of the set of objects that may be in the box according to it (or "premise set") and in assessing the truth value of a proposition by comparing it with the elements of that set. In the premise "There are only circles," the premise set may include a big blue circle, a small blue circle, a big green circle, etc., or a subset of those if memory limitations are hypothesized. It can be assumed for specificity that this mental representation is visual, although this is not essential for the present treatment. This procedure is referred to as "Procedure C" (for "concrete").

Various assumptions can be made as to how, specifically, the comparison between the proposition and the premise set is conducted. These, however, are not relevant to the design and data of Experiments I and II and are examined in the discussion of Experiment II and the introduction to Experiment III. Nevertheless, an important preliminary remark is that the premise set is a set of potential elements of the box, so that no simple mechanism involving scanning the premise set for the presence of the critical element can yield an appropriate evaluation of the propositions. In the example above, establishing that the premise set contains a blue circle does not imply that the proposition "There are some blue circles" is true.

2. In the process just outlined, a proposition is evaluated against a fully described representation of the set of objects, with all their physical characteristics. A similar, yet somewhat more abstract process involves evaluating the proposition against a coded or schematized representation of the premise, only involving the relevant aspect(s) of the objects (Procedure S, for "schematized"). In the case of the premise "There are only circles," such a representation may consist of a sizeless, colorless circle; the premise set then contains a single element. In this case, the response to undecidable propositions must be generated from an acknowledgment that the critical objects mentioned in the proposition (blue circles) have aspects that cannot be matched against the (colorless) referent representation. This is a more abstract procedure than the one described in (1) because it involves,

in fact, asserting the undecidability of a proposition on the grounds that it requires more information than is contained in the premise, which is analogous, for the imaginary objects dealt with here, to what a formal proof consists of for a symbolic material.

3. An intermediate mode of representation of the premise is one in which the objects are described more specifically than by their relevant aspects only (as in Procedure S) but not completely (as in Procedure C). In the example above, the premise set can consist of a blue sizeless circle, a green sizeless circle, etc. The pertinence of this alternative becomes apparent below. It is referred to as "Procedure SC." The representations corresponding to Procedures C, S, and SC are exemplified in Fig. 1.

4. Another mode of evaluation is worth mentioning for completeness and for its distinct theoretical connotations, although it is not distinguishable from Procedure S operationally in the present context. The child may carry on a procedure similar to a logical proof and use tautologies and deduction rules he or she knows to arrive at the conclusion. Specifically, what is hypothesized is that the child may have learned empirically the truth value of certain classes of statements by being exposed to various examples from these classes and their truth values and forming, by inference, concepts about these structures. For example, a 6-year-old may have learned empirically that if a Statement A is true, then Statement non-A is false and may apply this knowledge to many new statements without having to resort to imaginary verifications (of the type described above) on the referents of the statements. This putative learning process is of the same nature as any of the innumerable other concepts that the child has learned. Even if any truly formal capacity in children of that age is not

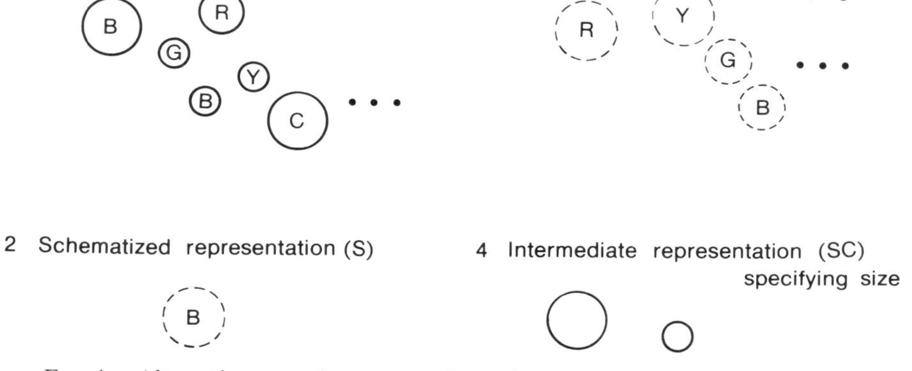

FIG. 1. Alternative mental representations of the premise "In the box there are only circles." Dotted lines indicate sizeless objects. Capital letters in the circles stand for colors.

assumed, the presence or such rules or concepts in their repertoire does not seem an unrealistic theoretical possibility. Such a knowledge is, for the practical purpose of performing deductions, very close to logical competence; whether such concepts are mediated by a symbolic representation or not appears to be largely irrelevant, for that matter, except perhaps for the greater generality of symbolically mediated concepts.

The various modes of evaluation described above are not necessarily exclusive. A reasonable assumption is that, regardless of the way in which the premise is encoded when originally presented, the various representations of the premise can be accessed to at all times when needed and that which representation and mode of evaluation are used at a given time depends on the proposition to be judged. Specifically, it is assumed that when a given proposition is presented for evaluation, the subject first encodes it at a purely linguistic level and then, depending on features of the proposition, switches to one or the other type of evaluation procedure by resorting to one of the available representations of the premise. If the pair premise–proposition evokes a conceptual deductive situation that is in his or her repertoire, the child may switch to a procedure of Type P and retrieve the relevant tautologies and deduction rules from long-term memory. If not, he or she may turn to one of the other modes of evaluation and bring up a mental representation of the premise of Type C, S, or SC. It may be hypothesized here that the specific representation used depends, among other things, on the difficulty of the judgement to be made and that more difficult propositions are likely to elicit procedures of Type C more often.

The switching mechanism, or the critical features in the proposition that bring up one or the other evaluation procedure, is obviously one of the most interesting parts of the process. The first study reported here was a pilot experiment aimed at revealing the potential occurrence of evaluation procedures of Type C or SC, as opposed to Type S or P. Experiment II is a followup of Experiment I, examining more specifically some aspects of the switching mechanism and aiming at distinguishing between the occurrence of Procedures C and SC, respectively. Experiment III was aimed at comparing two types of undecidable statements differing in their referential characteristics; the theoretical framework suggested by the results of the two former experiments has been used to account for the differences between these two cases in terms of latencies and types of errors.

EXPERIMENT I

A very simple discriminative prediction from the processes described above is that if Procedures C or SC are never used and if evaluation always conforms to Procedures P and S, then the number of items in the reference set, which are referred to implicitly in the premise, should not affect the latencies of responses. In the Procedure S case, this prediction stems from the fact that items in the premise set are only described by their relevant aspects and, therefore, the positive set associated to a given premise involves a constant number of (schematized) elements, irrespective of the size of the reference material. This holds whatever specific assumptions are made with regard to the detailed comparison mechanism involved. The same prediction is obvious in the case of Procedure P.

In contrast, when Procedures C or SC are used, then most assumptions about the comparison process should predict latencies to be positively related to the number of objects in the reference material, because the size of the positive set increases accordingly. The main purpose of Experiment I was to use this prediction to infer whether Procedures C or SC sometimes occur.

Method

Subjects. The subjects were 20 first graders from a Belgian public school attended by a mixed lower- and upper-middle class population. The children were between 6 years, 2 months and 7 years, 1 month when first tested.

Design. The experiment involved two sessions, approximately 8 weeks apart, only the second of which is reported here. The first session was mainly intended to explore this novel situation, how the children would respond to it, and whether a list of about 20 propositions to evaluate was a viable procedure. Latencies were not recorded on that session. Each session lasted for approximately 30 min.

Session II included two formally identical tasks, differing only by the reference set and given in a counterbalanced order at a few minutes interval. The reference set was composed of geometrical forms painted each on a 4 × 6-inch white card. The forms were triangles, circles, and squares, either big ($2\frac{3}{4}$-inch diameter) or small (1.25-inch diameter), and could take on either one of two colors (black or orange) in one of the tasks, or one of eight colors in the other one. The total number of objects displayed was the same in both tasks. The premises used were (*a*) "In this box all the drawings are small circles" for one task; and (*b*) "In this box all the drawings are big squares" for the other; a list of 20 propositions was then given verbally to the child for evaluation.

The two lists were identical, granted the appropriate vocabulary substitutions corresponding to the change in the premise, and the order within list was the same for both. For example, the proposition "In the box there isn't any circle" in the list related to the Premise (*a*) corresponds to the proposition "In the box there isn't any square" in the Premise (*b*) list.

The order of presentation was such that the three first propositions were the easiest ones of each response category, respectively, in order to familiarize the child with the mode of response.

Procedure

The various dimensions in the reference set were pointed out to the child and he or she was allowed to explore it for a few minutes. The material was then taken away from him or her, a few items were placed in a box (out of his or her view), the other ones were put in a pile face down on the table, and the box was shaken to make it obvious that it was not empty. The experimenter then gave the premise and told the child that the box would be opened later on. This was done to create an asymmetry in status between the premise (which had to be indubitable) and the propositions, which had variable truth values.

Three cards labeled "It is true," "You are lying," and "?" were placed on the table, and the experimenter and the child read them together during the instructions.

Each proposition was written on an index card. After reading the proposition, the experimenter handed it to the subject, who was then to say "It is true," "You are lying," or "Nobody could tell," and at the same time put the index card under the appropriate label on the table. This was to provide the child with an alternative way of responding in case of verbal inhibitions, and also to animate the task to some extent. Although the children were asked to give both responses, the experimenter only reminded them to do so once or twice, when it was necessary, and did not insist if they persisted in using one response exclusively. Latencies were recorded by means of a stopwatch, between the last syllable of the proposition and either the sorting response (i.e., the time the card was laid down) or the onset of the verbal response, whichever occurred first. The accuracy was within .5 sec. Both responses were consistent in most cases, and when they were not the latency was discarded. If the child made an error and spontaneously corrected it, this was considered as a correct response but the latency was discarded.

The experimenter emphasized the permissibility of the response "You are lying" by saying "Sometimes I will be lying, and then you will have to tell me that I am lying, to show that you do not let me trick you." The permissibility of the response "Nobody could tell" was likewise emphasized by saying "Sometimes I will say things such that the most intelligent person in the world would have no way of knowing whether I am lying or whether I am saying the truth; when I say things like that, you have to answer 'Nobody could tell.' " Then a number of examples in other situations were given until the child was convinced that some statements were indeed of that sort. If the first undecidable proposition was answered incorrectly, the experimenter interpolated a small discussion with the child, essentially repeating the instructions above and giving additional examples. (This directive procedure of introducing the child to the use of the undecidable category was motivated by the focus of the study on how the child came to the undecidable judgment when he or she did, rather than on whether he or she tended to do it spontaneously.) No other intervention was made thereafter. All responses were acknowledged with a (it is hoped) neutral, yet encouraging, nod. After completion of the list the box was opened, with the comment "See, there are only small circles (alternatively, big squares) here; but of course you could not know which ones they were."

Occasionally, once or twice during the list, the experimenter verified that the child remembered the premise, and in all cases he or she did. All the children understood the nature of the task immediately—save specific difficulties with the undecidable category—and answered without error to the easiest propositions. Most children asserted that it was easy and (surprisingly) that it was fun.

Results

Because of wide individual differences and because of the roughness of measurements in this pilot experiment, the analysis relies only on paired comparisons of latencies given by each subject to the various propositions of interest. Only the cases for which both responses are correct are involved in these comparisons. Table 1 shows the paired comparisons of individual latencies to (formally) identical propositions in the eight-colors condition and in the two-colors condition, respectively. There is an overall significant effect of the size of the reference set on latencies, indicating that a procedure of Type C or SC is sometimes used. When examined in more detail for propositions of various categories the effect seems to be mainly a result of undecidable (U) propositions. When undecidable affirmatives (UA) and undecidable negatives (UN) are considered separately, however, the effect appears to be much more sizeable in the former than in the latter propositions.[1]

The latter differential result does not have any straightforward interpretation within reasonable specifications of the framework proposed.[2] Until further replication of this differential effect, it is tentatively attributed to

[1] A similar split cannot be made for true (T) and false (F) propositions, because all but one T proposition are negative, the opposite holds for F, and both of these single propositions are simple, as opposed to the others.

[2] Two alternative assumptions can be made regarding the evaluation of negative propositions. (*1*) Evaluation of the corresponding affirmative proposition is

TABLE 1
Experiment I: Paired Comparison of Latencies to the Same Propositions, Respectively in the Eight-Colors Condition (I_8) and in the Two-Colors Condition (I_2)[a]

Proposition type	Proportion of cases where $l_2 < l_8$ (given $l_2 \neq l_8$)	p
All	.60	$< .01$
TN	.49	
UA	.72	$< .01$
UN	.59	
FA	.64	$< .05$

[a] Only pairs of correct responses are considered.
Total number of observations: 221.

the fact that latencies of negative propositions are longer and that the resulting increase in variability possibly masks the effect of the size of the reference set in UN latencies.

Discussion

The overall effect of the size of the reference set on latencies indicates that Procedures C or SC are used at least in some cases. The next step is then to try and assess which one is used and in which cases; in other words, which features of the propositions are relevant to the switching mechanism mentioned above.

An interesting result in Table 1 is the fact that the effect of the number of colors on latencies is much more sizeable for U (undecidable) propositions than for T or F propositions. Undecidable propositions have two distinctive characteristics in this pilot experiment: they are undecidable and

---

performed first, and the resulting truth value is subsequently transformed. (2) The information is processed under its negative form; that is, for each of the subsets of the positive set, the subject tests, for example, the validity of the statement "There is no blue circle." Under both assumptions, the number of subsets to be tested to attain two opposite instances is the same for UA and UN statements. Similarly, the fact that the hypothetical subsets tested are on the average larger in the eight-colors condition equivalently affects UA and UN propositions. Finally, the same remark holds for the fact that if a serial scanning of each hypothetical subset is assumed, the critical element (a blue circle) will, on the average, be reached later in the eight-colors condition, than in the two-colors condition, in the subsets that include it.

they mention the color of the object. Experiment II is aimed at replicating this result with materials that can distinguish these factors, and with more accurate latency measures, and at examining its implications for the switching mechanism.

EXPERIMENT II

In Experiment I, because the reference set was three dimensional and the premise involved a conjunction of two aspects, only one dimension could be irrelevant. All the undecidable propositions therefore mentioned the color of the objects. Two alternatives were therefore left open by the results obtained: (1) the number of colors in the reference set only affected the latencies of undecidable propositions mentioning the color of the objects or (2) the number of colors in the reference set affected the latencies of all undecidable propositions. These alternatives have different implications for the switching mechanism, as discussed below.

In Experiment II, the premises were simple and only specified one aspect to the items in the box (e.g., "In the box all the objects are circles"). Undecidable propositions could therefore refer either to the size of the items ("There are big circles in the box") or to their color ("There are yellow circles in the box") or to both. The list was constructed in such a way as to include comparable undecidable propositions of the two first types. Similar variations were introduced for the true and false propositions, within the truth-value restrictions, such as "There is no triangle . . . ," "There is no small triangle . . . ," "There is no blue triangle . . ." in the example above.

Method

Subjects. The subjects were 28 children from a first grade in a New York public school from a middle-class neighborhood. The children's ages at the time of their first session ranged between 6 years, 0 months and 7 years, 2 months.

Design. Each child had two sessions, at an approximately 3-week interval. Each session involved two "twin" tasks (as described for Experiment I), with a two-color reference set and with a six-color reference set, respectively. Except for the change from eight to six colors, the items of the reference set were the same as in Experiment I.

The premises used were, respectively "In the box there are only circles" and "In the box there are only squares" for the two tasks of Session I and "In the box there are only small things" and "In the box there are only big things" for the two tasks of Session II. Each list involved two types of propositions for each response category T, F, and U: propositions mentioning the color of a critical object (and labeled T_c, F_c, and U_c, respectively) and propositions mentioning its size (in the tasks of Session I) or its shape (in the tasks of Session II) but not its color (T_{nc}, F_{nc}, and U_{nc}, respectively). One list from Session I is shown in Table 2. Because most T propositions are bound to be negative and the inverse holds for F propositions, "dummy" propositions were introduced that were of no particular theoretical interest and simply served to help balance the subjective frequencies of these two forms in each response category.

Four different orders of presentation were used, with the constraint that the three first propositions be the easiest ones from each of the three response categories and that a given response category not be repeated more

TABLE 2
Experiment II, Session 1:
One Version of the List of Propositions

Premise: In this box there are only circles.

Identification nb (not rank)	Truth value	Proposition: In this box . . .
1	T	There is a circle
2	T	All shapes are circles
3	T	There is no triangle
4	T	There is no small square
5	T	There is no blue square
6	T	There is no big red triangle
7	U	There is something small
8	U	There is something orange
9	U	There is a big circle
10	U	There is a yellow circle
11	U	There is a big green circle
12	U	There is no small circle
13	U	There is no blue circle
14	F	There is a square
15	F	There is a big triangle
16	F	There is a black triangle
17	F	There is a small red triangle
18	F	There is no circle
19	F	There isn't any circle

than twice in succession. A given subject was presented both lists in the same order.

Procedure

The instructions and general procedure were the same as in Experiment I, with the difference that the subject gave his or her manual response by pushing one of three buttons labeled, respectively, "It is true," "?," and "You are lying," and connected to a timer. The accuracy of latency measures was within .01 sec.

Results

In addition to the paired comparisons of latencies (comparisons of pairs of correct responses) to formally identical propositions in the six-color and two-color conditions, respectively, mean latencies of responses (for the same data samples) are also considered. The bulk (90%) of latency distributions usually ranges from 1 sec to 8 sec, with a mode between 2 and 3 sec. Latencies longer than 12 sec are very rare and have been discarded from the mean latencies presented.

The results from the data of Session I are shown in Table 3. The paired comparison data clearly indicate that the number of colors in the reference

TABLE 3

Experiment II: Paired Comparison of Latencies to the Same Propositions, Respectively in the Six-Colors Condition (I_6) and in the Two-Colors Condition (I_2), and Mean Latencies in Both Conditions[a]

Propositions					Proportion of	
Type	Number	$\bar{I}_2$	$\bar{I}_6$	p	cases where $I_2 < I_6$	p
UN_{nc}	12	3.06	3.17		.50	
UN_c	13	3.30	4.50	<.05	.75	.01
UA_{nc}	7, 9	4.26	4.49		.50	
UA_c	8, 10	3.65	4.03		.66	<.05
U_{nc}	12, 7, 9	3.82	4.20		.50	
U_c	13, 8, 10	3.52	4.20	<.05	.69	<.00
F_{nc} ; T_{nc}	4, 15	4.06	3.80		.45	
F_c ; T_c	5, 16	4.29	4.29		.55	

[a] Only data from pairs of correct responses are considered.

set only affects (significantly) undecidable propositions mentioning the color. This holds both for affirmative and for negative propositions. Latencies of T and F propositions, whether mentioning the color or not, do not depend on the number of colors in the reference set. Table 3 also presents the mean latencies to the various types of propositions (only for the cases in which both responses were correct, that is, for the same data as those involved in the paired comparisons) and the results of the *t* tests on the difference between means.The results are consistent with those of the paired comparisons.

Discussion

That the size of the reference set does not significantly affect the latencies of T and F propositions suggests that a procedure of Type S or P is used to evaluate these. Furthermore, since the subject does not know in advance what the outcome of an evaluation will be, it is reasonable to assume that he or she first tries to use an S or a P procedure for U propositions as well, is unable to successfully complete it in that case, and subsequently switches to a more concrete procedure (as suggested by the effect of the number of colors on U latencies).

The reason Procedure S fails in the U case although it is used properly in the T or F cases quite naturally appears if the process of comparing a Representation S of the premise (e.g., a sizeless, colorless circle) and a given proposition is characterized in more detail. In the case of the (false) proposition "In the box there is a big square," such a comparison involves assessing whether a sizeless, colorless circle is a big square, concluding negatively, and therefore judging that the proposition is false. Similar operations underlie "True" judgments. When an undecidable proposition is presented (e.g., "In the box there are some blue circles"), Representation S (a sizeless, colorless circle) does not contain enough information to be matched against the critical object involved in the evaluation (i.e., a blue circle), and the subject switches to a representation of the premise specifically involving the missing aspect, that is, color in the present example.[3] That the child does not switch to a fully specified Representation C is indicated by the fact that the number of colors in the reference set does not affect the latencies of U propositions mentioning the size only (U_{nc}). It should be noticed that such a switch is not needed for T or F propositions mentioning an irrelevant aspect ("In the box there is a blue

[3] This switch is clearly not necessary on logical grounds. The very fact that the proposition cannot be matched against Representation S is sufficient to infer that it is undecidable. Instead, the occurrence of a switch is indicated by the pattern of latencies.

triangle"): a mismatch, in that case, can be established using the schematized representation; the referent, namely a sizeless, colorless circle, is clearly not a blue triangle (whereas it might be a blue circle in the U case).

Before more specific speculations are made about the way in which the new expanded representation of Type SC is dealt with, one remark is required. It is not too surprising that the child can recognize that some information is missing in his or her current representation, i.e., a sizeless, colorless circle (and switch to one more complete) and yet be unable to assess the undecidability of the proposition on that sole basis, in contrast to what an algorithmic procedure can do: the first judgment is a judgment of ignorance about objects, of the type "I don't know"; the second concerns the truth value of a quantified proposition and is of the type "Nobody would know whether the experimenter is lying or saying the truth." These clearly represent two distinct levels of sophistication, both formally and psychologically.

Various assumptions can be made about the mechanisms by which the new premise set (sizeless circles of various colors) is compared to the proposition (e.g., "In the box there are some blue circles"). It is worth emphasizing here again that the premise set is a set of potential elements of the box; each item in the premise set can be, but is not necessarily, in the box, according to the premise. Consequently, no simple scanning of the premise set for the presence or absence of the critical element (a blue circle) can be adequate. The following discussion is speculative at this point and only aims at providing a plausible mechanism for the subsequent steps of the process outlined so far.

Probably the most reasonable assumption is that the subject constitutes imaginary subsets of the premise set, thereby mimicking the potential manipulations performed by the experimenter, and assesses, for each of these subsets, whether the proposition is true or false (if this is the subset that happens to be put in the box). This process is exemplified in Fig. 2. Sampling of imaginary subsets goes on until either two opposite instances arise (in the present example, an imaginary subset containing a blue circle and one not containing a blue circle), in which case the proposition is judged undecidable, or conviction is attained after n congruent instances and the proposition is (wrongly) judged true or false. Errors can arise either from a failure to perform this "combinatorial" analysis or from too loose a criterion for conviction. It is hardly worth mentioning that this search is by no means assumed to be exhaustive or systematic, and that n is expected to be small.

It seems relevant to point out here that, as shown in the Results section, the latencies of responses in this situation usually extend over several seconds, which may add to the credibility of the mechanism described.

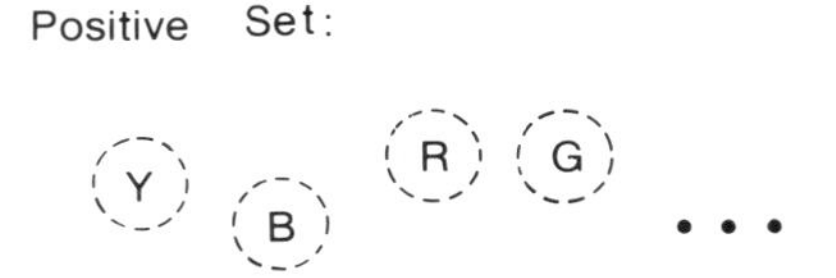

Test for each subset :
Is there a blue circle in this subset ?

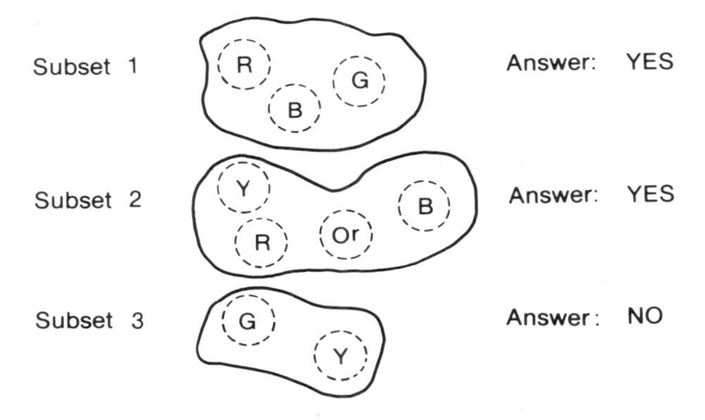

Conclusion: Proposition is undecidable

FIG. 2. Undecidable propositions: outline of the comparison mechanism after missing aspect (color) has been supplied, for the premise "There are only circles in the box" and the proposition "There are some blue circles in the box."

However, direct comparison of T, F, and U latencies cannot be made in this experiment because only one spatial order of responses (the one that seems intuitively easiest, namely, T, U, F) has been used, and the response component, particularly the discrimination between T and F, may be of importance. However, an experiment reported elsewhere (Falmagne & Porter, in preparation) has resolved this difficulty by only using one response key and concomitant verbal responses and has found latencies of U responses to be significantly longer than latencies of T and F responses.

An alternative class of comparison mechanisms involves scanning all the elements of the premise set for their compatibility with the proposition to be evaluated and computing the responses according to whether all of them are compatible with the proposition (as in the case of the proposition "There is no triangle" in the example above), in which case the proposition is true; whether none of them are, in which case the proposition is false;

or whether only some of them are, in which case the proposition is undecidable. This seems, however, to be a more sophisticated procedure than the previous one, and less plausible in the case of young children. The former mechanism, although complex, is in fact very close in its imaginary form to a concrete manipulation of real objects.

The pattern of results just discussed does not appear in the data of Session II, not presented here, and the number of colors in the reference set does not significantly affect any type of propositions. A number of interpretations of this are possible. A first is that the short practice with the task provided by Session I is sufficient to bring the subject to a more efficient (abstract) mode of evaluation. Such a possibility is highly interesting in terms of the learning process that has been hypothesized to underlie the acquisition of logic. A more restricted version of this interpretation is that the same dimension (color) is irrelevant in both sessions and that the subject may have learned to apply the more abstract procedure for color specifically ("I don't know which colors are in the box"). Although less interesting in terms of its general implications, such a shift involves some abstraction ability on the part of the child. Finally, a third open possibility relates to the specific premises used in Session II ("There are only big things in the box"), which refer to the size of the objects rather than to their shape, thereby have a lower imagery value than the premises of Session I, and may yield different evaluation procedures if it is assumed that the representation is visual. In relation to this, it is worth noting that the proportion of errors to U propositions is much higher on Session II than on Session I (.22 versus .13), which is particularly striking when contrasted with T and F propositions (.09 versus .20; .09 versus .08).[4] This may be partially related to the use of the term "thing," with which a number of children have had difficulties; yet the fact that the size of the object, rather than its shape, is relevant is likely to be the main source of difficulty.

These three interpretations cannot be distinguished with the design of this experiment but are interesting enough to warrant further systematic investigation.

EXPERIMENT III

In the two previous experiments, the data suggested that in order to evaluate undecidable propositions the subject first tried to use a Procedure S and subsequently switched to a more complete representation of the

[4] The high overall proportion of errors to T propositions on Session I as compared to U propositions is because the former involve more negative propositions.

premise. This switch was hypothetically attributed to the fact that the initial schematized encoding of the premise did not contain enough information for matching tests to be performed against U propositions. It was nevertheless adequate for judging T and F propositions.

The purpose of Experiment III was to devise a situation in which some U propositions would not require switching according to the present framework, whereas others would, and to test the differential predictions of the model for these two types of propositions. Accordingly, in contrast to Experiments I and II, the material in Experiment III was such that (1) the initial representation of the premise and the first step of all evaluations could be very likely assumed to be of Type SC and to involve a list of (partially described) items rather than a single schematized item, as in Experiment II, and (2) the relevant dimension could be classfied in two hierarchically related ways so that the premise could specify which "type" of items was in the box without mention of their specific category. For example, in one of the tasks used, the material included four different shapes: the letters A, E, and S and a square. Shape was used as the relevant dimension, and the premise given was of the type "In the box there are only letters." Two different types of undecidable propositions could be constructed with this material. "Intradimensional undecidable" propositions (U_i) refer to the objects according to the relevant dimension, but at a level more specific than the information given in the premise. In the example above, such a proposition could be "In the box there is an A." "Extradimensional U" propositions (U_e) refer to the objects according to a different dimension (e.g., "In the box there is something green," in the example above).

Within the framework proposed, and if it is assumed that the premise "There are only letters" is initially represented as a list (A, E, S, all sizeless and colorless) instead of by the abstract scheme of a letter (presumably less available to young children) there is a very meaningful psychological difference between the two types of U propositions compared. In the U_i case, the initial representation (the list A, E, S) is complete enough for the combinatorial analysis to be performed on it. In the U_e case, the initial representation must be expanded to include the additional dimension (color).

A number of predictions follow from this characterization. In the hypothetical evaluation process of Type SC described in the previous section, it is essential for the subject to keep in mind the potential status of the premise set, that is, the fact that it consists of potential elements of the box. Each subset examined in the subsequent combinatorial analysis is therefore a tentative content of the box, and the response must rely on the outcome of a sufficient series of tests rather than on the test of an individual subset.

One type of error is of particular interest within this framework: those errors that result from a failure to appreciate the potential status of the premise set or, equivalently, from a failure to perform the combinatorial analysis described (as combinatorial reasoning is by essence reasoning on potentialities). Such errors are here referred to as "radical errors." In the case of the premise "There are only letters in the box," if the representation currently used consists of a sizeless, colorless A; a sizeless, colorless E; and a sizeless, colorless S; and if the proposition to be evaluated is "There is an A in the box," a radical error yields a "True" response, which stems from a failure to realize that, although the premise set contains an A, the specific subset selected may or may not contain one.

If it is assumed that in this experiment the initial representation of the premise is a list of sizeless, colorless letters A, E, and S (in the example above), then it is natural to expect radical errors to be relatively more frequent in the U_i case than in the U_e case, because no switching is required during the evaluation of a U_i proposition in order to perform matching tests. These tests can be performed with the premise set (A, E, S) by which the premise was initially represented and which is used, furthermore, at a first step of all evaluations. The subject is therefore more likely to forget or disregard the potential status of the elements of the premise set. There is a stronger tendency to answer "True" to the proposition "There is an A" than to the proposition "There is something green" in the current example.

If radical errors consist in combinatorial failures, it is natural to expect their latencies to be short. All errors in the "radical" category, however, are not necessarily radical errors. Instead, the simplest hypothesis is to posit, in addition to the mechanism generating radical errors, a basic error mechanism (guessing or other) generating errors in the "radical" category or in the alternative category with equal probability. Because the "radical" category is a mixture of radical errors (with short latencies) and of other errors, its latency should be, on the average, shorter than the latency of the alternative response.

Furthermore, when the number of errors in the "radical" category increases relatively to the alternative error category, this inflation can be attributed to genuine radical errors (because the "basic" errors are distributed with equal probability between the two categories), and the difference in latencies between both types of errors should increase accordingly. It is worth noting that this prediction is not trivial but must be mediated by the framework proposed. In particular, if the "radical" response category contains more radical errors in the U_i case than in the U_e case, as predicted, the difference in latencies between the two types of errors should be larger in the U_i case.

Finally, if U_e propositions necessitate switching during the evaluation to an expanded positive set, the latencies of correct responses to these can be expected to be longer than latencies of correct responses to U_i propositions.

Method

Subjects. The subjects were 34 first graders from a New York public school in a middle-class neighborhood. The children were between 6 years, 1 month and 7 years, 1 month old at the time of the test.

Procedures. The instructions and general procedure were the same as in Experiment II. Each child was administered two tasks, at a few minutes interval, in counterbalanced order.

Material and tasks. The items in the reference set were, for one of the tasks (Task L), the letters A, E, S, and a square, each painted on a white index card. Each item could be large or small and blue, green, or red. For the other task (Task Sh, "shapes"), the items were a circle, a square, a triangle, and an E and were either large or small and either blue, green, or red.

For Task L, the premise was "In the box there are only letters." The list of undecidable propositions included three U_i propositions and three comparable U_e propositions, respectively, involving the quantifiers $\forall$, $\exists$, and $\neg\exists$. The complete list of propositions is shown in Table 4. For Task Sh, the premise was "In the box there are only shapes", and the list was formally identical to the Task L list, granting the appropriate vocabulary substitutions.

Results

The main latencies of correct responses and of the various types of errors to U_i and U_e, and $\forall$, $\exists$, and $\neg\exists$ propositions, and the corresponding frequencies, are shown in Table 5. It may be useful to point out that radical errors entail different responses for different propositions. In the case of the premise "There are only letters in the box," radical errors consist in judging the proposition "There is an A in the box" as true; the proposition "All the cards in the box are A's" as false, and "There isn't any A in the box" as false.

The category labeled "'radical' errors" in Table 5 refers to those responses that may have been generated by a radical error, that is, by a combinatorial failure. Clearly, as mentioned above, some responses from the same category may have been generated by other mechanisms, those also generating the alternative erroneous responses.

TABLE 4
Experiment III:
One Version of the List of Propositions

Material: A, E, S,
big, small
blue, red, green

Premise: There are only letters in this box.

Identification (not rank)	Truth value	Proposition: In this box . . .
1	T	There are some letters
2	T	There is a letter
3	T	All of them are letters
4	T	There is no square
5	T	There isn't any blue square
6	T	There isn't any small green square
7	U, i	There is an *A*
8	U, i	All of them are *S*s
9	U, i	There isn't any *E*
10	U, e	There is something green
11	U, e	There isn't any blue thing
12	U, e	All of them are red
20	F	All of them are squares
21	F	There is a square
22	F	There are no letters
23	F	There is a red square
24	F	All of them are small squares
25	F	There is no letter

For all types of propositions, errors in the "radical" category are more frequent than the alternative erroneous response, as is natural given the remark in the preceding paragraph. This difference is particularly large in the case of U_i propositions, as expected.

A related prediction concerned the shorter latencies of "radical" errors as compared to the alternative errors. This prediction is also verified for all types of propositions. The difference in latencies between the "radical" response category and the alternative errors is larger for U_i propositions than for U_e propositions, which lends further support to the notion that

TABLE 5
Experiment III: Mean Latencies of Correct Responses, of "Radical" Errors and of "Non radical" Errors, and Respective Frequencies

	Latencies			Frequencies		
Propositions	Correct	"Radical" error	Other error	Correct	"Radical" error	Other error
$\exists$	3.76	4.51	4.78	95	23	11
$\forall$	3.49	3.52	5.16	90	31	5
$\neg\exists$	3.86	4.73	6.86	88	27	10
e	3.73	4.40	5.52	147	28	13
i	3.67	4.09	5.74	126	53	13
All	3.70	4.20	5.63	273	81	26

the proportion of genuine radical errors within the "radical" response category is larger in the U_i case.

As can be seen in Table 5, the latencies of errors are in all cases longer than the latencies of correct responses. This is not surprising, because errors are more likely to occur for propositions that are more difficult for one reason or another. It is worth mentioning that the fact that latencies in the "radical" category are longer than correct responses is not in contradiction to the theoretical characterization of radical errors as combinatorial failures, because the "radical" category is a mixture of radical errors and other errors, the latencies of which are presumably longer, as indicated by the alternative error latencies.

The third prediction, according to which correct responses to U_i propositions should have shorter latencies than correct responses to U_e propositions, is not supported by the mean latency data shown in Table 5. However, paired comparisons of latencies given by the same subject to comparable propositions, respectively, of the U_i and in the U_e types (when both responses were correct) yield a significant proportion of differences in the expected direction (59 versus 37 cases, $p = .05$), which is encouraging.

Discussion

The error and latency data from this experiment follow the pattern expected from the theoretical characterization of propositions U_i versus U_e. However, this study has an illustrative rather than demonstrative value in terms of the framework proposed, as additional assumptions concerning the initial encoding of the premise have been introduced on intuitive grounds. Subsequent systematic variations of factors affecting the initial encoding are needed, especially regarding the availability, assessed independently, of a single imaginal or abstract code for the premise.

In addition to the rationale offered here, the difference between U_i and U_e propositions is worth studying because of their respective formal relationships to the premise: the set referred to by U_i proposition ("There is an A") is included in the positive set referred to by the premise ("There are letters"), in contrast to the case for U_e propositions ("There is something green"). The comparison of these two cases is therefore interesting in connection with Piaget's emphasis on the difficulties experienced by young children with class inclusion properties. U_i propositions should be expected, in this perspective, to yield more errors of all types than U_e propositions, which is indeed the case.

GENERAL DISCUSSION

The data analysis and speculations in this paper focus on the process operating in real time to generate deductions in the paradigm considered, and in particular on the mode of representation of the premise and the subsequent comparison mechanism between this representation and the proposition.

The results from Experiments I and II, related to the size of the reference set, support the hypotheses (1) that at least two evaluation mechanisms are possible, differing by the degree of abstractness of the encoding of the premise, (2) that the least abstract is specifically used for undecidable propositions after a first attempt to use the other one, and (3) that the more specific representation, in that case, selectively involves the aspects under evaluation, excluding other irrelevant aspects. The data from Experiment III, however, indirectly suggest that the degree of abstractness of the initial encoding depends (in a way as yet to be determined) on referential features of the premise.

When the positive set representing the premise contains more than one element, the comparison mechanism between that representation and the proposition has been hypothesized to consist (ideally) of a partial combinatorial analysis of the premise set. This process and its failures have proved to provide an adequate framework for interpreting the pattern of errors and latencies in Experiment III in a meaningful way.

In relation to many points developed in the former discussions, appropriate latency comparisons of, respectively, T, U, and F propositions are of relevance. This especially applies to the assumption that U judgments result from an unsuccessful attempt to use the abstract procedure and a subsequent shift to a more complete representation; taken by itself, this assumption predicts latencies of U propositions to be longer than latencies of comparable T or F propositions (although other parameters of the process, such as the stopping rule and timing assumptions, must be taken into account to generate definite predictions). As mentioned above, such prediction cannot be tested in the present experiments but has been supported elsewhere (Falmagne & Porter, in preparation).

Some qualifications are needed regarding the status of the mechanisms described here with respect to logical competence. In spite of the imaginal or apparent nonformal nature of the evaluation process in some cases, it must be emphasized that the sequence of operations described represents a "plan" (Miller, Galanter, & Pribram, 1960) rather than a mechanical sequence of transformations. The operations involved in choosing the representation of the premise and the mode of comparison are monitored by the subject's knowledge of which plan is appropriate and to that extent indirectly represent his or her formal understanding of the situation. The process exemplified in Figure 2 is illustrative in this respect: setting up the combinatorial analysis of subset and the appropriate calculus leading to the conclusion reflects, among other things, the subject's recognition of the potential status of the elements of the positive set; and conducting the appropriate test for each item ("Is this circle blue?") instead of, for example, asking the reverse question ("Is a blue circle a circle?") entails recognizing the similarly asymmetrical properties of the verb "to be" and of the implication.

In relation with the two-phase research strategy mentioned in the introduction to this volume, the general notions developed in this chapter suggest and provide a formulation for a number of questions of interest from a developmental standpoint. The most obvious one involves assessing those classes of situations to which the child is able to apply the more abstract procedure and their development, that is, identifying the features in the situation that govern the initial encoding, on the one hand, and the switching mechanism, on the other. The results from Experiment III, in contrast to those from Experiment II, are compatible with the notion that the premise, in that case, has been encoded according to a Representation SC, which is tentatively attributed to the unavailability of a schematic code for the premise (perhaps to be related to its lower imagery value). A developmental study of the range of application of both procedures would be of obvious interest in relation to the gradual building up of verbal logic in the child.

Other questions, less directly related to the specific results presented here, can be formulated in connection with the method used and with the theoretical framework. The first concerns the nature of the judgments obtained. Although a number of precautions have been taken to lead the child to give judgments about the truth value of propositions (labeling the responses "It is true," "You are lying," and "Nobody could tell whether you are lying or telling the truth," and preventing the child from saying "Yes," "No," "I don't know"), nothing of course insures that the judgments actually are of this type instead of statements about the objects themselves. The distinction is illustrated by contrasting the conclusion "You are lying" to the conclusion "There are no triangles in the box." In spite of their practical equivalence, distinguishing between such judgments is of importance, as the former is an application of propositional logic, whereas the latter is not. A major assertion advanced by Piaget is that it is only at around 12 years of age (stage of "formal operations") that the child acquires the ability to reason about propositions as opposed to factual matters or objects. As emphasized in the introduction to this volume, Piaget's theory has been developed in connection with a different empirical context and does not have immediate implications for the situations exemplified here (in addition to the general problem related to the identifiability of its concepts). However, this distinction must be retained, and a comparison of the emergence of propositional logic in both situations will be of unquestionable interest. The present paradigm lends itself to the study of this question, because the judgments can be made at either level. The problem is of a diagnostic nature and may not be insoluble if more relaxed instructions and systematic interviews are given.

A related question is evoked by the assumption that the subject performs a combinatorial analysis (although incomplete) of the positive set when more than one element is involved. This is another ability that has been assumed by Piaget to be lacking in the child's cognitive competence prior to the stage of formal operations. The same restrictive remark as above holds here, but it is natural to expect such a combinatorial ability to increase with age and in relation with its application in other contexts. If radical errors are taken as a symptom of the child's combinatorial incompetence in the present paradigm, a developmental study of patterns of errors and latencies in the vein of Table 3 is relevant to this question.

Finally, the formal connections between the two types of undecidability investigated in Experiment III and Piagetian class-inclusion tests have been indicated before and suggest joint studies of these two situations from a developmental point of view. The results from Experiment III have been shown to be compatible with general predictions stemming from Piaget's theory, although the present theoretical framework, being process oriented, yields additional, more specific predictions.

ACKNOWLEDGMENTS

This work was supported partly by the Fonds National Belge de la Recherche Scientifique and partly by Grant BM16735 from the National Institute for General Medical Sciences through Rockefeller University. The author wishes to express her appreciation to the principals and teachers of Ecole Berkendael in Brussels and PS 158 in New York for their cooperation.

REFERENCES

Falmagne, R. J., & Porter, G. Judgments of indeterminancy in children in verbal deductions, as a function of the referential nature of the problem. In preparation.

Hill, S. A study of the logical abilities of children. Unpublished doctoral dissertation, Stanford University, Stanford, California, 1961.

Le Bonniec, G. Étude genetique des aspects modaux du raisonnement. Unpublished doctoral dissertation, École pratique des Hautes Études, Laboratoire de Psychologie, Paris, France, 1970.

Matalon, B. Étude genetique de l'implication. In E. W. Beth *et al.* (Eds.), *Implication Formalisation et logique naturelle.* (*Etudes d'Epistemologie Genetique. Vol. XVI.*) Paris: Presses Universitaires de France, 1962.

Miller, G. A., Galanter, E., & Pribram, K. H. *Plans and the struture of behavior.* New York: Holt, Rinehart & Winston, 1960.

Neimark, E. D. Development of comprehension of logical connectives: Understanding of "or." *Psychonomic Science,* 1970, **21,** 217–219.

Neimark, E. D., & Slotnick, N. S. Development of the understanding of logical connectives. *Journal of Educational Psychology,* 1970, **61,** 451–460.

Paris, S. Comprehension of language connectives and propositional logical relationships. *Journal of Experimental Child Psychology,* 1973, **16,** 278–291.

Shapiro, B. J., & O'Brien, T. C. Logical thinking in children ages 6 through 13. *Child Development,* 1970, **41,** 823–829.

Suppes, P., & Feldman, S. S. Young children's comprehension of logical connectives. *Journal of Experimental Child Psychology,* 1971, **12,** 304–317.

Youniss, J., & Furth, H. G. Attainment and transfer of logical connectives in children. *Journal of Educational Psychology,* 1964, **55**, 357–361.

8

THE REPRESENTATION OF LINEAR ORDER AND SPATIAL STRATEGIES IN REASONING: A DEVELOPMENTAL STUDY

Tom Trabasso,
Christine A. Riley,
Elaine Gumer Wilson
Princeton University

INTRODUCTION

This chapter is concerned with two general questions on the study of thought and reasoning. First, how is that which is being thought about represented. By "representation" we mean the kind of symbol structure that the person uses to represent an external situation in solving a problem, answering a question, or making a decision (see Newell & Simon, 1972, for a more complete discussion of this view). Second, given that a problem representation has been constructed, how is it operated on in order to generate answers, decisions, deductions, or inferences? The concern here is with those processes which access or use a psychological structure.

The focus of this chapter is on a problem that has been studied in several contexts, developmental or otherwise, the ordered syllogism of the form

$$\begin{array}{r} A > B \\ \underline{B > C} \\ \therefore A > C \end{array}$$

Operationally, this problem is usually stated as two ordered premises, for example, "John is taller than Bill and Bill is taller than Fred," followed by a question, "Who is taller, John or Fred?"

Developmentally, this can be recognized as a "transitive reasoning problem" or "transitivity task." Beginning with Burt (1919), Piaget (1921, 1928), and subsequently Piaget, Inhelder and Szeminska (1960), this problem has been used largely as a diagnostic of intellectual growth. In particular, success on the task is used to decide whether or not the child has certain logical abilities, that is, whether he can coordinate the terms A and C via the middle term B, whether he appreciates the reversible nature of the order (e.g., $A > B$ implies $B < A$), and whether he can seriate long series of these asymmetrical, transitive relations (Piaget, 1970, pp. 29–30).

In research on older subjects, largely college students, the focus has been on task variables (e.g., premise and term orders as in DeSoto, London, & Handel, 1965) or linguistic factors (e.g., unmarked versus marked comparative adjectives as in Clark, 1969) or logical subject–object relations (as in Huttenlocher, 1968). In addition, process models or strategies have been offered to account for the order of difficulty of the various forms of the syllogism, ranging from use of spatial representations (DeSoto *et al.*, 1965; Huttenlocher, 1968) to decision trees (Johnson-Laird, 1972). We hope to extend these attempts in two ways: by reformulating the questions posed by these other investigators along the lines discussed above and by investigating them developmentally.

REPRESENTATIONS

An ordered syllogism may be represented and held in memory in at least two ways. In one, each premise is stored separately as an ordered pair of terms: A, B and B, C; in the other, the premises are integrated and stored as a linear ordering, A, B, C. The construction of both of these representations entails some knowledge of order, comparative adjectives, and physical continua. The differences between them is separate versus integrated storage and they differ in terms of what occurs when one is asked the inferential question.

If the premises are stored separately, they must be retrieved and coordinated at the time of testing; if they are stored as a linear order, then this order is retrieved and used in some way at the time of testing.

There is good reason to suppose that the integrated, linear order is a preferred representation (see Barclay, 1973; Potts, 1972) because this kind of "chunking" of ordinal information is more economical or efficient in storage than several separate units. However, we propose to provide empirical evidence that will allow us to decide these alternatives.

THE TASK ENVIRONMENT

Figure 1 schematizes the task structure. The numbers 1–6 refer to sticks of different lengths, with Stick 1 being the shortest and Stick 6 being the longest. Each stick is of a different color. In training, the subject learns

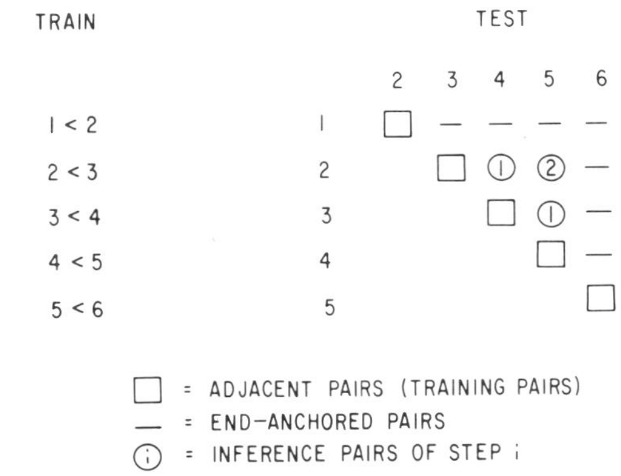

FIG. 1. Experimental paradigm for training adjacent pairwise relations and testing for all possible relations. Note that numbers refer to color-coded lengths, where 1 is the shortest and 6 is the longest member of the set.

TRAIN

1 < 2
2 < 3
3 < 4
4 < 5
5 < 6

TEST

	2	3	4	5	6
1	□	—	—	—	—
2		□	①	②	—
3			□	①	—
4				□	—
5					□

□ = ADJACENT PAIRS (TRAINING PAIRS)
— = END-ANCHORED PAIRS
ⓘ = INFERENCE PAIRS OF STEP i

the ordinal relation between adjacent pairs of sticks for which he must use the color codes to represent the sticks and predict their relation. That is, on a given training trial, the subject is shown a pair of sticks of equal length and asked one of two questions, either "Which is longer?" or "Which is shorter?" He then makes a choice of one of the colors and receives feedback. The feedback may be *Visual,* that is, he is shown the absolute lengths of the sticks, or *Linguistic,* that is, he is told the relation. The left-hand side of Fig. 1 shows that five adjacent pair relations are acquired. These pairwise relations constitute the premises for the inference problem.

After the subject has mastered these adjacent pairs, he is given tests on the relations for all possible pairs. On a given test trial, the relational question is asked first. Then a screen is raised, starting a clock, and the subject makes his choice by pressing one of two clear plastic panels located in front of each of the colored sticks with the response terminating the clock. Again, only the colors can be used to distinguish the sticks since they appear equal in length. In testing, no feedback of any sort is given. The matrix in Fig. 1 summarizes the kind of tests and information obtained. These aspects are discussed after consideration of what occurs in training.

SERIAL POSITION EFFECTS IN TRAINING

The first question of interest here is what occurs during training? In the course of training, each pair is first trained separately to a criterion. Then retraining is given on pairs, in a blocked, random order (i.e., all five pairs occur in an irregular order within a block of five trials) until the subject has met another criterion of mastery. The primary data of interest in training are how many errors or how many trials are required for mastery. Of particular interest is the pattern of errors that occurs over the five pairs. Note that the pairs can be ordered (1, 2), (2, 3), (3, 4), (4, 5), and (5, 6).

In our previous work on four pairs in training (Lutkus & Trabasso, 1974; Riley & Trabasso, 1974) it has been found that the errors distribute themselves according to a "serial position effect," with the maximum errors occurring on middle pairs. The importance of this empirical finding is that the occurrence of a serial position effect may be taken as *prima facie* evidence of the construction or use of an underlying linear ordering of events. Bower (1971) has reviewed the adult research on learning to associate names to positions on continua (cf. Murdock, 1960; Ebenholtz, 1965; DeSoto & Bosley, 1962). The consistent finding is that the distribution of relative errors over the continuum forms the well-known serial position curve.

Bower (1971) comments:

> . . . a simple principle exists for creating linear order among any new set of stimuli which previously were unordered. To induce a linear ordering onto a new set of unrelated elements, one simply associates them one to one with a second set of elements that were previously linearly ordered, perhaps on a 'primary sensory' basis. To be more explicit, the principle is this: If elements $a_1, a_2, \ldots a_n$ are linearly ordered in some primitive sense, and if we take any unrelated elements whatever, $b_1, b_2, \ldots b_n$ and associate the two series in pairs (a_1, b_1), then the set $b_1, b_2, \ldots b_n$ will acquire a derivative linear ordering. The critical implication of this derivative linear ordering is that stimulus generalization among the b_i's will now vary (in more or less degree) according to the proximities of the associated a's. That is, the proximity structure of the a set has been induced onto the b set, which were formerly unrelated elements.
>
> A corollary of these proximity relations is that a serial position curve will arise if we now try to use elements from the b set as stimuli for paired-associate learning. This is obviously an important principle, because it provides a possible way to think about how symbolic or conceptual linear orderings might have arisen from a history of analogical association to perceptually primitive orderings [p. 191].

The transitive inference task in Fig. 1 differs from the paired-associate tasks discussed by Bower (1971) in that (1) no obvious physical continua are provided for the subject's use in the task environment so that the subject must provide his own, perhaps spatial analogs, and (2) the subject must use ordered pairs of elements to induce a linear ordering; he does not have a prior linear ordering onto which he can map single members. The question, then, is how does the subject induce a linear ordering from such pairs?

One suggestion is given by Riley and Trabasso (1974). First, the subject isolates the end-anchor members (here, Sticks 1 and 6). This may be done in the following way: Find that stick which is only longer or only shorter, i.e., that stick which is only a logical subject or only a logical object (Huttenlocher, 1968). Then, imagine a linear, spatial array (either left–right or top–down), placing the shortest on the left (or right) and the longest on the right (or left). Once the end-anchor items have been mapped onto the spatial dimension, add other members to the array. This is done by first ordering the end pairs, (1, 2) and (5, 6), entering Sticks 2 and 5 into the array. Then pairs (2, 3) and (4, 5) are ordered, entering Sticks 3 and 4 to each end of the array. Finally, pair (3, 4) is ordered and the two ends of the array are joined. If errors are associated with each of these steps, this yields the serial position effect in acquisition of a linear ordering, which is repeatedly found in related, paired-associate, and psychophysical studies (see Moyer & Landauer, 1967).

If the subject is not inducing a linear order, spatial or otherwise, then a serial position effect with a maximum number of errors on pair (3, 4) is not expected. Instead, it may be expected either that all pairs are learned equally fast as an independent list of paired associates or that negative transfer via confusable responses occurs (e.g., Stick 2 is longer and shorter), yielding an end-anchor effect with pairs (2, 3), (3, 4), and (4, 5) equally confusable. Our training data thus allow a differential test of these possibilities.

THE TEST SITUATION

Following training on adjacent pairs (premises), the subject is tested on all possible pairs without feedback. The matrix on the righthand side of Figure 1, when filled with the proportion of correct responses or reaction times (RTs), tells us three pieces of information. The main diagonal (indicated by squares) gives us accuracy and speed of retrieving the relational information on the adjacent pairs of training and constitutes a test of memory. The first row and last column entries (indicated by lines) tell whether or not there are end-anchor effects since these tests involve endpoint (longest and shortest) sticks. The off-diagonal entries (indicated by circles) are inference tests. Here, distance or the number of inferential steps between sticks varies. The set (2, 4) or (3, 5) involves one step or one middle term; set (2, 5) involves two steps (Sticks 3 and 4 are middle terms).

The implications of each of the two methods of representation for the test data will now be considered. If each premise is stored separately in memory as an ordered pair and if at the point of testing the pairs are separately retrieved and coordinated, then certain patterns of RT s can be expected among the pairs. Assuming that the various retrieval and coordination operations are serial and require real time, then the RT for pair (2, 5) should be slower than those for either pair (2, 4) or pair (3, 5) because pair (2, 5) requires two coordinations and the other tests require only one. Furthermore, if the subject is retrieving pairs, then pairs (2, 3), (3, 4), and (4, 5) should be equally fast and faster than all inferential pairs because these are the ones on which the subject has received training and they require no inferential steps. The assumption that the subject stores separate pairs says nothing about end-anchor effects, that is, pairs involving Sticks 1 or 6 are faster.

If a linear ordering of the sticks is the representation at the time of test, the expected relations between RT and errors with distance between the sticks in the array can be predicted via a variety of models.

This can be illustrated using Bower's (1971) and Murdock's (1960) analysis of discriminability and errors. Assume that the sticks are odrered 1, 2, 3, 4, 5, 6. Then for Stick 1, the sum of the distances between it and the remaining sticks is $1 + 2 + 3 + 4 + 5 = 15$. For Sticks 2–6, these distances are 11, 9, 9, 11, and 15, respectively. The relative discriminability of Stick 1 is $15/(15 + 11 + 9 + 9 + 11 + 15) = .21$. For Sticks 2–6, they are .16, .13, .13, .16, and .21, respectively. Note that the relative discriminabilities give the serial position effect: Sticks 1 and 6 are most discriminable, while Sticks 3 and 4 are least. Note also that the difference in discriminability between Sticks 2 and 5 with Sticks 3 and 4 is not large relative to their difference with the end-anchor sticks, 1 and 6. To the extent that these distance measures predict errors and latencies, then, errors can be expected to occur the most and for RT's to be the slowest for pairs of sticks that are nearest to each other in the linear order. The predictions are that RT s are fastest for the most distant middle pairs (2, 5), intermediate for pairs of step size one (3, 5) or (2, 4), and longest for the adjacent, training pairs (2, 3), or (3, 4), or (4, 5). This model also predicts end-anchor effects because the ends of the scale are easiest to isolate. If linguistic factors operate (Clark, 1969), then the unmarked (long) end should be faster than the marked (short) end.

GENERAL RESEARCH PLAN

To test these alternatives and provide developmental data on the questions, subjects of different ages (6 years old, 9 years old, and college students) were tested in three conditions. Two groups were trained and tested as outlined above and they varied only in the kind of feedback they received in training. For one group, the feedback consisted of showing the actual sticks after a choice was made and this was called the "visual" condition. For the other, linguistic condition, the feedback was verbal and the subject was only told the correct relation (e.g., Red is longer than Blue).

In order to test the assumption that the linear order has spatial reference, a third group was added in which training was omitted and a physical display of ordered, colored sticks was present during the same test series given the other groups. This was called the Display condition.

METHOD

Apparatus and Materials

Thirty-six sticks (5, 6, 7, 8, 9, or 10 inches long), in each of six colors (blue, red, green, white, yellow, and orange) served as stimulus materials. For a given subject, a set of six sticks, each stick of a different length and color, was selected, counterbalancing the length–color combination over the group of subjects in a condition. In both training and testing, a pair of sticks was presented, one each behind one of two 3 × 4-inch clear Plexiglas windows. The windows were centered and hinged in a black box such that when the sticks were exposed they appeared equal in length (4 inches). A guillotine door covered the windows and, when it was raised, a Hunter Klockounter was started. When a window was pressed, the clock stopped. For the display condition, the sticks were placed in a Plexiglas rack in a staircase order. The left–right location of the longest end was counterbalanced over subjects, and the display was always placed to the left of the box.

Procedure

The subjects were run individually. Adults were able to complete all phases in one session of less than an hour; in conditions other than Display, some children occasionally required another session in order to reach the training criterion before being tested. All children were brought back for a subsequent session in which they were retrained and retested.

In the display condition, the display rack was set up next to the box and the test questions were administered without any preliminary training.

In the two training conditions, the children were given some preliminary testing on color naming of sticks of equal size, practice in operating the windows, and a demonstration of length differences using black, pink, and brown sticks of different lengths. They were also told that there were only six sticks and were allowed to feel them under a cloth. These preliminaries helped avoid confusion and made the task meaningful for the children; they were unnecessary for adults.

In training, each subject learned the comparative relations of five adjacent pairs, (1, 2), (2, 3), (3, 4), (4, 5), and (5, 6), Stick 1 being the shortest. For the children, training was first on each of the pairs separately and in order, starting with the shortest pair for half of the subjects with order of start counterbalanced over subjects within a group. The left–right position of the sticks in each training trial was random.

To start a trial, the subject was asked one of two questions, "Which is longer?" or "Which is shorter?" As soon as the question was asked, the experimenter raised the guillotine door, starting the clock. When the subject pressed the window in front of the color of his choice, the clock stopped. The two kinds of questions were equiprobable and randomized over trials according to a 50:50 sequence.

When the feedback in training was linguistic, it was stated by the experimenter of the form, "That's correct; the red stick is longer than the blue stick" or "No, that's wrong; the blue stick is shorter than the red stick." When the feedback in training was visual, the experimenter gave linguistic feedback and placed the pair of sticks in full view of the subject on top of the box.

For the children, the training criterion on separate pair training was eight out of ten correct choices on each pair. A concurrent training procedure followed and was used for all subjects in training. Here, all five adjacent pairs were presented in blocks of five trials with the pairs being randomized within each block. The subjects were trained to a criterion of four consecutive correct choices on each pair (four successive correct trial blocks). If the subject did not reach criterion in 120 trials (24 blocks), training was discontinued for that day. Training was resumed the next day, beginning with separate training on pairs. If the subject did not reach criterion in the concurrent phase after another 120 trials, he was not tested.

Testing followed immediately after criterion was reached in concurrent training. Test trials were administered in the same way as training trials except that no feedback was given. Each subject was tested four times on each of the 15 possible color pairs. These 15 pairs included the five adjacent pairs of step size 0, that is, pairs (1, 2), (2, 3), (3, 4), (4, 5), (5, 6) that were trained; two transitive inference pairs of step size 1, that is, pairs (2, 4) and (3, 5); one inference pair of step size 2, pair (2, 5); and seven end-anchor pairs, all of which involved Sticks 1 or 6, with step sizes of 1, pairs (1, 3) and (4, 6); 2, pairs (1, 4) and (3, 6); 3, pairs (1, 5) and (2, 6); and 4, pair (1, 6). The four test questions on each pair included two longer and two shorter questions. For each form of the question, the sticks were in both left–right positions. The 60 resulting test questions were presented in four blocks of 15, each pair of colors being presented in a block, and the 15 pairs were randomized in each block. The position of the colors and question asked were randomly assigned to a given pair over the four blocks.

Each subject was instructed that he would receive no feedback during testing and that he should respond as quickly as possible without making errors. At the end of the 60-test trials, subjects were retested on pairs on which they had erred.

Subjects

Eighty children were recruited via newspaper ads in the Princeton area and were paid $3 an hour for their services. Of these, 37 ranged in age from 8 years 5 months to 9 years 3 months (median = 9 years) and constituted the "9-year" sample; 43 ranged in age from 5 years 5 months to 6 years 6 months (median = 6 years 1 month) and formed the "6-year" sample. In addition, 36 college students from Princeton University served as paid subjects and constituted the "adult" sample.

Subjects were irregularly assigned to the three experimental conditions until six males and six females of each age met the training criterion and were tested. One 6 year old and one 9 year old did not reach criterion in the Visual condition; three 6 year olds did not reach criterion in the Linguistic condition. In addition, three 6 year olds refused to cooperate in training and were not continued.

Experimental Design

There were nine independent groups of 12 subjects, each formed by the combination of the independent factors of Age (6, 9, and Adult) and Condition (linguistic, display, and verbal). Question (Longer or Shorter) and Pair [(1, 2), (2, 3), (3, 4), (4, 5) and (5, 6)] were within-subject factors in training. Question and all pairs were within-subject factors in testing.

RESULTS AND DISCUSSION

Training

Mean errors are a negligible 0.9 in initial training with children and the errors are unrelated to condition, age, and pair. In concurrent training for all subjects, errors and the trial block in which the last error occurred for each adjacent pair are highly correlated ($r = .95$, $p < .01$). Further analyses are reported only on the trial block of last error.

Figure 2 shows the mean trial block of last error for all the significant ($p < .01$) effects: age, training pairs, and their interaction. No other main

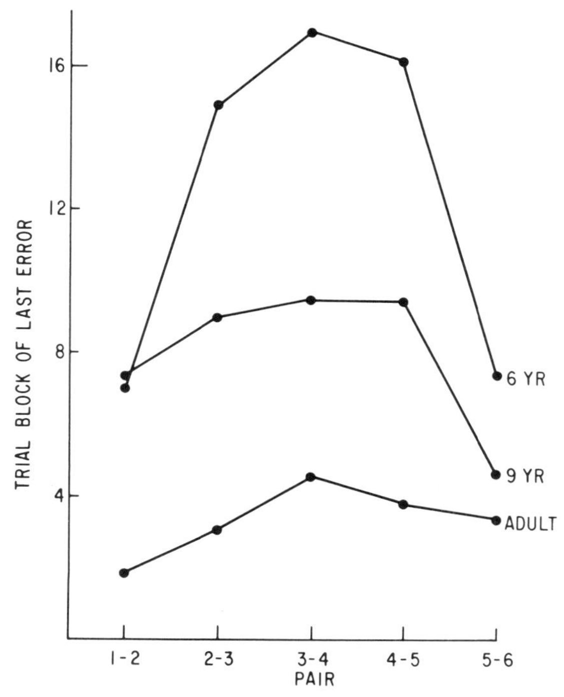

FIG. 2. Ease of learning adjacent pairs in concurrent training: mean trial block in which the last error on an adjacent pair occurs for each age group.

effects or interactions are significant. As can be seen in Fig. 2, the older subjects learn faster and show a less bowed but symmetrical serial position curve. Note that the curves peak at the (3, 4) middle pair. These serial position data are entirely consistent with the idea that the subjects have been constructing linear orders on the sticks during training (see Bower, 1971). Apparently, the subjects begin construction of the scale from the ends of the scale inward. End-anchor pairs, (1, 2) and (5, 6), are learned on average first, followed by the intermediate pairs, (2, 3) and (4, 5), followed by the center pair, (3, 4). The fact that the center pair is acquired last goes against an interpretation based on response competition (i.e., each stick other than 1 or 6 has two labels, longer or shorter, associated with it across pairs). The response competition hypothesis implies that all middle pairs are equally difficult.

The data in Fig. 2 have been recalculated as relative percentage of trials to reach criterion for each age group over the training conditions, to serve as indices of the relative difficulty of each pair. These are shown in Table 1.

TABLE 1
Relative Percent Trials to Criterion for Each Pair in Training

	Pair				
Age	(1, 2)	(2, 3)	(3, 4)	(4, 5)	(5, 6)
6	11	24	28	26	11
9	18	23	28	23	12
Adult	11	18	26	24	12
Observed average relative difficulty:	13	22	28	24	12

Note that the curves for relative difficulty are virtually identical for all three age groups. Therefore, although the younger subjects require more absolute trials to learn, their serial position curves are identical to those of older subjects when the curves are made relative to total trials. The suggestion here is that younger children are slower than adults but that the underlying mechanisms and sources of difficulty are the same. The developmental difference in acquisition is one of degree rather than kind; i.e., the younger children take longer to construct the linear order but they are prone to the same source of difficulty as older children and adults.

Testing

In analyzing the test data, we found that no major differences occurred between the two test sessions for the 6 and 9 year olds and the session data were pooled for each group and entered into the analysis along with the single-test data of the adult subjects.

The test series, it will be recalled, involved questions on all possible pairs, allowing separation and end-anchor tests (those involving Sticks 1 or 6), training pairs (step size = 0) and transitive pairs (step size = 1 or 2). Both speed (RT) and accuracy (proportion of correct responses) measures were obtained. The RTs are those from correct trials only and include those test trials added if a previous error occurred; the accuracy data are only for the first test series of 60 trials. Tables 2, 3, and 4 give the mean RTs for correct test responses and the proportion correct answers on the initial test series for each condition within each age group. The data are portrayed as a matrix of tests; the upper half diagonal gives the RT data for test pairs and the lower diagonal contains the proportions of correct responses.

TABLE 2

Speed and Accuracy of 6-year-old Subjects on Test Questions Mean Reaction Time (in msec) and Percentage Correct Responses on the 15 Pairs for Each Question and Condition

	Shorter?						Longer?					
S^a	1	2	3	4	5	6	1	2	3	4	5	6
Visual condition												
1	–	2323	3057	1982	2032	2025	–	2521	2800	2449	2368	1824
2	90	–	3174	2596	2645	2243	100	–	3163	3285	2890	1960
3	98	90	–	3497	3174	2202	100	96	–	3485	2992	2051
4	100	90	96	–	3270	2370	100	88	83	–	3008	2220
5	96	100	96	92	–	2148	96	96	92	94	–	2165
6	98	98	96	98	96	–	96	96	100	98	96	–
Display condition												
1	–	1950	1706	1808	1724	1685	–	2414	2340	2405	2275	1590
2	96	–	3688	3553	2991	1921	98	–	3837	3544	2814	1768
3	92	96	–	3779	3200	1926	96	96	–	3744	3286	1554
4	98	98	100	–	3547	2070	100	98	92	–	3416	1483
5	98	98	94	96	–	1908	96	96	100	96	–	1458
6	98	96	98	96	96	–	100	100	98	100	96	–
Linguistic condition												
1	–	3255	2893	3372	3047	2686	–	3053	4347	4045	3718	3560
2	88	–	3348	4570	4042	3399	96	–	3997	4612	3674	3396
3	75	83	–	4132	3994	2957	75	83	–	3537	3375	2448
4	69	60	88	–	3508	3060	81	71	81	–	4356	3499
5	83	75	83	77	–	2977	79	69	75	71	–	2715
6	85	83	88	81	96	–	88	83	79	90	96	–

[a] S = stick.

TABLE 3

Speed and Accuracy of 9-year-old Subjects on Test Questions Mean Reaction Time (in msec) and Percentage Correct Responses on the 15 Pairs for Each Question and Condition

	Shorter?						Longer?					
S^a	1	2	3	4	5	6	1	2	3	4	5	6
Visual condition												
1	–	1177	1442	1435	1369	1172	–	1378	1634	1569	1414	1104
2	98	–	1690	1570	1653	1303	92	–	1812	1726	1507	1149
3	94	92	–	2177	1660	1303	88	90	–	1853	1645	1140
4	94	96	94	–	2096	1421	85	98	83	–	1680	1053
5	96	96	90	85	–	1272	94	98	94	92	–	1079
6	96	96	96	96	94	–	94	100	98	92	98	–
Display condition												
1	–	1036	1053	972	991	871	–	1411	1516	1267	1328	856
2	98	–	2328	2250	1875	1326	100	–	2377	2163	1786	791
3	92	92	–	2546	2196	1166	94	85	–	2408	1810	911
4	100	98	92	–	2306	1267	92	96	96	–	1927	749
5	100	92	96	94	–	1296	96	98	98	98	–	822
6	96	98	94	94	94	–	96	100	96	96	96	–
Linguistic condition												
1	–	2732	3110	2459	2759	2315	–	2783	2986	2609	2637	2222
2	83	–	3862	2951	3216	2270	88	–	3248	3183	3381	2328
3	79	88	–	4208	4166	2101	81	94	–	3152	3673	2115
4	88	75	85	–	3571	2023	79	83	85	–	3385	2088
5	90	90	83	90	–	2079	85	90	90	85	–	2236
6	88	88	88	92	94	–	94	85	90	85	96	–

[a] S = stick.

TABLE 4
Speed and Accuracy of Adult Subjects on Test Questions Mean Reaction Time (in msec) and Percentage Correct Responses on the 15 Pairs for Each Question and Condition

	Shorter?						Longer?					
S^a	1	2	3	4	5	6	1	2	3	4	5	6
Visual condition												
1	–	955	926	852	791	843	–	1189	1246	1207	1016	808
2	92	–	1605	1204	1187	995	100	–	1685	1282	1022	884
3	92	83	–	1285	1309	1110	92	100	–	1291	1114	837
4	100	96	92	–	1657	1209	96	96	96	–	1203	812
5	96	100	96	83	–	1246	100	100	96	97	–	835
6	100	100	100	100	88	–	100	100	99	99	97	–
Display condition												
1	–	803	940	795	763	742	–	1339	1231	1130	971	722
2	92	–	1609	1279	1179	1055	92	–	1453	1430	1143	799
3	100	83	–	1476	1471	1049	96	96	–	1438	1178	754
4	96	79	96	–	1501	1034	100	96	100	–	1260	799
5	100	100	96	96	–	1256	100	100	92	88	–	778
6	96	100	100	100	100	–	100	100	92	96	96	–
Linguistic condition												
1	–	1029	1078	1079	1065	944	–	1442	1329	1292	1134	859
2	92	–	1544	1739	1469	1177	92	–	1645	1624	1432	1159
3	100	83	–	1784	1696	1242	100	96	–	1749	1373	1049
4	96	100	92	–	1638	1482	100	96	92	–	1808	866
5	100	100	100	96	–	1274	100	100	96	96	–	887
6	96	100	100	100	96	–	100	100	96	96	100	–

[a] S = stick.

Analyses of variance were performed on each subject's mean for a given pair, using Question and Pair as within factors and Age and Condition as between factors. All four factors and the Question–Pair interaction were statistically significant ($p < .01$).

We shall examine these and other factors in more detail below. However, scanning any matrix reveals obvious trends that bear on the models: the RTs generally, decrease and the proportion of correct responses increases with the distance or number of steps between sticks. End-anchor effects are apparent and interact with the comparative term used in the question: if the label of the stick corresponds to the question or if the pair contains a 1 or a 6 stick, RT is faster and answering is more accurate. These facts are consistent with Potts' (1972) finding on adults' inference times in a paragraph context as all his inferences contain end anchors; the interaction is consistent with Clark's (1969) congruence principle of question–premise matching in three-term series problems with adult subjects. A more detailed analysis of these effects follows.

Inference Tests

The RTs and proportion of correct responses on the tests that did not involve end-anchor sticks (1 or 6) were compared. Here the key variable was distance or inferential step size [0 for training pairs, 1 for pairs, (2, 4) or (3, 5), and 2 for pair (2, 5)]. Averaging over pairs of the same distance, the data strongly supported the assumption that subjects were using a representation involving a linear order during testing. The RT's decreased and proportion of correct responses increased as the number of middle terms between sticks increased. Only one slope out of the 18 (i.e., 0–1 and 1–2 slopes) failed to show this: the 6-year-old subjects responded more quickly (and made slightly fewer errors) on their training pair tests in the Linguistic condition. The 18 slope differences can be observed in Fig. 3 and Table 5, which shows the mean RT and proportion correct for each condition and age group as a function of step size.

The mean proportion of correct responses and mean RT for each subject for each pair having either 0, 1, or 2 inferential steps (excluding end-anchor pairs) were analyzed in an analysis of variance with Age and Condition as between factors and Step and Question as within factors. Both analyses yielded essentially the same results. Age, Condition, and Step were significant ($p < .01$). No interactions were significant in the RT data; an Age $\times$ Condition interaction ($p < .01$) was found for proportion of correct responses and is discussed below (see Table 6).

Returning to Table 5 and Fig. 3, it can be seen that RTs decline and correct responses increase with distance between sticks. This trend holds

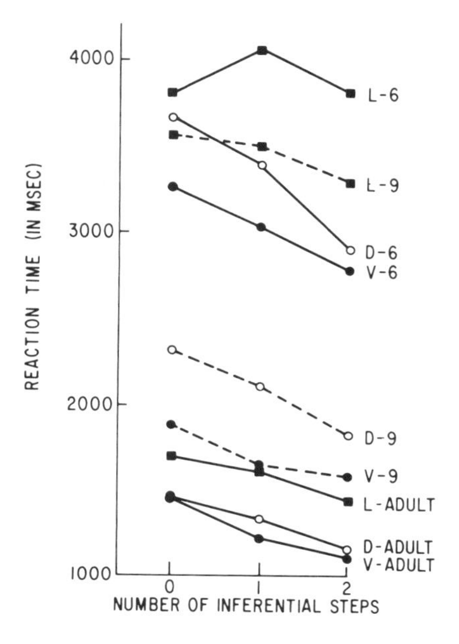

FIG. 3. Speed in answering inference test questions: mean reaction time for each condition and age group (L = linguistic, D = display, and V = visual).

TABLE 5
Percentage of Correct Responses for Each Age Group and Condition as a Function of the Number of Inferential Steps

		Number of steps		
Age	Condition	0	1	2
6 years	Linguistic	77	70	72
	Display	96	97	97
	Visual	91	91	99
9 years	Linguistic	88	80	89
	Display	93	97	95
	Visual	89	94	97
Adult	Linguistic	92	98	100
	Display	93	90	100
	Visual	89	96	100

TABLE 6
Percentage Correct Responses for All Test Trials: Age x Condition

	Condition		
Age	Linguistic	Display	Visual
6 yr	80	94	95
9 yr	87	95	95
Adult	97	96	96

across age groups: the visual and display conditions were processed both more accurately and faster than the linguistic condition.

The trends across the three conditions and ages for distance support the assumption of a linear order with spatial reference. Regardless of training, adjacent pairwise input led to the same kind of data as was obtained when subjects read information directly off of a physical display containing ordered size and distance information. The 6-year-old data and developmental implications are discussed below.

The Age $\times$ Condition interaction from the accuracy data analyses ($p < .01$) is shown in Table 6. The proportion of correct responses is very high and indistinguishable across age groups in the display and visual conditions. Only the linguistic condition shows a developmental trend. We suspect that the primary difficulty of the younger children in this condition has to do with an inability to generate a spatial representation from linguistic information alone. They clearly can map the language onto a physical referent for they succeed in all other conditions as well as older children and adults. Their failure, then, would seem to be from memory overload and isolation of end-anchor pairs. When the feedback is only linguistic, the only information available for the isolation of the ends of the scale are labels: find that stick which is called only shorter or only longer. This necessitates holding in memory several pairs, eliminating those elements that have two comparative functions, and narrowing down the set to the two colors that have one function. In the visual condition, this can be done by noting the absolute length or by linguistic analysis; in the display condition, spatial and length information are available. Many of the 6-year-old subjects in the linguistic condition claimed that they knew each pair but kept getting them mixed up. This suggests that at the point of testing, some 6 year olds were still in the process of integrating and were tested while they were trying to hold in memory five separate pieces of information. When they were provided with spatial reference, they performed as well as older subjects, indicating that mapping language onto a scale is not a mediation deficiency here (Flavell, 1971). As originally claimed by Bryant and Trabasso (1971), memory is one locus of difficulty in these tasks for young children.

End-Anchor Effects

If a subject integrates information into a linear order using spatial reference in his representation, certain "end-anchor" effects can be expected. In training, the end pairs, (1, 2) and (5, 6), should be more easily learned, and as seen in Figure 2 and Table 1, this has been found. In testing, end-anchor tests can be expected to be responded to more accurately and readily. This has also been found. Table 7 shows the mean percentage correct responding and mean RT s for end-anchor pairs (those involving Sticks 1 or 6), nonanchor training [(2, 3) or (3, 4) or (4, 5)] pairs, and inferential [(2, 5) or (2, 4) or (3, 5)] test pairs as a function of age group.

The end-anchor test RTs, excluding pair (1, 6), were analyzed by an analysis of variance with Age and Condition as between-subject factors and Anchor (Stick 1 or 6), Step (distances of 0, 1, 2, or 3 intervening sticks), and Question as within factors. The data for each subject were the RT to a given question averaged over left–right positions. The analysis yielded the same significant main effects on end anchors as on other pairs ($p < .01$): Age, Condition, and Step. In addition, an anchor effect was

TABLE 7
Accuracy and Speed of Responding on Types of Test Pairs for Each Age Group

Age	Type of pair		
	End anchor	Adjacent	Inferential
Percent correct			
6 yrs	93	88	87
9 yrs	93	90	92
Adult	98	92	96
Reaction time (msec)			
6 yrs	2466	3582	3402
9 yrs	1609	2590	2356
Adult	1021	1535	1341

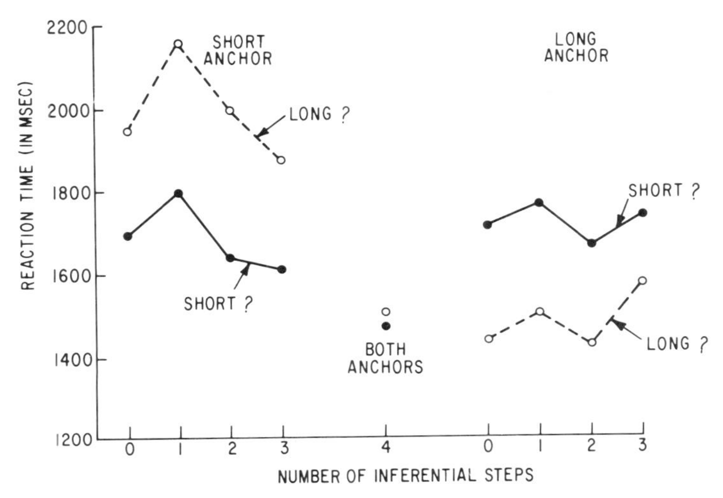

FIG. 4. End-anchor results: mean reaction time (RT) to answer different comparative questions on pairs varying in distance and as a function of which anchor was present.

found with the long stick being responded to faster by an average 333 msec than the short stick.

Three interactions were also significant ($p < .01$). The significant interactions were Anchor × Step, Anchor × Question, and Age × Condition. The first two interactions are displayed in Figure 4. When the anchor that was displayed in the test matched the question, RT was faster. This result is consistent with Clark's (1969) principle of congruence (when the question and premise comparatives match, the problem is easier for adults). This result constitutes the Anchor × Question interaction. Note, also, that when both anchors were present [pair (1, 6) or step = 4 in Figure 4], no difference was found as a function of question.

Unlike the inference tests referred to above, the training pairs or Step 0 pairs involving end anchors, (1, 2) and (5, 6), were faster than other, more distant, pairs. Furthermore, distance or step affected tests involving the short but not the long anchor. This is the Step × Anchor interaction.

The Anchor factor and the Anchor × Question interaction results suggest that linguistic factors (markedness) played a role in end-anchor tests. First, longer questions were answered faster. In addition, the colors were coded "long" or "short" and if the question matched the name of the end anchor present, processing was faster. If they mismatched, the long anchor might have been recoded, say as "not short," and a choice made since the times for this anchor were parallel and independent of distance. Although recoding may have occurred for the short anchor, the distance effect suggests that subjects used spatial information in answering the questions when it was present. This difference in processing suggests that the short end of the scale is not as clearly coded and although this variable is related to markedness, it is unclear why one would expect such a difference in processing.

The pattern of results suggests that subjects did not engage in deductive reasoning at the time of test in order to make comparative length inferences. The assertion that they integrate the pairwise relations into a linear order having spatial properties during training and then use this representation in testing is fully consistent with the data.

Memory and Reasoning

In discussing the one deviation in the data from the expectation of the linear order assumption, we noted that the 6-year-old subjects' retention of the premises was related to their success in making inferences. This relation, we noted, was consistent with Bryant and Trabasso's (1971) assertion that failure of "preoperational" children in transitive reasoning tasks could be a failure in retrieval of the premises rather than reasoning because their accessibility would be a precondition for either deductive coordination or integration. We examined this correlation for 16 conditions previously studied (Bryant & Trabasso, 1971, five conditions; three unpublished conditions on 4 year olds by Bryant and Trabasso, two of which were data from retraining of the 4-year-old subjects of their published study with visual feedback; Lutkus & Trabasso, 1974, two conditions; Riley & Trabasso, 1974, six conditions). The correlation between correct responding on the adjacent pairs and the one-step inference pair in testing was extremely high, $r = .89$ ($p < .01$).

At the very least, retention of the premises, in some form, is critical to inference behavior. Since this kind of memory has been shown here to be developmental, prior studies on transitivity clearly confound both memory and inferential processes.

Representation, Memory, and Inference Making

In order to avoid confusion about interpretation, we do not necessarily intend representation to mean "re-presentation" of sensory events. Instead, we intend to use "representation" in the sense used by information-processing theorists (Newell & Simon, 1972). An internal representation is a symbolic entity, containing elements that are related to one another in some defined way, which is constructed by the person in response to task demands and stored in memory for related purposes. This representation is constructed by processing stimuli and can be used to construct other representations, access descriptive information, and retrieve properties of elements in response to inferential questions.

Not all information is contained in this representation. For example, the fact that subjects were slower to retrieve adjacent pairs than to answer inferential questions suggests that they did not access by pairs even though they did so several times in training. In one sense, the pair alone information was not used during testing. This was presumably because the subjects integrated the pairwise information into a linear, spatial order and the form of the original information was no longer available. This result is consistent with Craik and Lockhart's (1972) depth of processing argument: the more elaborate and longer lasting memory representation is that which involved "deeper" processing.

Relation of the Present Work to the Adult Literature

The more recent work in prose contexts by Barclay (1973), Potts (1972), and Scholz and Potts (1974) strongly supports the assertion that adults use imaginal, linguistic, or spatial strategies to integrate and order premise information and that this is done in response to memory demands. Barclay (1973) has shown that this integration is subject controlled. He gives such information as: "The cow is to the left of the horse," "The elephant is to the right of the horse," etc. Under instructions to construct an integrated scheme, adults falsely recognized such sentences as "The elephant is to the right of the cow," whereas if they are told to rote memorize the premises, few false recognitions occur.

Potts (1972) independently derived a spatial integration model of the type presented here. In his study, subjects heard statements relating four elements: "The bear was smarter than the hawk; the hawk was smarter than the wolf; and the wolf was smarter than the deer." He found, using RT s, that the end-anchor (bear, deer) pairs were responded to faster than the middle pair (hawk, wolf). Although his data were consistent with the model, all nonadjacent pairs were also end anchored.

Scholz and Potts (1972) recognized this confound and used the procedure of presenting six terms rather than four. They report error data rather than RT, but the results are similar to ours. Subjects were more accurate in answering questions on elements further apart.

The Nature of Information in the Linear Order

The above data indicated distance (in terms of number of intermediate items) between the members in the linear order was a critical factor in the ease of making decisions about ordinal comparisons. Physical size and physical distance in the Display condition were correlated so that it could not be decided which property was used. Likewise, in the other conditions, it was possible that size rather than distance determined the decision time.

It is possible for subjects to store absolute size information separately and, when asked a question, to retrieve this information from separate stores, generate a pair of sizes, compare them, and respond. If so, then RT data similar to ours will be found but the mechanism will not be that operating on a linear order representation. A good example of this is found in a recent study by Moyer (1973), who has asked people to compare the sizes of different animals and has found that RT decreases linearly with an increase in the relative size differences between the animals. For example, the time taken to decide whether a bird is larger than a bee is shorter than the time taken to decide whether a dog is larger than a raccoon. Moyer interprets his data as supporting the idea that subjects use spatial images in comparison. It seems unlikely, however, that people have integrated all sizes of animals into a linear ordering; it is more plausible that we have size information stored in our knowledge of the world and can retrieve this (as images?) and generate comparisons. Variability in size may be a factor also, as dogs are more variable than bees. If so, the subjects may be slower because they would have to find an average, prototypic dog and this may take longer if the range of sizes is large.

It is possible, therefore, that in the visual condition, subjects retrieved absolute size information for each stick and compared these directly in their imagery rather than constructing a linear order during training. Although this is less likely in the linguistic condition, it is possible that subjects generated sizes for each color instead of ordering them and then used this generated size to make comparisons.

Because we did not have any psychophysical data for the sticks, used in this experiment, we examined the role that size and distance factors might have played in a simple experiment that varied these two factors independently. Two conditions were run with six college students serving as subjects in each condition. In both conditions, we presented the 60 test pairs of all possible colors, asking both kinds of comparative questions and controlling for position. In each condition, the size or distance information was physically displayed to the left of the apparatus. The procedure follows that used in the display condition of the main experiment reported above.

In the size condition, a pair of sticks was shown about 1 inch apart. The sticks differed in absolute height and were colored differently. Over the set of test trials, the difference in height varied from 1 to 5 inches, corresponding to the absolute size differences for the pairs in the display condition of the main experiment. Although for a given pair color was critical to decide which stick was longer (or shorter), over trials the pair of colors were uncorrelated with size.

In the distance condition, six differently colored sticks of the same height (all were 7 inches high) were displayed left to right, 1 inch apart, in a plastic case. This presentation was analogous to the display condition but with the size differences nonvisible. Subjects were told that the leftmost stick was the tallest and the rightmost was the shortest, or vice versa.

Subjects answered the 15 possible questions (based on the 15 combinations of the six sizes or six colors taken two at a time). In the Size condition, only a pair of sticks were compared on absolute height; in the distance condition, a pair of sticks were compared on imaginary height in a display of six equally high but ordered sticks so that only distance was correlated with height.

Table 8 gives the mean RTs (in msec) for the two conditions. For the distance group, these are shown separately for each question because that variable interacted with test pair ($p < .01$); it did not do so for the size group. Statistical analyses on step effects (0, 1 or 2) without end-anchor pairs showed that RTs decreased significantly ($p < .05$) in the distance (the respective means were 1551, 1370, and 1313) but not in the size (means = 803, 804, 817) condition. End-anchor effects for the distance were virtually identical to those found for the Display groups, whereas the size group showed no end-anchor effects except for step. In the size condition, unlike both the distance and display, Step 0 (the two adjacent pairs on the ends) took the longest; RT's for the other steps did not differ statistically in the size condition.

These results lend further support to the linear order assumption with a spatial reference. It is as if subjects scan an internal display and isolate pairs using distance information. Items that are close together are less discriminable than those further apart. The negative findings from the size condition argue against an interpretation that subjects retrieve or generate absolute lengths of the sticks from the colors, at least insofar as size differences do not produce the confusions that distance does.

Further Evidence on the Distance Relation and Linear Order

In order to show that an internal representation of a linear order is processed in a way similar to that of an internal, spatial, linear array, we ran yet another experiment on college students. There were two experimental conditions and each condition included six subjects. In order to increase the reliability of individual subject data, we increased the number of tests on the nonanchor pairs.

TABLE 8
Mean Reaction Time (msec) on the 15 Test Pairs for Each Question in the Distance Condition and on the 15 Pairs in the Size Condition

	Shorter?						Longer?				
Stick	2	3	4	5	6	Stick	2	3	4	5	6
Distance Condition											
1	696	754	759	711	690	1	1027	1283	1088	1046	700
2		1658	1286	1323	874	2		1465	1456	1305	684
3			1453	1507	988	3			1580	1233	644
4				1778	1066	4				1372	689
5					981	5					687
Size condition											
1	862	784	784	849	789						
2		764	783	837	780						
3			814	826	831						
4				831	841						
5					897						

In each condition, each subject received a total of 168 test trials, divided into eight blocks of 21 trials each. The 21 trials involved the same nine end-anchor tests as before but the non-end-anchor tests were repeated twice. Thus there was a total of eight tests per subject on each end-anchor pair and 16 tests per subject on each of the other pairs. The test series counterbalanced questions and positions of the colored sticks, as before. The trials were randomized within blocks.

We replicated the distance condition of the previous study. That is, during the test series, the subject saw displayed a row of six 8-inch sticks, each of a different color (blue, red, green, white, yellow, and orange), arranged in a Plexiglas holder, 1 inch apart. The position of the colors was counterbalanced via a Latin square design over the six subjects. Half of the subjects were told that the shortest stick was on the left and that the sticks increased in size from left to right but that they were sunken into the box so as to appear the same height. The other half of the subjects were told that the longest stick was on the left, etc. They were then tested using the same reaction-time apparatus as in the main experiment.

A second group of six subjects, called the Serial group, learned a list of six color names in serial order via the method of anticipation. The subjects were shown six 8-inch sticks, one at a time, and had to predict which color would come next.

Half of the subjects were told that the first stick was to be considered the longest and that each stick was progressively shorter; the other half were given the opposite instruction. After correctly anticipating the list once, each subject was asked to repeat the list. The six colors were counterbalanced in position over the subjects in a Latin square design. The subjects were tested as in the main experiment on the reaction-time choice apparatus. In both conditions, all subjects were given 15 practice test trials that were not analyzed.

The median RT of correct responses for each subject was used in the analysis in order to minimize effects of extreme scores. The mean of the medians for each cell and for each condition is given in Table 9.

The analysis of the data in Table 9 yielded the same reliable effects as in the main developmental experiment. Analyses of variance were performed on (1) pairs in the main diagonal of Table 9, (2) non-end-anchor pairs (steps sizes of 0, 1, or 2) and (3) end-anchor pairs. The first analysis showed that the main diagonal pairs differed significantly and these interacted with question ($p < .01$). When the question was "Shorter?" the order (from fastest to slowest) was (1, 2), (5, 6), (3, 4), (2, 3), and (4, 5); when "Longer?" it was (5, 6), (4, 5), (1, 2), (3, 4) and (2, 3). Thus end-anchor and congruence effects were found as well as serial position effects, with the exception that (3, 4) was faster than (2, 3) and (4, 5).

The distance analysis centers on the non-end-anchor pairs. Here a Question effect ($p < .01$) was found: "Longer?" was faster, and distance was statistically reliable ($p < .01$). Table 10 gives the mean RT for the median scores. In Table 10 it can be seen that RT decreased for both conditions as a function of the distance between sticks. All differences within a condition were reliable by individual comparisons ($p < .01$).

TABLE 9
Mean Reaction Time (msec) on Test Trials for the Serial and Distance Conditions

	Serial						Distance				
Stick	2	3	4	5	6	Stick	2	3	4	5	6
1	1206	1094	1124	978	876	1	1043	978	936	795	734
2		1703	1351	1148	1036	2		1318	1156	1035	888
3			1418	1101	960	3			1242	1094	816
4				1458	1006	4				1250	868
5					946	5					910

TABLE 10
Mean Reaction Time (msec) for the Serial and Distance Conditions

	Number of intervening sticks (steps)		
Condition	0	1	2
Serial	1526	1226	1148
Distance	1270	1125	1035

The end-anchor analysis yielded the same results as those shown in Figure 4 of the main study. It is not discussed further here.

The important finding is that the RT s pattern themselves very much like those in the main experiment when the input is (1) a linear order or (2) a spatial linear array without size information. This convergence of data suggests that subjects used the same underlying representation for processing all the order information, regardless of the form in which it had been encountered: (1) by adjacent pairs with only verbal comparative relation; (2) by adjacent pairs with visual feedback; (3) by spatial, linear arrays with size and distance information; (4) by spatial linear arrays with only distance information; (5) by strict serial, linear order; or (6) by differences in age across (1), (2), or (3) above.

This assertion was tested by comparing the test data for 12 conditions for the main and two lesser experiments (the average data for conditions in Tables 2, 3, 4, 8, and 9). Data from the size condition in Table 8 were excluded because they did not reflect linear order effects.

In order to show comparable relations among the test data across conditions, the following analysis was performed. First, we ranked the mean RT s for the 15 test cells in each condition from 1 to 15, where 1 was the fastest RT. Then we calculated a Kendall coefficient of concordance on the ranks for the 12 conditions. The coefficient was highly reliable: $W = .89$ [χ^2 $(14) = 150$, $p < .001$], showing strong agreement across the 12 different conditions on the order of the test pair RTs.

Figure 5 depicts this relationship pictorially and summarizes all the information that went into the coefficient computation. That is, Figure 5 shows the rank of the test pair for each condition plotted against the rank of the average rank across conditions for each test pair. The conditions are lettered by the order in which they are reported in Tables 2, 3, 4, 8, and 9, so that A = average 6-year visual condition tests and L = average distance tests for college students.

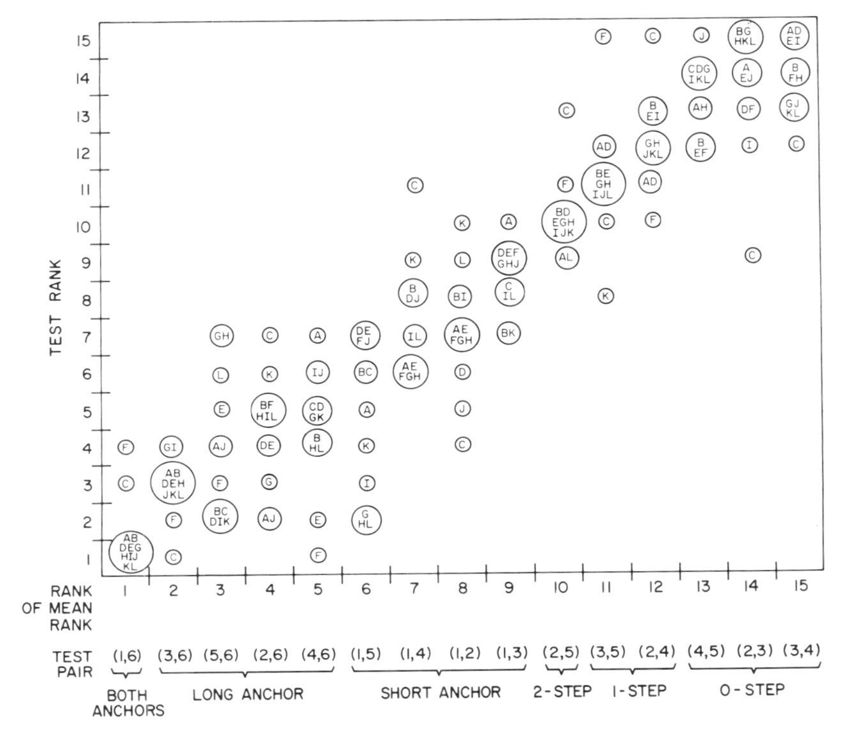

FIG. 5. The rank of each test pair for each condition, where test pairs are ranked in order of their average rank across conditions. The letters correspond to the conditions in the order in which they are reported in Tables 2, 3, 4, 8, and 9.

In Figure 5, one can see visually the strength of the relationship among the conditions, viz., the general linear relation in the graph and the relative small spread of the ranks for each pair across conditions.

The ranks of the average ranks of a test pair across conditions reveal the salient findings reported above in the several analyses of variance. Note that the order on the abscissa shows that (1) the end-anchor test pair (1, 6) is the faster pair overall, (2) followed by the four test pairs involving the long anchor, (3) followed by the four test pairs involving the short anchor, and (4) followed by the pairs of distance 2, 1, and 0, in that order, with the latter being the slowest pairs across all conditions.

Figure 5 thus, succinctly shows the end-anchor, unmarked anchor, and distance effects across the 12 different conditions. The clearest deviations are the 6-year-old (Condition C) and 9-year-old (Condition F) linguistic groups. Otherwise, the data attest quite strongly to the assertion made above, namely, that people use common, spatial, linear orderings to represent the ordinal information contained in these tasks.

Developmental Implications

We should like to conclude our discussion on a developmental note. We believe that we have shown that both children and adults use a common underlying representation—a linear order of a spatial nature—to integrate comparative relations among events. The central problem for the youngest children centers on their ability to find a representation for this information when it is only linguistic in form since they can easily map the relations onto displays or integrate adjacent pairs into a linear order when the feedback is visual.

The use of an underlying linear order for processing comparatives has been anticipated both by Bower (1971) and by Wales and Campbell (1970). Bower has also pointed out an important developmental question, namely, that the order of acquisition of comparative terms may depend on how directly they refer to actual physical dimensions. That is, children may acquire "bigger–smaller" and "taller–shorter" sooner than "happier—sadder" or "nicer–meaner" because the former have direct dimensional reference to physical objects whereas the latter do not. These comparatives are currently being studied by Christine Riley.

ACKNOWLEDGMENTS

This research was supported by Research Grant No. 19223 from the National Institute of Mental Health, United States Public Health Service to T. Trabasso. A paper based on this research was presented at the Eastern Psychological Association Meeting, May, 1973.

REFERENCES

Barclay, J. R. The role of comprehension in remembering sentences. *Cognitive Psychology,* 1973, **4,** 229–254.

Bower, G. H. Adaptation-level coding of stimuli and serial position effects. In M. H. Appley (Ed.), *Adaptation-level theory.* New York: Academic Press, 1971.

Bryant, P. E., & Trabasso, T. Transitive inferences and memory in young children. *Nature,* 1971, **232,** 456–458.

Burt, C. The development of reasoning in school children. *Journal of Experimental Pedagogy,* 1919, **5,** 68–77.

Clark, H. H. Linguistic processes in deductive reasoning. *Journal of Experimental Psychology,* 1969, **76,** 387–404.

Craik, F. I. M., & Lockhart, R. S. Levels of processing: A framework for memory research. *Journal of Verbal Learning & Verbal Behavior,* 1972, **11,** 671–684.

DeSoto, C. B., & Bosley, J. G. The cognitive structure of a social structure. *Journal of Abnormal & Social Psychology,* 1962, **64,** 303–307.

DeSoto, C. B., London, M., & Handel, S. Social reasoning and spatial paralogic. *Journal of Personality & Social Psychology,* 1965, **2,** 513–521.

Ebenholtz, S. M. Position mediated transfer between serial learning and a spatial discrimination task. *Journal of Experimental Psychology,* 1965, **65,** 603–608.

Flavell, J. H. Stage-related properties of cognitive development. *Cognitive Psychology,* 1971, **2,** 421–453.

Huttenlocher, J. Constructing spatial images: A strategy in reasoning. *Psychological Review,* 1968, **75,** 550–560.

Johnson-Laird, P. N. The three-term series problem. *Cognition,* 1972, **1,** 57–82.

Lutkus, A. D., & Trabasso, T. Transitive inferences in preoperational retarded adolescents. *American Journal of Mental Deficiency,* 1974, **78,** 599–606.

Moyer, R. S. Comparing objects in memory: Evidence suggesting an internal psychophysics. *Perception & Psychophysics,* 1973, **13,** 180–184.

Moyer, R. S., & Landauer, T. K. Time required for judgements of numerical inequality. *Nature,* 1967, **215,** 1519–1520.

Murdock, B. B., Jr. The distinctiveness of stimuli. *Psychological Review,* 1960, **67,** 16–31.

Newell, A., & Simon, H. A. *Human problem solving.* Englewood Cliffs, N.J.: Prentice-Hall, 1972.

Piaget, J. Une forme verbal de la comparison chez l'enfant. *Archives de Psychologie,* 1921, 141–172.

Piaget, J. *Judgment and reasoning in the child.* London: Routledge & Kegan Paul, 1928.

Piaget, J. *Genetic epistemology.* Translated by Eleanor Duckwork. New York: Columbia University Press, 1970.

Piaget, J., Inhelder, B., & Szeminska, A. *The child's conception of geometry.* London: Routledge & Kegan Paul, 1960.

Potts, G. R. Information processing strategies used in the encoding of linear orderings. *Journal of Verbal Learning & Verbal Behavior,* 1972, **11,** 727–740.

Riley, C. A., & Trabasso, T. Comparatives, logical structures and encoding in a transitive inference task. *Journal of Experimental Child Psychology,* 1974, **17,** 187–203.

Scholz, K. W., & Potts, G. R. Cognitive processing of linear orderings. *Journal of Experimental Psychology,* 1974, **102,** 323–326.

Wales, R. J., & Campbell, R. N. On the development of comparison and the comparison of development. In G. B. Flores d'Arcais & W. J. M. Levelt (Eds.), *Advances in psycholinguistics.* Amsterdam: North-Holland Publ., 1970.

9

INFERENCE AS A DEVELOPMENTAL CONSTRUCTION

James Youniss
Catholic University of America

There are several reasonable ways to approach the fact that young children generally do not make transitive inferences whereas older children do. In the present paper, inference making shall be looked at from a Piagetian developmental perspective. Inference is seen to follow from the logical property of transitivity and transitivity is viewed as consequent to the notion of serial order. In sum, "transitive inference" is described as a further step in a long-term structuring process that has a regularity and appears to be under the child's control.

This point of view is illustrated with empirical results of children's judgments of length. These data exemplify two general points about structuring. One concerns the idea that there is an interior order to the child's constructions. This is shown by contingency relations between serial order and transitive inference. The other concerns inference as an operational achievement. Data are presented suggesting a methodological criterion for this concept. Finally, results are reported with respect to children's measurement of length and its implication for the transition from qualitative to quantitative transitivity notions.

Before results of four experiments are presented, key elements of Piaget's theory are reviewed. These include ideas about the nature of mental objects and how they come to be known in their static and operative aspects. Second, transitivity is considered as a logical property of mental actions applied to the domain of length. Third, the concept of measurement is discussed in the context of operations. These points are first illustrated in an example observation from Piaget's study of geometrical concepts. They are then elaborated on with observations from this laboratory.

TRANSITIVE INFERENCE

Piaget has discussed inference in several works; this chapter draws mainly from Piaget, Inhelder, and Szeminska (1960), Beth and Piaget (1966), and Piaget and Inhelder (1971). The study of transitivity has generally been restricted to length so that content area will be dealt with here.

In one common situation, Piaget showed children two lines that were not clearly discriminable in length from visual inspection alone. Children were asked to decide which of the two lines was longer or taller. In another situation, children were shown two towers made of blocks—one tower stood on a short table and was composed of large blocks; the other tower stood on a higher table and consisted of smaller blocks. Again the children were asked to determine the relative heights of the two.

In these experiments children were given a variety of opportunities to use a middle or common term to evaluate the relative lengths. They were given string, cardboard, or paper. In one case they were asked to use their fingers "to walk along the two lines." In other cases, they were given such measuring devices as index cards—one line was compared with a card marked off in 3-cm steps and the other line was measured against a card marked off in 6-cm steps. These middle terms were supplemented with such verbal interchanges as: "Can you be certain just by looking?" "Count the number of steps it takes to walk along both lines." "Would it help to use the string?"

The general observations were as follows. Some children were content to judge relative length by using only visual inspection. Others employed their own body as a middle term, employing arm or finger span or gauging one length with a hand spread and carrying it over to the other tower. All of these devices, of course, fall short of producing precise and certain length judgments. In distinction, other children utilized the materials offered as middle terms and undertook kinds of measurements that could be transferred without change across two heights and therefore could serve as logical middle terms. That is, using these materials children could arrive at a sure judgment of the form: $A < M$, $M < B$, therefore $A < B$.

LENGTH AS A MENTAL OBJECT

Piaget has discussed children's understanding of length from two aspects. The first is in terms of length as a physical feature of things, perceptible in configurations. The child can experience length directly, abstract and generalize it, and learn names and functions for it from adult mentors. Length can also be known in a logical–mathematical sense. The child abstracts from his actions and coordinates these abstractions into length, producing mental transformations. Length, in this nonconfigurational sense, is a mental object constructed by the child.

The transformations that produce length are guided by two factors. One is the coordination of the mental actions, which produces intensive properties. This structuring process is called "reflective abstraction" (Piaget, 1971, p. 320). The other guide is the configurational feature of length themselves; to be adaptive, a child's mental structuring should be in line with extensional length as it appears in objects. The properties of the transformational structure must be consistent within themselves and also applicable to objects in the environment.

The knowledge of length, which begins in logical–mathematical abstractions from actions, is called the operative aspect (Piaget, 1966). It is differentiated from the configural aspect in the same way that transformation is distinguished from state. This distinction recognizes that objects are known both according to the actions that bring them about and according to their static appearances.

Piaget's study of length has stressed the operative aspect. He has looked at the child's constructions of logical operations. In focusing on intensional changes, Piaget has attempted to describe the development of the child's knowledge in an orderly sequence as it might be autonomous or self-directed rather than due to exogeneous factors of instruction, language, and the like.

This viewpoint puts length in the category of other mental objects, such as relations in general, for example, order, number. The child's knowledge of them develops as he reflects on his own actions and how they come to produce certain extensional situations. This development can be found in identifying structures or operations that the child initially applies to concrete situations and later formalizes at a propositional level. It follows from this viewpoint that these mental objects are not simply in the external environment to be identified and discriminated. The child puts them there by reflecting on his actions and understanding how he can bring objects into being. As his structurings of these abstractions change so do the objects themselves.

TRANSITIVITY

Piaget has discussed transitivity in several different contexts. The most familiar one concerns "spontaneous measurement" in his study of geometrical conceptions (Piaget *et al.,* 1960). Piaget (1971) discusses the operational grasp of transitivity in terms of two characteristics of logical–mathematical structures—"closure" and "necessity" (p. 316). In Beth and Piaget (1966) "transitivity" exemplifies "self-evidence" and "invention" (pp. 191–192).

Empirical evidence from children indicates that the property of transitivity comes late in the development of relations. For example, young children recognize length as a relation between two terms but fail to understand an order or series. Given lengths to seriate, they work with individual pairs. Each pair represents a length relation but relations between pairs are ignored.

Subsequently, older children recognize order and can construct a complete series of an asymmetrical relation. Given rods to seriate, the child can put them in order from shortest to tallest. Any pair of rods correctly exemplifies a consistent length relation and so do the transitional steps between any two pairs.

Transitivity enters into this relational structuring when the passage among three terms in a series is understood. A particular term in the series is no longer viewed as having a one-way relation but is recognized as bearing on two directions simultaneously. For example, term B is seen as being taller than term A and shorter than term C. In effect B has the character of a middle term. More generally, each term in a series is recognized as a potential middle term since it is taller than all items preceding it and shorter than all terms that follow.

Two Types

Transitivity is an ordinal qualitative property. It has a logical character because terms in the domain of this property bear necessary relations with each other. Given parts of a series two terms at a time with an overlapping middle term, the person can make an inference which must be true for the relations among all the terms.

Qualitative transitivity is an achievement of concrete operational structuring. It is dependent upon earlier structuring including, among other things, a kind of conservation of the middle term. For instance, in applying a middle term B to other terms, the child must view it as maintaining itself as it is compared alternately with other terms. He could do otherwise, for example, by treating B as taller in the relation $A < B$ and as shorter in $B < C$. In this case the relation of A to C is not ascertainable because B's length is variable and contingent on discrete comparisons with other terms.

There is a second type of transitive relation that enters developmentally with the idea of "measurement." With measurement it is presumed that the child mentally decomposes length into units so that each individual length to be evaluated is composed of these units. The middle term then takes on the features of a measuring implement. Inferences made from its comparisons with other terms rest on transitive inequalities, which can be abbreviated as "quantitative transitivity."

The ideas of closure of a relational structure and necessity are seen more clearly at this level. Not only are terms in a series definitely related as a whole but each term has an internal relationship—it is composed of N units—which is applicable to all others. For instance, term B can be known as term $A + X$ and term C can be known as $B + X$, etc. It would follow that C must have more units than A in that B is the middle term in a logical sense because it has an intermediate number of units.

MEASUREMENT

Measurement is a pervasive concept in much of Piaget's work on concrete operational intelligence. It represents a kind of precision which enters into thinking once operations become formed. Its appearance cooccurs with children's recognition that relations among objects must be true. Measurement, however, remains an empirically undertappad area that may yield insights about the further development of formal operations.

With respect to length and transitivity, measurement seems to rely on the basic idea that length is a product of unit iteration. The child who can decompose a given length into unit form and then see the unit as moveable yet maintaining its constancy is open to the quantification aspect of operations.

The notion of unit pertains to the internal relations of an object as well as to comparisons among such objects as a measuring rod and another rod. With a stable idea that a given length can be generated through unit iteration, an object being measured and the measuring device need not even look alike but need only share a common internal unit. The child combining transitivity with measurement is able to determine with precision how discretely presented terms are related through a common term. The internal composition of all terms can be a shared frame of reference that allows congruent units to change position yet stay constant. Inference about two terms not directly compared then becomes knowable in a precise way (Piaget *et al.*, 1960).

PREVIOUS EMPIRICAL FINDINGS

Of the several options open for a structural analysis the work in this laboratory focused on three aspects of operative development. An attempt was made to track the development of length in children's structurings from understanding of ordinality, to transitivity, to transitivity plus measurement. This sequence represents a single line of development from a preliminary notion of length to a relatively complete structure. In Piagat's terms, this sequence represents movement into the concrete operational phase of intelligence.

It is admittedly difficult to assess this structural position precisely. There are no standardized procedures or a single criterion to indicate levels of structuring. Moreover, to find a sequence in the technical sense, children should be observed longitudinally.

Three points in the presumed development were examined as follows. The relation between serial order and transitivity as properties of length is clear in Piaget's reasoning. Transitivity should follow seriation sequentially. Transitivity of length requires passage between nonadjacent terms through the intermediary of a common term. Before a particular length can be used as a common term, however, the child must recognize that it bears a dual relation between all terms that precede it and all subsequent terms. Serial ordering requires something less. The child need only recognize that length can be arranged in a continuous asymmetric series. In fact, as he builds an order, let us say, from shortest to tallest, each successive placement adds to a configurational "good figure." The child need only view length as going in one direction so that each term is taller than the term that just preceded it.

This relationship was tested by assessing each child on both properties of length. It was expected that children who would succeed on transitivity should come only from the sample who had also shown success on serial order. Both tasks were arranged, in a pass–fail four-cell contingency table and the cell of "fail seriation but pass transitivity" was expected to contain zero frequency. Put another way, subjects who were successful on transitivity should have come only from the sample who had also shown success on serial order.

Second, an attempt was made to asses transitivity in a manner that could be called operational. A criterion was chosen whereby a subject would have to manifest a transitive inference in more than one material length situation. This was done by employing different kinds of length comparisons as premises when a definite inference could be made about nonadjacent terms. The particular situations are described below. The three variations were (1) $B > C > D$, (2) $B > C = D$, and (3) $B = C > D$. In all three cases, C is a common term for a transitive relationship although the specific length relations vary. Operational transitivity was defined by success in all three situations.

Finally, the point in structuring when qualitative would be followed by quantitative transitivity was examined. The child's measurement of length was employed as the criterion. A child had to make measurements one at a time and then draw an inference about the correct location for a term in a given series. It was expected that children who could do this successfully would come from the sample who had also shown transitivity in a qualitative sense.

Methodology

In our investigation of serial order, a child was presented with five to seven rods differing in length by unequal increments. He was asked to put them in a row. If he did not make a complete serial order, he was shown the complete order by the experimenter. It was taken away and he was asked to replicate it.

Production of an order with either instruction was followed by a second assessment. The child was asked to reconstruct a series in the reverse direction by beginning with the rod which he had previously placed last. A final assessment followed success on these previous steps. With the child's construction before him, he was told to insert a new rod in its correct location in the series. He could insert the rod wherever he thought it belonged.

The rationale for this assessment was to tap understanding of the asymmetrical order of length and the dual directionality of any term. The former was reflected in seriation and its physical reversal, whereas the latter was reflected in the insertion trial.

Transitive inference was tested as follows. The child was presented two rods, *B* and *D*, differing by approximately $\frac{1}{8}$ inch. They were placed on a wooden board in an L shaped form. Both rods touched a 1-inch square block in the bottom-left corner. Both rods were painted blue. The child was asked to estimate which rod was longer or taller and told, "It's hard to tell so I am going to help you."

He was then shown other rods in comparison with *B* and *D*. These comparisons provided premises from which inference about *B*'s and *D*'s relative lengths could be drawn. For example, rod *A* was placed next to *B* so that the child could see and say that $A > B$. Next he was shown $D > E$. Then the middle term, *C*, was placed next to *B* and rotated 90° next to *D*. Here the child saw $B > C$ and $C > D$. The test trial for inference asked the child again which of the two rods remaining on the board was taller, *B* or *D*?

The three material situations used were: (1) $A > B > C > D > E$, (2) $A = B > C = D > E$, and (3) $A > B = C > D = E$. The transitive relation involved in the test trial is underlined. In all three situations *B* can be known as longer than *D* through their relation with the common term, *C*.

This procedure provided a control for the child's possibly designating *B* or *D* in absolute terms as a "tall" or a "short" rod. If *B* and *D* were only compared with *C*, *B* would have been shown to be tall and *D* would have been shown to be short. To call *B* tall again on the test trial the child would not have to understand the transitive relation. To avoid this possibility four premise trials were used that equalized size designations for *B* and *D*. In Situation (1), for instance, *B* is short with respect to *A* and tall with respect to *C*. Furthermore *D* is short with respect to *C* but tall with regard to *E*. Therefore, neither choice term has a biased designation, although they are logically relatable via the common term. The procedure for measurement is described in the last experiment below.

Observations

Two of the experiments have yielded data pertinent to the relation between serial order and transitivity. In Murray and Youniss (1968) 51 children between 5 years 6 months and 8 years 1 month of age met a criterion for operational transitivity while 93 children failed the same criterion measure. Of the 51 successful children, 43 also succeeded on the independent task of seriation; thus, eight children violated our expectation. Looked at from a more general view, a total of 91 children succeeded on all steps in the seriation task. Of these subjects, 43 went on to succeed with transitive inference.

In Youniss and Dennison (1971) only subjects between 5 years 6 months and 7 years 1 month of age showed errors in seriating. Thirty-two children passed the three steps and 32 children failed. The 32 seriators gave the following proportions of correct inferences in two trials each for Situations (1), (2), and (3): .72, .81, and .62. Respective proportions for the nonseriators were: .55, .58, and .61.

Although these data are not exact with respect to the predicted sequence, they illustrate a strong relation between serial order and transitivity. The former can be called a prerequisite for the latter. In both studies, the combined result was that 67 children met criteria for operational transitivity and of these only eight children (all in the first experiment) failed to manifest success on seriation.

With respect to transitivity as a concrete operational achievement three experiments yielded relevant data. In Murray and Youniss (1968) each subject made four test trial judgments in Situations (1), (2), and (3). A criterion of success of at least three correct judgments in each situation ($p = .031$) was set. In Youniss and Murray (1970) each subject made five test trial judgments in each of the three situations. The criterion of success was four correct judgments in at least two of the three situations; 37 of 64 subjects achieved criterion. Twelve subjects were successful in all three situations. In Youniss and Dennison (1971) each subject made two test trial judgments in each of the three situations. Success was defined as six correct inferences in six attempts.

The common age span for these experiments was 7 years 6 months to 9 years 2 months. In the three respective experiments the numbers of subjects who passed the criteria of success in this age span were: 25 of 48; 17 of 32; and 16 of 32. It appears that about 50% of the 112 children seen within this span were capable of manifesting transitivity in an operational sense. In complement, serial ordering taken in our operational sense was passed by about one-half the subjects at around 6 years 6 months of age.

NEW EMPIRICAL FINDINGS

In the scheme followed here, the operative development of length exemplifies how the child's structurings include logical characteristics in a progressive way. Asymmetrical serial order is followed by qualitative transitivity, which is succeeded by quantitative transitivity.

The data reported now focus on this last relation in structuring. We attempted to obtain a better approximation to the assessment of measurement than can be gotten from the premise–conclusion kind of situations described above. The task chosen asked children actually to measure length and then to draw an inference from their own measurements. It was expected that systematic measurement would be manifested by subjects who already understood transitivity in a qualitative sense. Subjects who did not comprehend transitivity were expected to perform measurements in systematically different ways.

The subjects were 9- and 12-year-old Costa Rican rural and urban school children; two ages and two milieus gave four groups with 20 subjects in each. Children were seen in two consecutive sessions. On the first task transitive inference of length was assessed as in the experiments described above; Situations (1) and (2) were used in which the experimenter made all the length comparisons described above as premises. The child made an estimate before and a judgment after the premises. Two test trials with each situation were given for a total of four inferential judgments.

The second problem also involved inference but was set up so that the child had to provide himself with measurement information in order to arrive at an inferential judgment. The task is depicted in Fig. 1; rod *X* was set on the 1-inch block; nine other rods were to its right in serial order. These rods were of differing colors and arranged in unequal sized increments varying from 1 to 3 mm. The child's task was to determine the proper location of rod *X* in the series, and he had to do this under the restriction that rod *X* could not be moved off the block. He was told to take rods out of the series one at a time and, by comparing them one

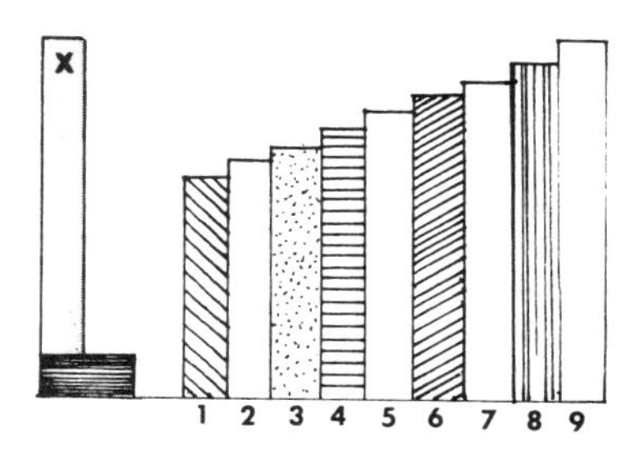

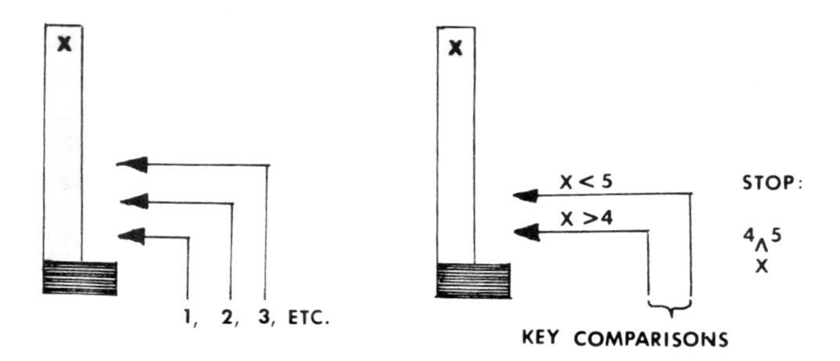

FIG. 1. Description- and information-producing task.

at a time with *X*, to determine *X*'s proper location. On Trial 1, *X* belonged between rods 5 and 6; on Trial 2, *X* belonged between rods 8 and 9.

The task used in this experiment is distinct from the previous studies in important respects. In the prior studies, insertion is part of the seriation procedure. The child is allowed to move the rod across the series and find where it fits. This allows for direct empirical evaluation of the rod's height compared with other rods. He need not be systematic in the same sense as above nor does he have to infer because he looks directly at the "gap" into which the rod fits. In this study, since rod *X* cannot be moved, other rods from the series must be brought to it. Furthermore, because they are brought to *X* one at a time, the child must make comparisons in systematic order and integrate information from two separate comparisons in order to find *X*'s proper location.

Results

Several discernible strategies were observed and they can be summarized into four categories. In Strategy A the child took rods out of the series in no systematic order; he might compare X with rod 1, then with rod 7, then with rod 9, etc. At some point in these mixed comparisons, the child would designate a location, seemingly on an arbitrary basis. In Strategy B a child typically took rods from the series in systematic order starting with rod 1, usually but not always ending with rod 9. He would then locate X's position some distance backward from the end. The approach in Strategy C might be labeled as locating X's position by means of approximation. The child began as in Strategy B to compare rods 1, 2, 3, etc., in order. As he did so, he saw the length differential between X and each succeeding rod getting smaller. He would then, usually after four comparisons, approximate X's location as the next rod or some steps forward. He did not check this out by actually making further comparisons. This strategy can be further broken down into two subcategories; it occurred 50 times in Trials 1 and 2; 23 times it resulted in a wrong location for X while 27 times it resulted in the correct location. The first result will be called "C1" and the second "C2." Although the approaches looked similar, C1 quite often meant that the child had stopped making comparisons at least two steps from X's location or that he overshot the correct position by two steps. In distinction C2 showed a greater control insofar as the child waited until there was almost an equality between X and the last comparison rod.

The remaining Strategy D was unequivocally related to a clear understanding of length. Here, the subject systematically proceeded one by one until he saw, for instance, $X >$ rod 5 and $X <$ rod 6. He then stopped and indicated X's location between rods 5 and 6. Two subcategories were also evident. In one, the child seemed to reconfirm his preceding comparison: When he saw $X > 5$ and $X < 6$, he went back to rod 5, checked that $X >$ rod 5, and then indicated the correct location. In the other, the child not only followed the logical sequence of Strategy D, but he was more efficient from the outset. Instead of beginning the sequence with rod

TABLE 1
Frequencies of Children Employing Different Strategies on the Length Location Task

	Trial 1 strategies					Trial 2 strategies				
Age (yr)	A	B	C1	C2	D	A	B	C1	C2	D
9	4	10	8	4	14	3	4	6	7	20
12	3	12	6	4	15	3	3	3	12	19

TABLE 2
Percentages of Children Using Each Strategy According to Correct Number of Judgments on the Standard Inference Situations

Number of inferences	(*N*)	Trial 1				Trial 2				Better trial			
		A/B	C1	C2	D	A/B	C1	C2	D	A/B	C1	C2	D
0/1/2	(25)	.40	.32	.08	.20	.32	.16	.20	.32	.28	.12	.24	.36
3	(22)	.50	.09	.05	.36	.18	.05	.23	.55	.14	–	.27	.59
4	(33)	.24	.12	.15	.48	.03	.12	.27	.57	.03	.09	.18	.69

1, he estimated X's location in the series and began his first comparison with a rod further in the series, proceeding systematically until he could make an exact location.

For purposes of this chapter, rural and urban children have been grouped. The frequencies of children who followed the various strategies are reported separately for Trials 1 and 2 in Table 1. No age differences are evident on either trial. A between-trial effect is evident in the shift from about a .50–.50 division between incorrect and correct location of X on Trial 1 (A, B, and C1 versus C2 and D) to .25–.75 division on Trial 2. The improved performances on Trial 2 may indicate that for some children the first trial was instructional and that Trial 2 represents more their capability to measure.

The relationship between use of strategies and performance on the standard inference Situations (1) and (2) is reported in Table 2 for Trial 1, Trial 2, and the "better" of the two trials—i.e., the trial on which a particular child showed a more logical strategy. According to our position, transitive inference should be a prior structural condition for the generation of measurement strategies. Subjects catagorized as using Strategies A and B exhibited behavior that gave no indication of transitive understanding of length, whereas Strategy D included patently logical approaches.

The percentages in Table 2 follow a pattern representing this expectation. Children who made fewer (0, 1, or 2) correct judgments on the standard inference task tended to use Strategies A, B, and C1 on Trial 1. They also employed Strategy C2 on Trial 2. Children who made four correct inferences tended to use Strategies C2 and D on Trials 1 and 2 and the best-trial measure; very few of these subjects used strategies that gave no obvious indication of measurement or transitivity after Trial 1.

Although these data are by no means exact as to the inference–measurement relation, they do illustrate the suggested sequence of structuring with respect to length: Serial ordering is an early construction; inference follows later; and still later a capacity for inference with attendant strategies of measurement is evident. Viewing length in this way, the structuring aspect takes on a dominant role of controlling such processes as measurement. In this case measurement includes providing oneself with length information in a systematic way so that a conclusion regarding relative length can be made.

CONCLUSIONS

The data of the four experiments held to make explicit the structuring process outlined by Piaget. The operative aspect of length apparently undergoes development in which certain logical–mathematical properties manifest themselves sequentially. Although the methods used in the present studies are not longitudinal, they yield results depicting contingency relations congruent with Piaget's ideas.

The structuring sequence from serial order to transitivity to inference and to measurement holds up across the present findings. It presumably represents the child's coming to grips with the results of his own actions as he attempts to organize them into a coherent system of transformations. Clearly, while the child is constructing he is also being instructed by adults about refined adjustments to make on the physical world. Such directives from others cannot be discounted. However, it is important to recognize that order across different groups of subjects and cultural milieus speaks forcibly for self-direction in development.

This point remains one of the more interesting in Piaget's position. If logic is neither innately given nor induced from an objective environment, it must come from a third source. Piaget has identified the child himself as the constructing agent who builds logic into his mental action systems by reflecting on each prior step in operational development.

The example of length shows progression from ordinality to transitivity to discovery of units to measurement. Each step in the general structuring relies on its predecessors but not in a causal or linear chain. Rather the idea of coordination with respect to transformations, on the one hand, and their extension to reality, on the other, makes for a joint determination of the logical (Piaget, 1971).

This work represents a beginning step toward understanding the place of logic in psychological processes. In the current literature, there is a strong trend to look more closely at the person's ways of processing information to reach logical conclusions. These efforts have focused on ways in which information is represented by the subject to himself in light of task demands (e.g., Huttenlocher & Higgins, 1972).

As yet the structural perspective and information processing view have not been integrated. These two approaches are clearly not incompatible and, indeed, share many assumptions about the person as a constructor and thinking as a self-directed activity. It seems most important that Piaget's insights into the nature of logic in the psychological domain be at least attended to by contemporary theorists (Youniss & Furth, 1973). It is hoped that the present analysis will aid that endeavor.

ACKNOWLEDGMENTS

The research reported in this paper was partially supported by NICHHD grant No. 02026 and by the Boys Town Center for Youth Development at the Catholic University of America.

REFERENCES

Beth, E. W., & Piaget, J. *Mathematical epistemology and psychology*. Dordrecht: Reidel, 1966.

Huttenlocher, J., & Higgins, E. T. On reasoning, congruence, and other matters. *Psychological Review*, 1972, **79**, 420–427.

Murray, J. P., & Youniss, J. Achievement of transitivity and its relation to serial ordering. *Child Development*, 1968, **39**, 1259–1268.

Piaget, J. Response to Brian Sutton-Smith. *Psychological Review*, 1966, **73**, 111–112.

Piaget, J. *Biology and knowledge*. Chicago: University of Chicago Press, 1971.

Piaget, J., & Inhelder, B. *Mental imagery in the child*. New York: Basic Books, 1971.

Piaget, J., Inhelder, B., & Szeminska, A. *The child's conception of geometry*. New York: Basic Books, 1960.

Youniss, J., & Dennison, A. Figurative and operative aspects of children's inference. *Child Development*, 1971, **42**, 1837–1847.

Youniss, J., & Furth, H. G. Reasoning and Piaget. *Nature*, 1973, **244**, 314–315.

Youniss, J., & Murray, J. P. Transitive inference with nontransitive solutions controlled. *Developmental Psychology*, 1970, **2**, 169–175.

10

OVERVIEW: REASONING, REPRESENTATION, PROCESS, AND RELATED ISSUES

Rachel Joffe Falmagne
Clark University

At the risk of temporarily misrepresenting factual truth but with the benefit of coherence in exposition, I want to state what seems to have been, for some of us, the conceptual framework underlying the study of reasoning. This intuitive rationale is the notion of the child or the adult as having some logical knowledge, identifying how it applies in a specific reasoning task, and, in that case, using a set of rules determined by his present knowledge to transform the initial information he is given into a conclusion. These transformations may correspond to processes of various sorts that will be examined later but need not concern us here. The important points in this conceptualization are that: (*a*) it distinguishes a function of representation of the information (of the verbal problem or, more generally, of the situation to be reasoned about) from the subsequent transformations applied to that representation; (*b*) further, it takes those transformations to be generated in one way or another by the subject's logical knowledge. The obvious analogy is with a machine that operates in a certain code (formal, pictorial, set-theoretic, or other), so that the information has to be encoded or formalized, as is argued below, in the suitable format in order to be processed. Such a conception does not per se preclude feedback loops to be assumed between representation of information and logical processing, but the two functions retain their conceptual separateness even if they cannot be identified strictly with serially organized stages in the process. The theoretical focus then is to characterize those rules and operations used by the subject as reflecting his logical knowledge. Within this perspective, there is an obvious similarity between what studies of reasoning are aiming at and the psycholinguistic enterprise of inferring the subject's linguistic competence. It therefore can be anticipated that the issues pertaining to both contexts will parallel each other.

Although this perspective is not adopted unanimously by all contributors to this volume, it is used as an anchor for organizing empirical results, for recapturing the various processes that have been hypothesized here, and as the first element of a contrast to be outlined later, when an alternative conception is described. A number of distinct, yet related, questions arise from the above formulation and will be discussed in the following sections. The first issue concerns the empirical validation of competence models of the sort outlined above. The second question refers to which type of knowledge, or rules, we should qualify as being logical. More general questions addressed to the conceptual scheme itself will be discussed in the final section.

THE LOCUS OF ERRORS

A familiar methodological facet of the enterprise is that the subject's performance only gives us indirect access to his logical knowledge, granting at this point that he has such knowledge: the relation between competence (as well as any hypothetical construct) and behavior has to be mediated through retrieval, utilization, and response assumptions. Overlooking this distinction led earlier studies to test the validity of Boole's "laws of thought" by examining their adequacy as a description of subjects' performance, a hopeless enterprise as Osherson points out. Confusions of that sort have pervaded the disputes in the earlier literature on reasoning, of which Revlis, Johnson-Laird, and Staudenmayer present a selective review.

With this awareness in mind, the question about competence can be reformulated. Given that subjects do make errors in logical tasks, should those errors be blamed on the input and representation process or on the deductive process (or more generally, in Johnson-Laird's terms, on the process of transformation of information)? Suitable empirical evidence of the type given below can be used to answer that question, although the issue is only partly empirical.

In terms of the framework proposed, data presented in this volume and elsewhere indicate that our a priori analysis of the initial information does not necessarily fit what actually enters the "machine." Scribner (this volume) in a syllogistic task and Bryant and Trabasso (1971) in a situation involving transitivity of length, among others, have shown that the subject may distort or forget the information given. It is interesting to note that the same type of distortion in memory occurs in these two widely different situations (one highly verbal, the other only minimally so). The present point about the uncertainties in the input process is thus clearly relevant to these two traditionally distinct contexts. Bryant and Trabasso's results and results reported by Trabasso, Riley, and Wilson (this volume) indicate that, when memory encoding is secured, the performance of young children in transitivity problems is far superior to what is usually found in developmental data. Relatedly, Scribner points out that the pattern of error in recall of syllogisms parallels the usual pattern of error in solution to similar problems. Such results suggest that at least part of the errors on logical problems may be due to memory deficiencies during encoding of the information. The matter is not that simple, however. If, as Barclay (1973), Paris and Carter (1973), and Piaget and Inhelder (1966) have suggested, memory is to be seen as a constructive process, it may be hypothesized that these failures of encoding in memory occur precisely because the inferential process that would have led to a structured memory representation has not been operative. This is one of the potential feedback loops mentioned above between representation and logical processing. It is the first challenge to the radical notion that these constitute independent functions. Other perplexities for this notion are found below, but it must be noted that such considerations do not disprove the (essentially conceptual) notion of two distinct functions, but only the assumption that they operate independently in the psychological process.

Another distortion in input consistently found in the literature, and reported in this volume by Scribner is an empiric bias whereby the subjects tend to rely on the factual information contained in the premises, rather than on their formal characteristics, to reach the conclusion. A closely related factual bias is interestingly discussed in Revlis' introduction: the subject may fail to discriminate between information given in the propositions and associated information in long-term memory. Factual distortions of this sort are clearly linked to the use of meaningful propositions with familiar content, and it is interesting in that respect to note that Staudenmayer (this volume) has found more consistency in interpretation of abstract propositions than that found for problems with meaningful content. Coming back to the comparison made in the introduction to this volume, between Piagetian tasks and tasks in the "propositional" tradition, a parallel may be drawn between the empiric bias observed in this context whenever "empirical" reasoning is possible, and the similar bias that has been hypothesized to operate in the "scientific" situation, when the child is presented empirical information exclusively. The similarity of these phenomena and the fact that the "empiric" attitude observed in adults in propositional situations is readily seen as a bias rather than as a symptom of logical incompetence, may lead us to reconsider the implications of this phenomenon concerning children's logic in the alternative task domain.

These are distortions in what could be characterized as a primitive stage of encoding, namely, input of "untransformed" information. Subsequently, however, the information has to be converted into the form in which it will be processed to generate the conclusion, whatever that process may consist of. In Osherson and Johnson-Laird's models, the deductive process operates on symbolic material. The logical form of the verbal premises must therefore be abstracted before the deductive transformations can be applied. Revlis proposes a deductive process operating on a set-theoretic (or functionally equivalent) representation of quantified propositions. For similar situations, Johnson-Laird describes a process in which the subject constructs hypothetical examples representing the stated relations. Thus, rather than engaging in a set-theoretic calculus proper, the subject manipulates prototypical exemplars from each area of the would-be Venn diagram. In the models described by Trabasso, Riley, and Wilson (this volume) for transitive inferences about length and by Huttenlocher (1968) for ordering syllogisms in general, the information is assumed to be translated into a spatial representation isomorphic (ideally) to the system of relations stated verbally. In fact, Trabasso, Riley, and Wilson's result that young children understand and use "long" and "short" rather than the comparative form is of interest here, because categorical descriptions cannot be translated into spatial relations in a univocal way.

Clearly, the "secondary" encoding, or translation, is an important part of the problem-solving process and distinct from the primary verbal encoding. What is involved here is a formalization process whereby a subject possessing a given mode of representation and a set of logical rules operating on it recognizes that the situation at hand is an example of that logical structure.

Formalization is a process of wide generality. Among other instances, it mediates (imperfectly, as any teacher knows) statistics with its application in practical problems. Similarly, a child may master arithmetic notions and computations, yet be at a loss when faced with a problem involving "apples that cost so many pennies, and what is the total amount spent," because of a failure to realize that the problem ought to be formalized into a multiplication operation. In the present case, the subject may know, in some symbolic or otherwise abstract mode, the biconditional connective "$\leftrightarrow$" and the corresponding patterns of inference; yet, when presented with statements such as "*a* and *b* always cooccur; *b* happens if and only if *c* occurs," he has to formalize these appropriately, that is, he has to recognize that this compound statement is an example of the structure "$a \leftrightarrow b$; $b \leftrightarrow c$; therefore, $a \leftrightarrow c$." In other words, in addition to logical knowledge per se, the deductive system also must include a pattern recognition device that identifies the logical structure in complex verbal (or nonverbal) inputs. The cues used in this pattern recognition process must be valid in order for the formalization and subsequent deduction to be acequate. Reliance on surface cues that correlate positively but imperfectly with the valid cues may lead to phenomena such as the "atmosphere effect" in which the response will turn out to be correct quite often, but for the wrong reasons, so to speak.

In the usual sense, the notion of formalization applies when a situation (for example, a proposition in this case) is represented in the terms of a formal system (for example, logic) the properties of which are isomorphic to the relevant properties in the original situation. Such a notion naturally extends to representations such as those invoked in Osherson and Johnson-Laird's models, which, although they depart from a strictly logical system in important respects, share with it the property of offering a formal representation of sentences. It is important, however, to realize that a formalization process is similarly involved when the subject chooses the appropriate spatial representation, or more generally the appropriate concrete model to deal with a reasoning task. A spatial representation of ordering syllogisms, mapping the information in the comparative propositions (*A* older than *B*) onto a straight line, indeed involves formalization because it rests on the identification of an isomorphism between the comparative statement and the order on the line, so that the transitive inference warranted by the comparatives can be achieved via the corresponding property on the line. A similar remark applies to the set-theoretic representation postulated by Revlis. The ramifications of this point will be discussed in the next section; its relevance here is to emphasize that a subject may encode and recall the information perfectly, in a task such as Scribner's, for example, yet incorrectly formalize that information into the spatial (or formal) representation. Neimark (this volume) has specifically investigated the translation of quantified statements into a pictorial set-theoretical representation, and identified failures in encoding at this level. Such failures could be responsible for part of the frequent errors in deductions with quantified propositions (granting, of course, that the Venn diagram model really is what the subject uses to perform the deduction), and the specific misrepresentations identified by Neimark do indeed corroborate findings common in syllogistic reasoning tasks (for example, treatment of "some" as "some but not all"). Also, it is interesting to note that her result showing the error rate for compound statements to be almost entirely predicted by the error rates to the corresponding individual propositions, lends support to the assumption made by Revlis on this point in the context of his syllogistic reasoning model: namely, the main burden of errors would lie in the initial formalization stage, and composite representations and subsequent deductions would be generated by an essentially errorless process.

Errors of the sort described above now are widely documented in the literature with respect to connectives and quantifiers; they have been discussed in several of the preceding chapters and need not be reviewed further. These errors are usually referred to as errors of interpretation (of quantifiers or of connectives). Conceptualizing them as errors in formalization gives this phenomenon a slightly different perspective in that it emphasizes the fact that it is the whole proposition which is represented, or formalized. This notion does not presuppose that the representation of the various terms is set up in isolation from the atomic propositions which they connect or quantify. Such a conceptualization seems to more easily handle findings such as Staudenmayer's, indicating that the representation of "if . . . them" is context dependent. It also permits us to take into account semantic relations between the elementary propositions, such as synonymy: synonymous propositions presumably will be assigned the same representation in the formal model (the same symbol if the representation is symbolic, the same position on the line if the representation is that of a spatial array, the same set in the case of Venn diagrams). Errors in formalization may occur at that level if the reasoner overlooks those relations that pertain to lexical inference (see Johnson-Laird, this volume, for an interesting discussion of lexical reasoning).

Finally, the notion that the representation function essentially involves a formalization of the information given in the premises, emphasizes the cognitive process involved in constructing the appropriate formalization, and suggests the interdependence between representation and subsequent processing, a point argued to be important in the next sections.

The discussion so far addressed questions regarding the possible locus of errors in a reasoning process and argued that such errors do not necessarily disqualify the assumption of an underlying logical competence. A related but somewhat different issue concerns the variability of reasoning performance as a function of the verbal formulation of problems, the abstractness of the premises, the nature of the phenomenon in "scientific" situations, and a multiplicity of other task variables. Such findings, exemplified in this volume in Staudenmayer's chapter and elsewhere by Wason and Johnson-Laird (1972), raise an important issue about the generality of the logical competence that a model may assume. This question, if asked in its general form, is readily answered negatively on the basis of such results. The question can be reformulated more clearly, however, if we conceptualize the reasoning process in the way outlined above, as involving an initial formalization of the situation—for example, of the verbal information—and a subsequent deduction process. We then may ask whether it is possible to identify a deductive component which operates in a standard way on a standard translation irrespective of content or other linguistic factors, although these may affct other components of the process. Such a question cannot be settled on an empirical basis only. It is unquestionable that the subject's performance depends heavily upon the content and formulation of otherwise identical problems. Imputing this variability to the notion that deductive rules are necessarily language bound (or, more generally, content bound) or, alternatively, to occasionally imperfect formalization of natural language input into an abstract system in which the subject is competent, is a matter of theoretical predilection and investment. Thus, when a subject is able to perform transitive inferences about length but unable to deal with other transitive situations, he may be said to possess the formal apparatus required but to use cues of insufficient generality in the pattern recognition process, or, alternatively, to only possess a content-bound inferential scheme.

THE REASONING PROCESS AND THE LOCUS OF LOGIC

In the preceding chapters, a variety of deductive processes has been proposed that differs widely in appearance, and perhaps in basic features. It is of interest to examine the ingredients of which the reasoning process is made in these respective models, in particular with regard to the second question raised at the beginning of this discussion, concerning the status of the various processes with respect to logical knowledge.

The views on the reasoning process can be divided conveniently into those models that are essentially linguistically based and those that invoke a concrete or schematic model of the situation, such as an imaginal representation or selection of examples. Accounts of the first type have been proposed by Osherson and by Johnson-Laird for propositional reasoning. Speculations about a similar mechanism to account for acquisition of logic in children have also been made by Falmagne, although not documented by the studies presented: it was suggested that children may learn facts about logic (valid deductions, inference schemata) by being exposed to verbal situations exemplifying those, and learning to recognize the structures involved by abstracting the relevant cues. The process invoked is then a gradual structuring of the linguistic environment, analogous to the mechanism of acquisition of grammatical rules documented in the area of language development.

A reasoning process of the same, linguistic sort is spelled out by both Johnson-Laird and Osherson. As noted above, there is a strong commonality between the mode of representation postulated by these authors and what a strictly logically based model of reasoning would involve: natural language input is formalized into well-formed expressions containing propositional symbols and connectives (or some functional equivalent of this symbolization) on which formal rules then apply. Regarding the deductive process proper, Osherson questions the psychological validity of standard logic and proposes instead a series of inference schemata, or rewrite rules sanctioned by, but not exhaustive of, the theorems of standard logic. The sequence of operations is governed heuristically: operations are selected at each step of the deduction process in such a way as to reduce the discrepancy in surface form between the obtained expression and the conclusion to be evaluated. In terms of the question raised above, it is clear that the set of rules, or inference schemata, can be taken in a natural way to represent the subject's logical knowledge. This is also the case in the model proposed by Johnson-Laird, in which the subject's logical knowledge is encapsuled in a set of "primary" and "secondary" patterns of inference. A noteworthy feature of Johnson-Laird's model is the powerful executive function which monitors the sequence of those inferential steps through a hierarchy of goals and subgoals. A subgoal for inference is formulated when the system identifies chunks of information that have to be supplied for the inference currently attempted to be possible. In other words, the system not only formalizes natural language input but identifies missing slots in this formalization in regard to what the available inference schemata would require. The executive component of the deductive system is interesting theoretically in providing an efficient utilization of logical knowledge. The fact that it is explicitly incorporated into the model is also interesting from a metatheoretical point of view: the discussion below will indicate that an executive function that transcends the deductive process per se has to be invoked even when it is not spelled out explicitly.

Processes of a seemingly quite different nature have been described in the previous chapters by Trabasso, Riley, and Wilson for transitive inferences and by Revlis for syllogistic reasoning. In these models, information is formalized into a spatial model; once this translation is effected, all the subject has to do is to read off the answer from the representation that has been constructed. This step—computation of the answer—is quite straightforward, is assumed by both authors to be errorless, and clearly does not qualify as logical in the usual sense. A closer examination of the entire process, however, indicates that logic is not absent from it; it is simply hidden in the formalization process. Clearly, in order for a subject to select the appropriate representation—the straight line—in a transitive inference task, he must be aware of the formal similarity between the terms of the problem and the properties of the line, namely, in this case, transitivity. It is important here to realize that the representation invoked by Trabasso, Riley, and Wilson (this volume) and Huttenlocher (1968) is not a direct image associated with the premises, as would be the case if "A longer than B" were to be represented imaginally as two rods of different heights. Rather, the subject is assumed to map A and B onto a straight line, in such a way that order on the line corresponds to the stated inequalities in length. A crucial step in this process is the choice of the straight line as the vehicle for inference. The import of this point appears if one realizes that the subject was entirely free to choose to map the information onto a circle, for example. The formalization of the problem thus clearly entails recognizing that comparative terms have formal properties isomorphic to order properties of points on the line, namely nonreflexivity, noncommutativity and transitivity. This kind of knowledge pertains to what Johnson-Laird has described as lexical reasoning. Johnson-Laird's discussion makes it clear that knowlege of such properties must be considered to be part of the meaning of the term and stresses that lexical entries must be assumed to be tagged with their logical properties, that is, with the inferences they permit. This points at the intricacy of the connections between logic and language, to which we turn later.

It has been proposed above that formalizing a situation into a given representation involves a pattern recognition mechanism whereby the subject assesses that the situation at hand (the syllogism) is an exemplar of some conceptual representation (a line or array). Developmentally, this pattern recognition process can be assumed to be based on increasingly valid cues, and cues of increased generality. Thus young children may be able to perform transitive inferences about length but fail on transitive tasks involving other comparative terms, because they have not yet abstracted the more general cue ("comparative") indicative of transitive patterns. Trabasso, Riley and Wilson mention the interest of developmental studies of this sort. It may be noted that the notion that children possess the formal machinery for transitive inferences but have to learn its range of application, is closely similar, though from a different perspective, to Piaget's notion of horizontal *"décalage."* The difference in perspectives lies in the explicit emphasis made here on the leanring process involved in pattern recognition.

The model proposed by Revlis for syllogistic reasoning is subject to the same comments as those raised above concerning transitive inference. Revlis assumes each of the verbal premises to be formalized into a Venn diagram representation; a composite representation of both premises is then formed, from which the answer is read off. Clearly, the initial formalization step and the final decoding or "reading off" do, as in the previous case, entail an awareness of the isomorphism between the meaning (i.e., the logical properties) of "some" or "all" and the corresponding properties of the diagram representation (overlap, inclusion). This awareness is not a trivial matter: Piaget and Inhelder (1964) have shown the difficulties encountered by children in coordinating the extension of a set (as represented in the diagrams) with its definition in comprehension. For this reason among others, it would be misleading to confer to Venn diagrams the status of a direct, imaginal representation. Considered in their "achieved" state, Venn diagrams could be said to pertain to imagery: once translation has been performed, inspection of the spatial properties of the diagrams can be used to generate the response (with the proviso mentioned above). However, Venn diagrams are conventional representations of a formal theory, and to that extent might be regarded as a symbolic material, in a weak sense. Such an intermediate (or ambiguous) case is useful in suggesting that there may be no essential difference in terms of "logicality" between a process such as this one and the apparently more formal, linguistically based processes discussed above.

In addition to the implicitly logical nature of the formalization step, the process described by Revlis also clearly involves logical processing while the composite representation is formed. Construction of this composite representation from the representation of both premises is indeed a deductive process, both in a technical and in a psychological sense—in a technical sense, because it consists in deriving new information from the original information. It is deductive in a psychological sense because the process allows for errors: for example, "A overlaps B" (as representing "some A are B" and "B overlaps C," can be combined erroneously to show "A overlaps C" if the subject fails to realize that this is only one of several possibilities. This example makes it clear that the same knowledge is involved in setting up the composite representation as would be required to deal with the verbal statements themselves. Revlis does not describe this process in detail, but postulates it to be errorless, an assumption interestingly (and surprisingly) supported by Neimark's results on the representation of compound statements.

The process hypothesized by Johnson-Laird for syllogistic inferences is of a somewhat different nature, and the difference is interesting for reasons mentioned below. Instead of assuming a set-theoretic representation of the quantified statements, Johnson-Laird postulates that the subject sets up, in symbolic or other form, imaginary elements exemplifying the stated relations. For example, the statement "All artists are beekeepers" is represented by an arbitrary artist *a* (element of the set A), who is also a beekeeper *b* (element of B), where the fact that *a* is a *b* (and not the converse) is represented by a (metaphorical) arrow from *a* to *b*. That some beekeepers may not be artists is represented by an isolated *b*, unreached by any arrow. The information in the second premise is appended to this representation in a cumulative way. Once the composite representation is formed, the answer to the syllogism may be read off by proceeding in the direction of the arrows. The process thus consists in constructing a series of prototypes ranging over the possible cases. An interesting feature of the model is its proposing a representational "language" (the arrows) that fits the psychological properties of the verbal statements (that is, the arrows reproduce the asymmetrical properties of the verb "is" for which subject and predicate are not generally interchangeable), and the advantage of the model over set-theoretically based processes is advocated on this basis by the author. In the context of the present discussion, it must be noted that because of this very similarity between the format of the verbal input and that of the representation, much of the logical burden rests on the mechanism by which prototypes are selected, mappings are established, and the answer is computed. The executive process that generates the appropriate range of prototypes and the rules governing the setting up and reading of arrows must utilize some knowledge paraphrased by " 'All A are B' and 'Some B are C' means that there may be Bs that are not A, and there may be C that are not B and B that are not C . . ." among other things. Also, reading off the answer by proceeding in the direction of arrows presupposes awareness of the transitive properties of the verb "is" when used to denote class membership. It is thus clear that the model only superficially resembles a process of reasoning by examples. It is worth emphasizing here the distinction between a reasoning process operating on concrete examples (such as the process proposed by Chapman & Chapman, 1959) and a process operating on prototypes, the construction of which entails the abstraction of essential features or cases.

As mentioned above, the comparison between this model and the set-theoretic model proposed by Revlis is interesting in indicating two different notational schemes, which are apparently intertranslatable if the appropriate assumptions are made, despite the fact that one model relies on a formal representation of the premises whereas the other invokes a reasoning process using prototypes. This similarity in structure raises to a particularly obvious degree the general question regarding the identifiability of alternative, structurally similar mechanisms, and the psychological reality of the modes of representation invoked.

In the models discussed above, the logical burden (or most of it) lies in the formalization process, as has been argued. The case is somewhat different for the process hypothesized by Falmagne to underlie "undecidable" judgments in the situations considered. There, the child was assumed to bring up a representation of the premise ("there are only circles in the box") consisting of the relevant objects under their concrete form. If this representation is assumed to be visual, this is indeed direct imagery (in contrast to the formalized representations discussed above and to the alternative, schematized representation postulated in Falmagne's chapter for true and false propositions). It then is assumed that the child samples various subjects of this set of potential elements of the box (as a way of mimicking the possible manipulations performed by the experimenter), and reaches a conclusion about the truth value of the proposition ("there are some blue circles in the box") according to whether all, some, or none of the subsets sampled verify the proposition. As noted before, this procedure is close in its imaginary form to what a concrete manipulation of objects would involve. Because of the concrete nature of the imaginal representation and subsequent sampling, such a procedure could be viewed as substantively different from (and opposed to) a logically based procedure. However, it is important to acknowledge that the process as a whole does not consist in a mechanical sequence of operations, but rather represents a "plan," the adequacy of which must, again, be sustained by some implicit logical knowledge. At the core of this plan is the knowledge that the proposition is false if and only if no subset is compatible with it, true if all of them are, and undecidable otherwise. Logical knowledge is thus embodied here in the heuristic function that monitors the whole process.

LOGICAL COMPETENCE: DEFINITIONAL ISSUES

The discussion above has pointed at the difficulty of distinguishing, at the conceptual level, "logically based" from "concretely based" models of reasoning. It has been argued that logical knowledge can be embodied in various ways in the reasoning process, either in the deductive operations themselves, in the case of linguistically based models of reasoning, or, for models relying on a spatial or concrete mode of representation, in the heuristic function governing the choice of the appropriate representation and the operations performed on it.

Such an issue is consonant with Piaget's conception about the interrelations between operative and figurative knowledge, especially with regard to imagery (Piaget & Inhelder, 1966): images are not seen as a direct or approximative copy of the object, but, in a very real sense, as the product of a construction. The issue is also reminiscent of corresponding difficulties, in models of memory, to formally and functionally characterize propositional encoding as distinct from imaginal coding (e.g., Bower, 1972; Simon, 1972).

The notion of logical competence needs reconsideration, in the light of these issues. When should the subject be said to reason logically? Although such semantic issues may not be the most useful ones, they are worth examining here briefly because of the fact that "logical" versus "nonlogical" modes of reasoning tend to be argued for polemically (the latter being usually characterized as information processing strategies, or reasoning by examples). A number of ambiguities are resolved by distinguishing between three different roles that can be assigned to logical models. On the one hand, the model can be a structural model characterizing essentially the class of tasks that the subject is able to perform successfully, regardless of the process by which he performs these (for example, a three-year-old might be unable, either by using imagery or any other resource, to deal with information involving double negation). This approach leads to an operational definition of competence; logic is seen as our symbolism as investigators, is used to characterize the task, and is not introjected into the subject's mind. The question about which reasoning process qualifies as logical clearly does not apply in this case.

Alternatively, logical competence can be defined as the set of concepts, or facts about logic, that a person may know, regardless of how this knowledge is actualized. This is a structural definition of competence, analogous to the one now traditional in linguistics. Thus, a subject will be said to reason logically if he performs operations of any kind as long as their validity is sanctioned by some logical rule that the subject is assumed to know, as has been argued to be the case for deductive processes operating on prototypes (Johnson-Laird for reasoning with quantifiers) or on samples of concretely represented objects (Falmagne).

A third alternative is to incorporate logic into the process which is assumed to operate in real time to generate conclusions in a reasoning task. Competence is then defined as logical knowledge together with logically based operations generating the responses. Thus, a reasoning process would qualify as logical only if the steps used in real-time deductions are of a logical nature. Models of deduction such as Johnson-Laird's or Osherson's clearly are of that sort.[1] Similarly, in order for a language user to be considered competent in that language, he would have to not only emit judgments of synonymy or well-formedness consistent with the rules of grammar (thereby indicating his knowledge of those rules) but also show evidence that the steps in the process leading to his judgments of synonymy (for example) correspond to the transformational rules of the grammar.[2]

[1] The process described by Revlis is an ambiguous case, relying as it does on a representation that pertains both to imagery and to the formal system of set theory; its characterization would depend on the process leading to the composite representation, which has not been made explicit.

[2] An interesting radical version of this view on competence, is found in models proposing a procedural definition of knowledge (e.g., Papert (1972), for geometry; Winograd (1972) for syntax and semantics; Baron (1973) for semantics) whereby knowledge is represented and stored in the form of procedures, or operations, rather than in structural form. The distinction between knowledge and process therefore collapses in such a representation, since knowledge is defined in process terms. Within such a conceptualization, it is a truism that a subject logically competent by the "structural" criterion also possesses processlike logical competence.

These considerations purport to emphasize that characterization of a reasoning process as logical or nonlogical is contingent upon the notion of competence adopted, and that arguments about whether subjects have demonstrated logical competence (as opposed to concrete or other "nonlogical" mode of reasoning) must be qualified accordingly. Coming back to the conceptual framework outlined at the beginning of this chapter, this discussion indicates that the assumption according to which information processing is governed by the subject's logical knowledge, is not as stringent as it appears to be. The second feature of that general scheme, namely the conceptual separation between representation of information and logical processing, is discussed in the next section.

REASONING AND LANGUAGE COMPREHENSION, OR LOGIC AND SEMANTICS

Nothing is more comfortable for the mind than clear-cut distinctions in concepts and time. Two-valued logic, and more recently process models with serial nonoverlapping stages, perhaps owe their impact and popularity to that property, fortunately confounded with the technical advantage of tractability. The framework presented at the beginning of this discussion is also of that sort: it proposes a sharp conceptual separation, borrowed to a large extent from the computer simulation culture, between encoding of information (in particular, of verbal information) and logical processing, and furthermore assumes these to be distinct components of the psychological process, although not necessarily serial stages.

But we have seen along the way a number of difficulties encountered by this simple notion. These are of various sorts. First, the implicit logical knowledge involved in the representation of information had to be recognized: modes of representation apparently straightforward such as examples, prototypes, or visual arrays have been argued to presuppose a knowledge of the logical properties of the situation represented. This leads to a first weakening of the notion that representation and logical processing constitute independent functions—or operations.

A closely similar issue, more general because it is not restricted to the context of a reasoning task, has been raised in the discussion of lexical reasoning. The meaning of a number of lexical items has been argued by Johnson-Laird to incorporate logical properties of various sorts. Thus, the meaning of a connective can be said to consist of the inferences it permits (what would it be, otherwise?) (Paris, 1973). The meaning of comparatives can be said to include their nonsymmetrical property. The meaning of concrete nouns can be said to intrinsically involve set theoretical properties of their denotations; part of the meaning of "canary" is the fact that it is a bird, with the implicit class inclusion relation involved between their referents. It is clear that in this context, as in the more specific context of a reasoning task discussed above, logic is one of the architects of representation.

Another difficulty for the "separability" notion is created indirectly by results indicating that verbal connectives, or quantifiers do not have a fixed representation, nor do structurally identical sentences containing those terms. Rather, context, presuppositions, and extraneous factual information control the way in which the sentence is formalized. Thus, Staudenmayer showed that *if . . . then* could be construed either as a conditional or as a biconditional, depending on the pragmatic relation between the antecedent and the consequent (when these are meaningful propositions). Similarly, Revlis showed that *All* A*s are* B*s* could be encoded in different ways, depending on extraneous information about the sizes of the sets A and B. If such variables as context and presuppositions affect encoding, these differences must be mediated by the recognition, somehow, that the situations described have a different logical structure. Staudenmayer's results indeed suggest that the literal connective has very little to do with the way in which the statement is construed: the formalization is governed primarily by the semantics and pragmatics of the terms connected. This clearly precludes the notion that translation into the language of the "logical machine" is standard.

The arguments above resemble in many ways those advanced by generative semanticists to challenge syntactically based linguistic theories, and so will the rest of this discussion. It may be appropriate, therefore, to recapture the parallel that has been indicated earlier, between models of reasoning and linguistics. At the heart of the issue is the assumption, advanced in connection with standard generative transformational grammar (Chomsky, 1965, 1971; Katz & Fodor, 1963) that language can be characterized in a basically syntactical way, in terms of syntactical categories and of rewrite and transformational rules based exclusively on those; semantic information is inserted at one privileged stage (the deep structure) to confer meaning to the sentence. Semantics is, therefore, an interpretive component of the system, in the sense that the grammatical derivations, the rules of well-formedness and the resulting structures are formally based, and once achieved can be "interpreted" (in the technical sense) in various lexical realizations. Two notions are essential here. First, syntactical categories are assumed not to be semantically based, that is, a conceptual separation is established between syntactic and semantic properties. Second, in the course of transformations, there is a sequence of transformations (from deep to surface structure) which is exclusively syntactically based. Separability of semantics and syntax is thus assumed in a second sense, namely in the sequence of derivations or (if the sequence is interpreted that way) in the production or comprehension process.

The analogy with the framework proposed at the beginning of this chapter is evident, particularly regarding the second of these aspects. This framework proposed the notion that natural language input is formalized into an appropriate format, on which a "logical machine" then operates in a standard way. The comments above, concerning the "separability" question, have stressed the implicit logical operation underlying representation of the information: symmetrically, the assumption may be questioned that once representation is established, the subsequent sequence of operations is based exclusively on the formal rules of the propositional calculus. For example, in Johnson-Laird's model of propositional reasoning, when the deductive process is operating and primary inferences are attempted, many of the auxiliary inferences that have to be called upon are, in fact, lexical (rather than propositional) inferences, that is, of a semantic rather than formal nature. This challenge to the "separability" assumption concerning the reasoning process, is analogous to the argument and examples offered by Lakoff (1971) against the appropriateness of syntactically based linguistic theories, especially if these are considered to be psychological models as well. Lakoff points out that, in a number of cases, it is not possible to find a sequence of transformations from meaning to surface structure which would be exclusively syntactical; rather, various lexical items have to be inserted at various points in the sequence if the meaning of the sentence is to be preserved. Similar to this interaction between syntax and semantics in the dynamics of linguistic transformations, what seems to emerge with regard to reasoning is an interactive relation between the logical and semantic (or representational) functions, that governs all steps of the process.

The other crucial feature of syntactically based theories concerned the conceptual separation between syntactic and semantic properties of logical items or sentences, which Lakoff (1971) and Fillmore (1971) among others have convincingly questioned. Fillmore's case structure grammar provides a characterization of lexical items which is undistinguishably grammatical and conceptual (or semantic): that the verb "write" admits as complement (grammatically) an instrument is also an intrinsic part of its meaning. Along similar lines, the difficulty of establishing a sharp conceptual distinction between reasoning and language comprehension has been emphasized above in the context of lexical reasoning with respect to the meaning of individual lexical items and to the relations between those meanings. The same remarks apply, perhaps even more convincingly, to the logical nature of sentence comprehension as a whole. McCawley (1971) has stressed this point from a linguistic viewpoint by proposing a notational scheme for the meaning (and/or the structure) of sentences that is logically based—expressed in terms of predicates, quantifiers, and variables—with an organization paralleling (with some differences not relevant here) that of logical expressions. A similar view has been actualized by Winograd (1972) in a computer model of language understanding, via a logically based characterization of meaning and the functional dependences between the semantic processor and the logical processor. Finally, the interdependence of meaning and logic has been illustrated by Barclay (1973) and Paris (1973) among others in psychological tasks.

In view of these remarks, it appears that the interface between representation and logical processing (or between semantics and logic) is so intricate and so overwhelming, that their identity as components of the psychological process tends to disappear. Similarly, at the conceptual level, the difficulty of assessing the respective provinces of language comprehension and reasoning, or of semantics and logic, seems to call for a scheme focused on the common, rather than disjoint, territories. The conceptual framework originally proposed, with its stress on distinct functions and separable components of the process, appears to be, at best, inefficient and, at worst, inadequate in that respect. Though this scheme retains its usefulness as an anchor for categorizing empirical findings (and for establishing distinctions before they are questioned), a more dialectic scheme seems called for, in which language comprehension and logical reasoning are seen as alternative perspectives on the same object rather than complementary ways of slicing it.

REFERENCES

Barclay, J. R. The role of comprehension in remembering sentences. *Cognitive Psychology,* 1973, **4,** 229–254.

Baron, J. Semantic and conceptual components. *Cognition,* 1973, **2,** 299–317.

Bower, G. H. Mental imagery and associative learning. In L. W. Gregg (Ed.), *Cognition in learning and memory. New York: Wiley,* 1972.

Bryant, P. E., & Trabasso, T. Transitive inferences and memory in young children. *Nature,* 1971, **232,** 456–458.

Chapman, L. J., & Chapman, J. P. Atmosphere effect re-examined. *Journal of Experimental Psychology,* 1959, **58,** 220–226.

Chomsky, N. *Aspects of the theory of syntax.* Cambridge, Massachusetts: M.I.T. Press, 1965.

Chomsky, N. Deep structure, surface structure and semantic interpretation. In D. Steinberg & L. A. Jakobovitz (Eds.), *Semantics.* Cambridge, England: Cambridge University Press, 1971.

Fillmore, C. J. Types of lexical information. In D. Steinberg & L. A. Jakobovitz (Eds.), *Semantics.* Cambridge, England: Cambridge University Press, 1971.

Huttenlocher, J. Constructing spatial images: a strategy in reasoning. *Psychological Review,* 1968, **75,** 550–600.

Inhelder, B., & Piaget, J. *The growth of logical thinking from childhood to adolescence.* New York: Basic Books, 1958.

Katz, J. J., & Fodor, J. A. The structure of a semantic theory. *Language,* **39,** 1963, 170–210.

Lakoff, G. On generative semantics. In D. Steinberg & L. A. Jakobovitz (Eds.), *Semantics.* Cambridge, England: Cambridge University Press, 1971.

McCawley, J. D. Where do noun phrases come from? In D. Steinberg & L. A. Jakobovitz (Eds.), *Semantics.* Cambridge, England: Cambridge University Press, 1971.

Papert, S. Teaching children to be mathematicians vs. teaching about mathematics. *International Journal of Mathematical Education in Science and Technology,* 1972.

Paris, S. G. Comprehension of language connectives and propositional logical relationships. *Journal of Experimental Child Psychology,* 1973, **16,** 278–291.

Paris, S. G., & Carter, A. Y. Semantic and constructive aspects of sentence memory in children. *Developmental Psychology,* 1973, **2,** 105–113.

Piaget, J., & Inhelder, B. *The early growth of logic in the child.* New York: Harper & Row, 1964.

Piaget, J., & Inhelder, B. *L'image mentale chez l'enfant.* Paris: Presses Universitaires de France, 1966.

Simon, H. A. What is visual imagery? An information processing interpretation. In L. W. Gregg (Ed.), *Cognition in learning and memory.* New York: Wiley, 1972.

Wason, P. C., & Johnson-Laird, P. N. *Psychology of reasoning: Structure and Content.* Cambridge, Massachusetts: Harvard University Press, 1972.

Winograd, T. *Understanding natural language.* New York: Academic Press, 1972.

AUTHOR INDEX

Numbers in *italics* refer to the pages on which the complete references are listed.

A

Abelson, R. P., 50, *52*
Amarel, S., 16, *52*
Aronson, J. L., 59, *78*
Austin, J. L., 68, *78*

B

Barclay, J. R., 106, *129,* 171, *172*, 202, 221, *228,* 249, 263, *263*
Bar-Hillel, Y., 9, *52*
Baron, J., 259, *263*
Begg, I., 99, 100, 111, 120, *129*
Bendix, E. H., 19, *52*
Beth, E. W., 15, *52,* 232, 234, *245*
Blumenthal, A. L., 59, *78*
Boole, G., 55, *78,* 81, *90*
Bosley, J. G., 204, *228*
Bourne, L. E., Jr., 85, 87, *90*
Bower, G. H., 204, 206, 210, 228, *228,* 258, *263*
Bransford, J. D., 50, *52*, 106, *129*
Bryant, P. E., 218, 220, *228*, 248, *263*
Burt, C., 201, *228*

C

Campbell, R. N., 228, *229*
Carnap, R., 9, *52*
Carroll, L., 109, *129*
Carter, A. Y., 171, *173,* 249, *264*
Ceraso, J., 37, *52,* 75, *78,* 97, 104, 110, 124, 129, *129,* 136, 148, *150,* 170, *172*
Chapman, J. P., 36, 43, *52,* 95, 97, 99, 100, 106, 107, 111, 116, *130,* 257, *263*
Chapman, L. J., 36, 43, *52*, *95*, 97, 99, 100, 106, 107, 111, 116, *130,* 257, *263*
Charniak, E., 51, *52*
Chase, W. G., 98, 111, *130*
Chomsky, N., 261, *263*
Church, A., 8, *52*
Clark, H. H., 10, *52*, 98, 99, 107, 111, 114, *130,* 202, 206, 215, 219, *228*
Cohen, M. R., 95, 96, *130,* 155, 165, *172*
Cole, M., 154, 156, *172*
Collins, A. M., 10, 50, *52*
Craik, F. I. M., 221, *228*
Cresswell, M. J., 89, *90*

D

Davey, M., 77, *79*
Dawes, R., 105, 114, *130*
De Morgan, A., 110, *130*
Dennison, A., 238, *245*
Denny, J., 99, 100, 111, 120, *129*
DeSoto, C. B., 202, 204, *228, 229*

Dowty, D. R., 14, *52*
Doyle, A. C., 7, *52*

E

Ebenholtz, S. M., 204, *229*
Eifermann, R., 99, *130*
Erickson, J. R., 36, 42, *52,* 104, 110, *130*
Eisenberg, K., 100, *131*
Evans, J. St. B. T., 21, *53,* 58, *78,* 128, 129, *130,* 156, *172*

F

Falmagne, R. J., 197, *199*
Feather, N. T., 94, 105, *130*
Feigenbaum, E. A., 106, *130, 132*
Feldman, S., 136, *151,* 175, *199*
Fillmore, C. J., 60, *78,* 262, *263*
Flavell, J. H., 135, *151,* 218, *229*
Fodor, J. A., 261, *264*
Franks, J., 106, *129*
Frase, L. T., 95, 96, 103, 105, 110, *130, 132*
Frege, G., 106, *130*
Frick, F., 94, 105, *131*
Fujii, M. S., 58, *79*
Furth, H. G., 136, *151,* 175, *199,* 244, *245*

G

Galanter, E., 26, *54,* 197, *199*
Garcia, R., 75, 77, *79*
Gay, J., 154, 156, *172*
Geis, J. L., 128, *130*
Geis, M., 76, *78*
Gibbs, J. L., Jr., 156, *172*
Glick, J. A., 154, 156, *172*
Glucksberg, S., 98, *130*
Gödel, K., 22, *53*
Goldman, N., 51, *54*
Goldstein, S., 94, 105, *131*
Goodman, N., 89, *90*
Gordon, D., 108, *131*
Gordon, R., 94, 105, *131*
Gough, P. B., 99, *131*
Greene, J. M., 99, *131*
Grice, H. P., 107, *131*

H

Handel, S., 202, *229*
Harrison, C., 77, *79*
Hatano, G., 136, 144, *151*
Hayes, J. R., 103, 104, 113, *132*
Henle, M., 55, 56, 58, 76, 77, *78,* 81, *90,* 94, 97, 103, 105, 110, 121, *131,* 156, 165, *172*
Hewitt, C., 9, *53*
Heyting, A., 21, *53*
Higgins, E. T., 10, *53,* 244, *245*
Hill, S. A., 135, *151,* 157, *173,* 175, *199*
Hintikka, J., 43, *53*
Horn, L. R., 108, *131*
Hughes, G. E., 89, *90*
Huttenlocher, J., 10, *53,* 100, *131,* 202, 205, *229,* 244, *245,* 250, 254, *263*

I

Inhelder, B., 2, 3, *6,* 143, *151,* 201, *229,* 232, 233, 235, *245,* 249, 256, 258, *264*

J

Jackendoff, R., 37, *53*
Janis, I., 94, 105, *131*
Johnson, D. M., 105, *132*
Johnson-Laird, P. N., 8, 10, 14, 19, 20, 37, 45, 49, 51, *53, 54,* 77, *78,* 88, 89, *90, 91,* 97, 100, 114, 128, *131, 133,* 135, 136, *151,* 166, *173,* 202, *229,* 252, *264*

K

Kant, I., 55, *78*
Karttunen, L., 19, *53*
Katz, J. J., 261, *264*
Kaufman, H., 94, 105, *131*
Keenan, E. L., 24, *53*
Kevin, R. C., 171, *173*
Kintsch, W., 60, *79,* 113, *131*
Klahr, D., 110, *131*
Kneale, M., 22, 41, *53*
Kneale, W., 22, 41, *53*
Koob, H. F., 115, *132*
Kowalski, R., 9, *53*

L

Lakoff, G., 37, *53,* 56, *79,* 108, *131,* 262, *264*
Lakoff, R., 18, *53*
Landauer, T. K., 10, *53,* 205, *229*
Langford, C., 81, *90*
Le Bonniec, G., 175, *199*
Leech, G. N., 37, *53*
Lefford, A., 94, 105, *132*
Legrenzi, M. S., 77, *78,* 128, *131*
Legrenzi, P., 40, *53,* 77, *78,* 128, *131*
Levy-Bruhl, L., 154, *173*
Lewis, C., 81, *90*
Lipkin, S. G., 104, *132*
Lippman, M. Z., 102, *132*
Lockhart, R. S., 221, *228*
London, M., 202, *229*
Lukasiewicz, J., 96, *132*
Lunzer, E. A., 77, *79*
Luria, A. R., 154, 155, *173*
Lutkus, A. D., 204, 220, *229*
Lynch, J. S., 128, *130*

M

Matalon, B., 88, *90,* 175, *199*
Mazzocco, A., 40, *53*
McCarrell, N. S., 50, *52*
McCawley, J. D., 262, *264*
Meyer, D. E., 10, *53*
Michael, M., 94, 97, 105, 110, 121, *131*
Mill, J. S., 55, 56, 77, 78, *79*
Miller, G. A., 14, 26, *54,* 197, *199*
Montague, R., 7, *54*
Moore, W., 100, 111, 112, *132*
Morgan, J. J., 94, 105, 116, *132*
Morton, J. T., 94, 105, 116, *132*
Moyer, R. S., 205, 222, *229*
Murdock, B. B., Jr., 204, 206, *229*
Murray, J. P., 238, *245*

N

Nagano, S., 136, 142, *151*
Nagel, E., 55, 59, *79,* 95, 96, *130,* 155, 165, *172*
Neimark, E. D., 85, 87, *90,* 136, 142, 144, *151,* 175, *199*
Newell, A., 26, *54,* 85, 86, *90, 91,* 97, *132,* 201, 220, *229*
Nilsson, N. J., 85, *91*
Nitta, N., 136, 142, *151*

O

O'Banion, K., 85, 87, *90*
O'Brien, T. C., 175, *199*
Osherson, D. N., 83, *91*

P

Papert, S., 259, *264*
Paris, S. G., 136, *151,* 171, *173,* 175, *199,* 249, 260, 263, *264*
Parrott, G. L., 94, 105, *132*
Parsons, T., 7, *54*
Peel, E. A., 136, *151*
Peirce, C. S., 95, *132*
Perchonock, E., 99, *132*
Pezzoli, J. A., 96, 105, 110, *132*
Piaget, J., 2, 3, *6,* 15, *52,* 81, *91,* 143, *151,* 154, *173,* 201, 202, *229,* 232, 233, 234, 235, 244, *245,* 249, 256, 258, *264*
Porter, G., 197, *199*
Potts, G. R., 202, 215, 221, *229*
Pribram, K. H., 26, *54,* 197, *199*
Provitera, A., 37, *52,* 75, *78,* 97, 104, 110, 124, 129, *129,* 136, 148, *150,* 170, *172*

Q

Quillian, M. R., 10, 50, *52*
Quine, W. V. O., 82, *91*

R

Ramsey, F. P., 25, *54*
Reich, C. M., 50, *52*
Reichenbach, H., 57, 75, *79*
Reiter, R., 16, *54*
Rescher, N., 96, 110, *132*
Revlis, R., 100, 103, 104, 105, 111, 112, 113, *132*
Richter, M., 97, *132*
Rieger, C. J., 51, *54*
Riesbeck, C., 51, *54*
Riley, C. A., 204, 220, *229*
Rips, L. J., 10, *54*
Roberge, J. J., 111, *132*

Robinson, J. A., 8, *54*
Rollins, H., 98, *133*
Roncato, S., 40, *53*
Ross, B. M., 136, *151*
Ryan, S., 105, 110, *133*

S

Savin, H., 99, *132*
Schaeffer, B., 10, *54*
Schank, R., 51, *54*
Scholz, K. W., 221, *229*
Sells, S. B., 36, 38, *54*, 58, *79*, 93, 115, 120, *132*, *133*, 154, *173*
Seuren, P. A. M., 37, *54*
Shapiro, B. J., 175, *199*
Shapiro, D., 76, 77, *79*, 128, *133*
Sharp, D. W., 154, 156, *172*
Shaughnessy, E., 98, *133*
Shaw, J., 85, *90*
Shoben, E. J., 10, *54*
Simon, H. A., 26, *54*, 85, 86, *90*, *91*, 97, 106, *132*, 201, 220, *229*, 258, *264*
Slotnick, N. S., 85, 87, *90*, 136, 144, *151*, 175, *199*
Smith, E. E., 10, *54*
Stalnaker, R. C., 26, *54*, 57, *79*
Staudenmayer, H., 58, 75, 77, *79*, 87, *91*, 128, *133*, 135, 142, *151*
Strauss, S., 100, *131*
Strawson, P. F., 57, 75, *79*
Suppes, P., 19, *54*, 82, *91*, 136, *151*, 175, *199*
Szeminska, A., 201, *229*, 232, 233, 235, *245*

T

Taddonio, J. L., 128, *133*, 135, 142, *151*
Tagart, J., 88, *90*
Tannenbaum, P., 100, 103, *133*
Taplin, J. E., 58, 75, *79*, 87, *91*, 97, 128, *133*, 135, 142, *151*
Tarski, A., 23, *54*
Terwilliger, R., 94, 105, *131*
Thouless, R., 105, *133*
Trabasso, T., 98, *130*, *133*, 204, 218, 220, 228, *228*, *229*, 248, *263*
Tridgell, J., 20, *53*

V

van Fraassen, B. C., 8, *54*

W

Wald, J., 98, *130*
Wales, R. J., 228, *229*
Wallace, J. G., 110, *131*
Wallace, R., 10, *54*
Wason, P. C., 8, 45, 51, *53*, *54*, 58, 75, 76, 77, *79*, 89, *91*, 97, 128, *131*, *133*, 135, *151*, 166, *173*, 252, *264*
Werner, H., 154, *173*
Whimbey, A., 105, 110, *133*
Wilkins, M. C., 39, *54*, 72, *79*, 94, 97, 99, 101, 105, 107, 116, 117, 126, *133*, 166, *173*
Williams, F., 100, 103, *133*
Wilson, D., 50, *54*
Wilson, W. R., 65, *133*
Winograd, T., 9, *54*, 259, 263, *264*
Winthrop, H., 94, 105, *133*
Wittgenstein, L., 57, *79*
Wohlwill, J. F., 135, *151*
Woodworth, R. S., 36, 38, *54*, 58, *79*, 115, 120, *133*, 154, *173*

Y

Youniss, J., 136, *151*, 175, *199*, 238, 244, *245*

Z

Zwicky, A. M., 76, *78*, 128, *130*

SUBJECT INDEX

A

Age, 1–4, 6, 19, 29, 135, 138–149, 175–198, 201–202, 206, 209–211, 217, 220, 227–228, 231–244, 249–250, 253, 255, *see also* Concrete operations; Formal operations
 concept of measurement and, 231–232, 234–240, 243–244
 as factor in reasoning, 1–4, 6, 19, 29, 135, 138–149, 175–198, 201–202, 206, 209–211, 217, 220, 227–228, 231–244, 249–250, 253, 255
  development of serial order, 231, 234, 236–239, 243–244
  memory and, 29, 249
  propositional logic and, 1–2, 6, 19, 175–198, 250, 253
  with quantifiers, 135, 138–149
  with transitive inferences, 201–202, 206, 209–211, 217, 220, 227–228, 231–244, 249–250, 255
Artificial intelligence approaches to inference, 8–9

B

Bias, 4, 39–42, 45, 48, 58, 105–109, 111–112, 114–115, 117–127, 129, 141–143, 167, 169, 204–206, 210–211, 215, 218–221, 223, 225, 227, 238, 249–251, *see also* Pragmatic factors
 atmosphere effect, 39–40, 58, 114–115, 120, 251
 conversion, 107–109, 114–115, 117–120
 empiric, 4, 105–106, 109, 167, 169, 249–250
 end-anchor, 204–206, 210–211, 215, 218–221, 223, 225, 227, 238
 form of conclusion, "figural" effect, 39–42, 48
 against "indeterminate" responses, 45, 111–112, 118–127, 129
 matching, 58
 number of response alternatives and, 141–143
Biconditional statements, 25–26, 55, 58, 61–64, 67–68, 71–74, 76, 128–129, 250, 261, *see also* Conditional statements

C

Causality, 14, 59–62, 68–69, 72–73, 76
 definition of physical, 60–61
 lexical, 14

Causality (*contd.*)
in reasoning with propositions, 59–62, 68–69, 72–73, 76
Competence, 2–9, 82–90, 135–136, 176, 179, 190, 196–198, 201–202, 231–244, 247–250, 252–254, 258–260
development of operativity in Piagetian tasks, 6, 231–244
linguistic, 248
logical, 2–9, 82, 85, 88–90, 135–136, 176, 179, 190, 196–198, 201–202, 247–250, 252–254, 258–260
issues about definition and assessment of, 82, 85, 88–90, 247–250, 252–254, 258–260
standard logic and, 7–8, 82–87, 89, 248–250, 252, 258–260
versus performance, 2, 5, 7–9, 82–90, 247–250, 252–253
Concrete operations, 142, 220, 238–239, *see also* Formal operations
transitivity and, 238–239
versus "preoperational" children in transitive inferences, 220
Conditional statements, 15–16, 20–21, 24–26, 55–78, 83–90, 127–129, 261, *see also* Biconditional statements; Material implication
biconditional statements and, 25–26, 56, 61, 128–129
formal representation of, 20–21, 24, 83–87
interpretation of, 24, 56–63, 69, 74, 76, 88–90, 261
pragmatic factors in, 60–62, 69, 74, 76, 261
material implication and, 15–16, 24–25, 62, 127–129
subjective truth value of, 24–26
Connectives, 5, 14–20, 23–26, 56–59, 68–69, 72–73, 75, 83, 85–86, 88, 136, 142–146, 175, 250, 252, 254, 260–261, *see also* Conditional statements
definition in terms of conjunction and negation, 17
interpretation of, 5, 23–24, 56–59, 72–73, 75, 136, 142–146, 175, 250, 252, 260–261
development of, 175
lexical conjunction, implicit, 14
Connectives (*contd.*)
logical representation of, 15, 23, 88, 254
propositional reasoning and, 14–16, 18, 20, 24, 59, 68–69, 83, 85–86
semantics of, 24–26, 250, *see also* Semantics
topicality constraints, 14, 16, 18–19
Content, 2, 5–6, 8, 13, 24, 50, 55–78, 89, 105–106, 109, 117, 121–127, 177–179, 182–183, 190, 196–197, 248–254, 256–259, 261
factors in reasoning, 2, 5, 8, 13, 50, 55–78, 89, 105–106, 109, 117, 121–127, 249, 252–253, 257, 261
abstract material, 13, 68, 72–74, 77–78, 105, 117, 121–127, 249, 252
concrete material, 2, 13, 68, 72–74, 105–106, 109, 121–127, 249, 257
events, 59, 68
meaningful statements, 8, 50, 55–78, 89, 249, 261
representation of, 5–6, 24, 177–179, 182–183, 190, 196–197, 250–254, 256, 258–259
abstract, 5, 24, 177–179, 190, 196–197, 250, 252–254, 256
concrete, 6, 177–179, 182–183, 190, 196–197, 251, 253, 258–259
verbal versus nonverbal tasks, 2, 248–253, 256–257
Conversion of premises, 43, 87, 107–109, 111, 114–115, 117–129, 138–139
bias toward, 107–109, 114–115, 117–120
errors resulting from, 43, 87, 107–109, 115, 117–119
process of, 111, 114–115, 117–129, 138–139
Culture, 153–173
cognitive differences and, 153–173
reasoning and, 153–155, 169
recall of premises and, 160–163, 167

D

Deduction, 7–9, 26, 30–33, 85–87, 109–110, 177–178, 248–249, 252–254,

Deduction (*contd.*)
257–258, *see also* Propositional reasoning; Quantifiers; Syllogisms
error, the deductive process as a source of, 248–249, 252–253
heuristic factors in, 8, 26, 30–33, 109–110, 254, 257–258
natural procedures for, 7–9, 85–87, 177–178
formal proofs and, 8–9, 177–178

E

Encoding, *see* Representation
Errors, 4, 20, 39–43, 49, 55–56, 82–90, 97, 107–109, 114–115, 117–121, 127–129, 136–149, 155, 164–167, 169–172, 177, 182–184, 187–198, 202–206, 209–211, 215, 219–220, 225–227, 238–239, 247–253, *see also* Bias
assessment of source of, 82–90, 247–248
competence versus performance, 82–90, 247–248
locus of errors in deduction process, 247–253
propositional calculus as standard, adequacy of, 82–85, 87, 89, 248, *see also* Logic, relevance to reasoning, systems of, standard
guessing due to, 120–121, 192
in interpretation of quantifiers, 136–149, 252
with invalid syllogisms, 114–115, 118–119
with linear syllogisms, 203–206, 209–211, 215, 219–220, 225–227, 238–239
end-anchor effect, 205–206, 210
linguistic factors, 206, 215, 219–220
memory factors, 220
serial position effect, 204–206, 210–211, 215, 225–227
logical versus semantic, 55–56
in Piagetian transitive inference and seriation tasks, 238–239
with propositional inferences, 20, *see also* Undecidable propositions

Errors (*contd.*)
with quantified statements, 188, 191–198
radical, 191–195, 198
in recall of premises, 43, 87, 97, 107–109, 115, 117–119, 155, 164–167, 169–171, 249
conversion of premise, "illicit," 43, 87, 107–109, 115, 117–119
conversion to factual, 109, 167, 169
displacement of terms, 165
omission of premises, 164–165
quantifiers, changes in, 165–167, 170–171
in representation of syllogisms, 41–42, 49, 115, 127–129, 171–172, 202, 251–252
with undecidable propositions, 39–40, 120, 177, 182–184, 187, 189–191, 196–197

F

Formal operations, 12, 135, 142–143, 149, 198, *see also* Concrete operations
Formalization, 3–4, 247–257, 261–262, *see also* Representation, modes of, formal

I

Inference schema, 11–13, 16–22, 24–33, 85–86, 250–254, 262
auxiliary, 19, 22, 26–30, 32, 254, 262
natural deduction procedure, 16–17, 20, 25–26, 28–30, 85–86
primary, 19–22, 26–33, 254, 262
semantic bases and, 24, 250–251, 253, 262
Interpretation, *see* Representation; Semantics

L

Lexical factors, 5, 9–14, 17, 23, 50, 252, 255, 260–262
in reasoning, 5, 9–14, 255, 260–262
Lexical inference, 9–11, 13–14, 17, 23, 50, 252

Linguistics, 3–5, 7–17, 23–24, 36–38, 50, 55–57, 61–62, 75, 78, 89–90, 136–137, 141, 145, 147, 149, 179, 202–206, 215, 217, 219–221, 225, 227–228, 248–257, 259, 261–263
factors in reasoning, 4–5, 7–17, 23–24, 36–38, 50, 55–57, 61–62, 75, 78, 89–90, 136–137, 141, 145, 147, 149, 179, 202–206, 215, 217, 219–221, 225, 227–228, 248–257, 261–263
interpretation
of linear syllogisms, 202, 204–206, 215, 219–221, 225, 227–228, 250
of propositions, 4, 7–8, 14–16, 23–24, 50, 55–57, 89–90, 179, 262
of quantifiers, 36–37, 136–137, 141, 145, 147, 149
lexical inferences in ordinary language, 7–14, 16–17, 23–24, 37–38, 253–255, 261–263
sentence structure, 56, 61–62, 75, 78, 262–263, *see also* Semantics; Syntax
models of reasoning, 3, 253, 256, 259, 261
study of reasoning and, parallel between, 260–263
Logic, 1, 5, 7–9, 11, 15–16, 23, 25, 37–38, 55–58, 75, 77–78, 81–90, 93–97, 109, 136, 138–147, 149, 175–178, 188, 190, 196–198, 201–202, 227–228, 231–244, 253–254, 258–262
development of, 11, 175–176, 178, 188, 190, 196–198, 201–202, 227–228, 231–244, 253
of classes, 175–176, 178, 188, 190, 196–198, 253
propositional, 175–176, 178, 188, 190, 196–198
of relations, 11, 201–202, 227–228, 231–244, *see also* Transitivity
interpretation of logical terms and, 88, 136, 138–147, 149, 260–261, *see also* Conditional statements; Connectives; Quantifiers
Logic (*contd.*)
relevance to reasoning, 1, 5, 7–9, 25, 37–38, 55–58, 75, 77–78, 81–90, 93–97, 109, 175–178, 197, 253, 258–259, 262
systems of, 1, 5, 7, 15–16, 23, 37–38, 81–82, 93–97, 109, 253–254, 259–262
standard propositional calculus, 1, 5, 7, 15–16, 23, 37–38, 81–82, 93–97, 109, 253–254, 259–262

M

Material implication, 15–16, 24–25, 62, 88, 127–129, *see also* Conditional statements
conditionals and, 15–16, 24–25, 62, 127–129
language and, 24
paradoxes of, and standard logic, 88
Memory as factor in reasoning, 9–10, 29, 87, 97, 99, 105–107, 112–113, 121, 127–128, 138, 141–143, 156, 158–163, 168–169, 179, 182, 205, 217–218, 220–221, 248–249, 251, 258
inferential constructive factors for sentences, 171–172, 249, 258
long-term, 97, 105–107, 112–113, 121, 127–128, 179, 249, *see also* Pragmatic factors
recall accuracy, 156, 158–163, 168–169, 182, 205, 251
in relation to recall procedure, 156, 158–159, 168
semantic, and logical reasoning, 9–10
short-term, 29, 87, 97, 99, 107, 113, 141–143, 217–218, 220–221, 248–249
data base and, 97, 107, 113
syntactic complexity and, 99

N

Negation, 18, 20–22, 24, 37, 43–44, 46, 48, 83, 99, 182–183, 187
of antecedent, 24
in conditional statements, 83
conjunctions and, 18

Negation (*contd.*)
double, and inference, 21–22
errors of inference and, 20
quantifiers and, 37, 43–44, 46, 48
as syntactic feature, 99–100
in undecidable propositions, 182–183, 187

P

Pragmatic factors, 3–5, 9, 18, 25–26, 50–51, 55–57, 60–62, 68–69, 73–78, 88–90, 107–109, 155, 159–160, 163, 165, 167, 169–172, 175, 249–250, 253, 261, *see also* Bias; Errors
in interpretation of premises, 3–5, 56–57, 60, 68–69, 74–75, 107–109, 167, 169, 170
personal knowledge in reasoning and, 5, 9, 18, 25–26, 50–51, 55–56, 61–62, 73–74, 76–78, 88–90, 155, 159–160, 163, 165, 167, 169–170, 175, 249–250, 253, 261
in sentence memory, 171–172
Propositional reasoning, 1–8, 14–37, 50, 55–61, 64–68, 71–73, 76–77, 81–90, 175–198, 249–250
with abstract material, 57–59, 72–73, 76–77, 177–180, *see also* Content, abstract material
development of, 1–2, 6, 19, 175–198, 250–253
interpretation of propositions and, 4, 7–8, 14–16, 23–24, 50, 55–59, 88–90, 179, 262
with meaningful material, 249–250, *see also* Content, meaningful material
models of, 14–36, 81–90
Piaget's theory and, 1–4, 249
task domain of, versus scientific tasks domain, 2–3, 175–176
truth tables as model of, adequacy of, 58, 60–61, 64–68, 71–72, 84–85
Psycholinguistics, 3, 248, 253, 259, 261
models of reasoning and, 3, 259, 261

Q

Quantifiers, 6, 12, 36–50, 83, 87–89, 91–110, 127–129, 135–152, 162, 165–167, 169–171, 175–176, 178, 188, 190, 196–198, 252–253, 259, 261, *see also* Syllogisms
conditional representation of quantified statements, 83, 87–88, 127–129
interpretation of, 12, 36–38, 41, 43, 89, 97–110, 135–149, 169, 252, 261
development of, 135–149
psychological adequacy of standard representation of, 103, 136, 138–147, 149, *see also* Logic, relevance to reasoning
reasoning with, 6, 36–50, 91–98, 109–111, 138–139, 141, 143, 175–176, 178, 188, 190, 196–198, 253, 259
development of, 91–98, 175–176, 178, 188, 190, 196–198, 253
errors for positive versus negative quantified statements, 138, 141, 143, 149
for universal versus particular quantified statements, 138–139, 149
recall of, 162, 165–167, 170–171

R

Representation, 3–6, 11–36, 38–50, 55–61, 75–78, 97–115, 120–121, 124–125, 127–129, 136–137, 148–149, 169, 171–172, 176–184, 186–188, 190–193, 196–198, 201–202, 204–207, 210–211, 215, 217–218, 220–223, 227–228, 247–262
of connectives, 13–36, 55–61, 75–78, 252, 261
errors and, 41–42, 49, 115, 127–129, 171–172, 202, 248, 251–253
of linear syllogisms, 201–202, 204–206, 210–211, 215, 217, 220–223, 227–228, 248, 251, 254
by absolute magnitudes, 222–223
linear, integrated representation of, 202, 204–205, 210, 217, 220–223, 227–228, 251, 254

Representation
of linear syllogisms (*contd.*)
premises stored separately, 202, 205–206, 211, 215, 221
modes of, 4–6, 11–13, 24, 36, 38–50, 57–58, 97–115, 120–121, 124–125, 127–129, 136–137, 148–149, 169, 176–184, 186–188, 190–193, 196–198, 202, 204–205, 207, 217–218, 220–223, 227–228, 249–262
abstract representation, 5, 24, 177–179, 190, 196–197, 250, 252–254, 256
concrete, 6, 177–179, 182–183, 190, 196–197, 251, 253, 258–259
by diagrams, Venn and Euler, 42, 48–49, 109–110, 114, 136–137, 148–149, 250–252, 255–256
by examples, 5–6, 57–58, 253, 257–260
formal representation, 12, 57–58, 250–254, 257, 261–262
schematized representation, 177–180, 182–183, 187–188, 190–191, 253, 258
spatial representation, 202, 204–205, 207, 217–218, 220–223, 227–228, 250–252, 254
switching between alternative, 179, 183–184, 187, 190–191, 193, 197–198
visual representation, 4, 6, 177, 190, 197, 251, 253–258, 260
of propositional statements, 36, 176–180, 182, 187–188, 190–192, 196–197
of quantified statements, 43, 176–177, 179–180, 182–184, 186–188, 191, 193, 196–197, 251
of quantifiers, 6, 12, 38, 41, 43–50, 97–111, 169, 250–251, 256, 261
of relational terms, 106
semantic, 11, 24, 38, 260–262
of spatial relations, 12–13
of syllogisms, 6, 38–41, 99–109, 111–115, 120–121, 124–125, 127–129, 249–250, *see* Representation, linear syllogisms, *see also* Errors, in representation of syllogisms

S

Scientific reasoning, 3–5, 175–176, 198, 249–250, 252
versus reasoning in "propositional" task domain, 3, 249–250, 252
Semantics, 4, 9–16, 23–26, 36–38, 55–56, 59–62, 68–69, 73–75, 77–78, 99–103, 106–109, 127–129, 136–137, 141, 145, 147, 149, 252, 256, 260–263
generative semantics and, 261–263
and interpretation
of causal statements, 14, 62, 68–69, 73–74, 77–78, *see also* Conditional statements
of logical terms, 14–15, 25–26, 256, 260, *see also* Connectives
of propositional calculus, 4, 15–16, 23–24, 262
of quantifiers, 36–37, 136–137, 141, 145, 147, 149, *see also* Quantifiers
of relational terms, 106–109
reasoning and, 55–56, 59–61, 75, 99–103, 127–129, 260–263
relations between words and, 9–14
synonymity and lexical inferences, 23, 37–38, 252
Syllogisms, 5, 36–55, 93–133, 143–153, 174–198, 201–244, *see also* Deduction; Error; Quantifiers; Representation; Transitivity
atmosphere effect in, 40, 114–115, 120, 251
development of syllogistic inference, 174–198, 231–244
encoding in, 43, 99, 169, *see* Representation, of syllogisms, of linear syllogisms
inference, syllogistic, 93–133
interpretation of, 143–153
linear, 201–230
types of class, 38, 94–97
Syllogistic reasoning, models of, 42–48, 97–99, 111–117, 254–256
Syntax, 56, 61–62, 75, 78, 99–103, 127, 261–263
as factor in reasoning, 99–103
negation, 99–100

Syntax
as factor in reasoning (*contd.*)
voicing, 100–103
word order, 102–103
logic and, parallel between, 261
semantics and, 56, 61–62, 75, 78, 261–263

T

Theorem-proving machines, 5, 8, 16
Transitivity, 6, 10–13, 45, 47, 68, 201–228, 231–244, 248–251, 255, 257
bias toward, 45, 47
development of, 6, 231–244
of length, 202–228, 231–237, 239, 241, 243–244, 250, 255

Transitivity (*contd.*)
in lexical reasoning, 10–13, 68, 257
memory and, 248–249
representation of, *see* Representation, of linear syllogisms

U

Undecidable propositions, 39–40, 45, 111–112, 118–127, 129, 177, 182–184, 187, 189–197, 257–258
bias against "undecidable" responses, 45, 111–112, 118–127, 129
errors with, 39–40, 120, 177, 182–184, 187, 189–191, 196–197
intradimensional versus extradimensional propositions, 191–196